The Heartmates®
Meditation Journal
A Companion for Partners of People with Heart Disease

Advance Praise for...

The Heartmates® Meditation Journal:
A Companion for Partners of People with Heart Disease

Thank God; *The Heartmates® Meditation Journal* is a blessing. It provides gentle guidance to sojourners through valleys of illness, crisis and faith. The journal offers both travel markers of growth and rest stops for grieving. The meditation focal points and the affirmations will be particularly useful for heartmates of all faiths to chart their course toward healing, hope and understanding.

> – The Reverend Jewelnel Davis, M.Div., M.S.W.
> Chaplain

A great gift to heartmates everywhere! With compassion and insight, this *Journal* will help you and your loved ones know what you are feeling and what you need to do to cope with the emotions that come as you live with heart illness.

> – Wayne M. Sotile, Ph.D.
> Author of *Heart Illness and Intimacy: How Caring Relationships Aid Recovery*

The Heartmates® Meditation Journal is a great concept! A resource I will reach for to share with "my" cardiac families. I heartily endorse this gift of hope I can extend to them as I care for their loved one.

> – Carolyn Lawson, R.N.
> ICU, Education, Cardiac Rehabilitation
> Harris Regional Hospital, North Carolina

The Heartmates®
Meditation Journal
A Companion for Partners of People with Heart Disease

by Rhoda F. Levin, M.S.W.

MinervaPress
Minneapolis, Minnesota

The Heartmates® Meditation Journal:
A Companion for Partners of People with Heart Disease
©Copyright 1995, Rhoda F. Levin

The trademark, Heartmates® consisting of the word and the logo, is registered in the U.S. Patent and Trademark Office, and in other countries, to Heartmates Inc., Minneapolis, Minnesota, U.S.A.

Library of Congress Cataloging-in—Publication Data

Levin, Rhoda F.
      The Heartmates® Meditation Journal: A Companion for Partners of People with
      Heart Disease

ISBN 0-9637795-2-4

Cover and text design: Cottage Communications
Cover and interior art: "New Reality" © 1994 Bonnie S. Barland

Heartmates® books and other resources are available at special discounts for bulk purchases for educational use and fund-raising. For details, contact:

Special Sales Director
MinervaPress
P.O. Box 16202
Minneapolis, MN 55416
(800) 9HM-3331
Fax: (612) 929-6395

Grateful acknowledgment is made for permission to quote from MAINSTAY, ©1988 by Maggie Strong, Little, Brown & Co., and FEAR OF FIFTY, ©1994 by Erica Jong, HarperCollins.

This book is printed on an acid-free paper that meets the American National Standards Institute Z39.48 Standard. The text paper is made from 50% de-inked, recycled fiber including 10% post-consumer waste.

First MinervaPress Edition 1995
Printed in the United States of America

ΔΔ 10 9 8 7 6 Δ 5 4 3 2 1

<u>Important Information</u>

<u>Important Phone Numbers:</u>
    Emergency   **911**
    Family Doctor
    Cardiologist
    Hospital
    Favorite Nurse
    Clergy/Chaplain
    Cardiac Rehab
    Pharmacy
    Heartmates® Helpline   **(612) 929-3331**
    Other

<u>Prescriptions:</u>
    Drug Name
    Prescription Number
    Dosage
    Side Effects

    Drug Name
    Prescription Number
    Dosage
    Side Effects

    Drug Name
    Prescription Number
    Dosage
    Side Effects

<u>Doctor/Rehab Appointments:</u>

Date		Date	
	Dr.		Dr.
Date		Date	
	Dr.		Dr.
Date		Date	
	Dr.		Dr.
Date		Date	
	Dr.		Dr.

My Questions:

(for the doctor, hospital personnel, clergy, other cardiac spouses, etc.)

Question/date:

Question/date:

Question/date:

Question/date:

Question/date:

Books/Reading Recommendations:

Things & People to Remember:

(New friends, helpful hospital personnel, stores that stock healthy foods, recipes, etc.)

Table of Contents

Author's Request:

My work on behalf of heartmates and cardiac families continues. I wou
appreciate hearing your unique experiences and stories. I am especially i
terested in your opinions about the usefulness of this book in general, a
how specific quotations or weekly topics were beneficial to you. I wou
also like to know about any of your personal recovery needs that I did n
address the book. Please write me at the address below or via e-mail.

Rhoda F. Levin, MSW
MinervaPress
P.O. Box 16202
Minneapolis, Minnesota 55416

e-mail address: heartmates@aol.com
To be on our Internet Mailing list send heartmates@giz.com
a message saying, "I want to join."

For information about other Heartmates® resources,
professional training or motivational speaking,
contact Heartmates® Inc.
Call: (800) 9HM-3331
Fax: (612) 929-6395

INTRODUCTION

I wrote *Heartmates® A Survival Guide for the Cardiac Spouse* in 1986. Since then, I have become even more interested in addressing the emotional and spiritual core of cardiac recovery, something as vital as the medical protocol for healing the cardiac spouse, patient, and family.

Our culture still holds a narrow definition of healing. We've grown accustomed to methods that isolate the patient, focusing on treatment technology and the physiological aspect of disease. A broader view of both illness and recovery identifies illness as a tear in the fabric of family life. We tend to focus on the illness, the tear itself. Since the illness can't be undone, we need to reweave the fabric so that it is once again whole, though different than before. The whole family has been wounded by and thus suffers from heart disease. The goal is healing and the whole tapestry of family health and human feelings must be addressed, not just the part that shows the damage.

Studies indicate that social support is essential to a full recovery. Yet once heart patients and heartmates return home after a brief hospitalization, they are on their own, often isolated, and apart from others who share their concerns. Many heartmates live far from the hospital where cardiac care was given and cannot participate in new and often limited outpatient educational and support programs. Heartmates' recoveries are complicated further by the fact that the physical illness is not theirs, but their mates'. Society eagerly but erroneously believes that family life has "returned to normal" because the patient has survived.

In my production of the videotape series, *Portrait of the Heartmate*, (available now for home viewing—see coupon at the end of this book) I described my personal experience which was so different from everyone's expectations: that our family would be untouched and would bounce back because Marsh had recovered from two heart attacks and by-pass surgery.

"I didn't know what to do, what was expected of me, so I did what many women do in a crisis, I jumped right into my SuperWoman suit and tried to handle everything.

It was only when my husband was...discharged...that I stopped to take a breath, and then it hit me! I was relieved and grateful that he was well enough to come home, but I was also very frightened, because I didn't know exactly what I was supposed to do for him. At the same time I felt responsible for making him healthy and keeping him alive. And then it was on to recovery and more unknowns.

I came to realize that we, the heartmates, are also in recovery. We have been so busy caring for our spouses that we haven't paid enough attention to ourselves. We have to find the right balance of caring for our spouses and ourselves so that recovery can be as full as possible."

i

With these realities in mind, I have written *The Heartmates® Meditation Journal: A Companion for Partners of People with Heart Disease* to help combat the isolation and lack of support that so hampers long-term recovery. The journal differs from *Heartmates® A Guide for the Spouse and Family of the Heart Patient* in that it invites heartmates to participate in their own recovery, to learn how to help themselves heal, by reading, journal writing, and meditating. Weekly entries provide options and practical techniques to support heartmates coping with the ongoing changes in their lives due to their mate's heart disease.

The Heartmates® Meditation Journal will enhance the recovery of heartmate readers wherever in the recovery process they find themselves. I expect that most heartmate readers will be women, and since our society has us well-trained to take care of our men and our children and not ourselves, self-care is an important focus of this book. Some women may know about taking care of themselves through diet and exercise, others may have a friend or a therapist to talk with, and still others may be comforted by their religious faith. As a result of the lack of education about self-care, few heartmates understand about balancing needs during healing. Their bodies, feelings, minds, and spirits need attention. It is as necessary to address needs for privacy and quiet as needs for social connection, support, and stimulation. And further, heartmates need support in relation to their needs for meaning, and service.

Ruth Fram, a very experienced heartmate, wrote me about her recovery:

> "I have had many years of coping with the traumas of life. I'm made of tough stuff. I have learned to be more philosophical about life and I take one day at a time and cherish that day. I am happy to report that I still have the ability to laugh and I make sure that some laughter is part of my day....Even though I take my responsibilities very seriously, I am not a martyr. I am the caregiver and perhaps I don't get out socially as much as I might want to, but I keep a part of me for just me. If I give all of me then I can be destroyed as an individual and then I have nothing to give. I am 67 years old and still learning....everyone should have another interest that they are passionate about. For me it is needlework."

It is my sincere wish that *The Heartmates® Meditation Journal* will help heartmates heal so they can live fully and with great optimism like Ruth and so many others.

One purpose of this book is to comfort and support heartmates who feel alone and frozen in place by fear. Heartmates can't take advantage of the positive opportunities of the cardiac crisis until they are liberated from the deep freeze, can feel again, and return to the rest of the world.

Another purpose is to teach and challenge heartmates to accept where they are — the first step to further growth. I am not a person who believes we are given illness in order to grow, but I do believe that once we are touched by life-threatening illness, it is normal and natural to question much of what we have taken for granted. This includes questions of priorities and values, the meaning of life, particularly our own lives, and questions about God and spiritual purpose. I hope this book will lead each heartmate to make that all-important connection of body and personality with soul, and of self with others.

HOW TO USE THIS BOOK

The Heartmates® Meditation Journal is designed for your personal use as an interactive year-long recovery resource. At the beginning of the book there is an organized section to write down specific concerns and to help remember all the things you are responsible for during recovery: important phone numbers, prescriptions, questions for your doctors, special recipes, personal notes.

The body of the book is organized by the week, rather than every day. Daily entries are too overwhelming, too much to take on when you are grieving and healing. The book follows the course of a year, but it is your own calendar of recovery, rather than January through December. You'll find a balance of messages, thoughts and information, and space for you to record your recovery. Each weekly entry contains: a quotation; a short explication or pertinent illustration applying the quotation to heartmates' issues; an affirmation; suggestions for thinking and writing that relate to the weekly topic; and three pertinent qualities for meditation. The entries are short and to the point, because, particularly in the early months of grieving, heartmates may experience difficulty concentrating for any length of time.

I have tried to provide guidance that is both general enough to mean something to all heartmates, and specific enough for you to apply to your personal situation and circumstance. There are several additional pages of quotations in Appendix B to help you make the book work for you. These quotations invite you to choose a different focus for any week; they can become more meaningful than other weekly assigned quotations, or they can be used as additional readings anytime during this year of recovery, or beyond.

Although I have chosen the qualities for meditation that I believe fit the focus of the week, and are appropriate to issues in a particular phase of recovery, you may occasionally wish to replace my choice of qualities with your own. For that reason, I have provided a very complete list of qualities in Appendix D to give you that option. The affirmations are in Appendix C as well, so that you can see them in order, read them, and mark ones that are especially important to you.

The format:
Part I: "Help, I Don't Get It!" — the first 20 weeks, or "Early Recovery"
Part II: "The Long Haul" — the next 20 weeks, or "Mid-Recovery"
Part III: "I Can See The Light" — the final 12 weeks of a calendar year, or "Toward Full Recovery"

Each part contains self-care, feelings, isolation and support, meaning and values, spiritual issues, and "re-pair" of the couple's relationship including physical intimacy, partnership, and family concerns.

Each time a topic is readdressed in a later part in the book, the focus goes deeper. Early months stress recognition and acknowledgment; middle months focus on acceptance, once a reality is acknowledged; the later months aid integration and encourage celebration.

THE CHAOTIC COURSE OF HEALING

Although the book is divided into three parts, corresponding to three distinct phases, I warn you, there is no straight path in healing. Each of us, unique and beautiful, must chart and follow our own course. So although Part I, a 20 - week section, focuses on issues that occur mainly in the acute months of the recovery process, you may find you want to return to Part I and tend to some of those issues even as you near the end of the book.

I wish I could predict an orderly, straightforward recovery for heartmates, but I know from my own experience and that of many others, chaos reigns! Remember that if you try to match your recovery path with the orderly structure of the book. It is to honor chaos that I have not dated the weeks. Number the weeks of your recovery in the way that best suits you or feel free not to number the weeks at all.

Because books are linear, one page follows another. You may want to read along until you come upon an entry that fits your immediate need or interest, and then write and meditate about it. Certain topics may interest you for only a few days, and others you may choose to write about for a month or even longer. Some people open books randomly, believing that what they open to is what they need, and proceed accordingly, using the Journal in a most personal way.

CELEBRATION

Because we are a culture that stresses speed and efficiency and has little patience for mourning and the lengthy process of healing, we have few rituals to celebrate healing. When progress is made, goals are met, and anniversaries lived through, these special moments deserve to be marked by celebration. In the recommended reading list (Appendix A), I have included books about ritual, although none apply specifically to your family or your recovery from heart disease. Talk with each other and design your own personal celebration practices. Enjoy them as often as you can define something to celebrate.

HUMOR

While it may be difficult to be playful or tell jokes without disturbing, confusing, or insulting some one, humor is a great contributor to the healing process. It shifts perspective, and allows us to see with fresh clarity, an important component of healing. That's why you'll find humor throughout, including a wonderful Mel Brooks line from the *2000 and 13 Year Old Man* album.

One of the most difficult conversations that my husband Marsh and I had was just prior to his bypass surgery when he was 46, and I was 45. He told me that he was putting his future in my hands, giving me the responsibility, if something went wrong in surgery, to make sure that he wouldn't live interminably as a vegetable. You may know from having a similar discussion how intense a situation it was; if not, imagine the awesome power of that moment. Holding my breath, I asked him to define "vegetable." My question was the perfect "straight line" for Marsh's comedic sense. He responded without a second's hesitation, "If I can't eat barbecued ribs." The two of us laughed until we cried.

Humor can be a recovery tool; use it as much as you can. It lightens the weight of your pain; it puts your situation in perspective, and laughter may be as physiologically therapeutic as tears.

JOURNAL WRITING

For many people writing is the ideal medium of expression. Some heartmates lack a confidante to share their pain and joy; others hold privacy as a higher priority than social connection; still others find it difficult or impossible to share in a group.

Read the weekly entry. Then, if you take a few minutes daily or a couple of times a week to write in the journal, you will be exercising self-care. You'll be caring enough about yourself to give yourself time to think and write about your concerns. You will find suggestions each week to stimulate your thinking and writing. You may have a different response to the quotation than my comments present, or the reading may evoke a deep, personal memory that you prefer to write about. Remember, the suggestions are just that, suggestions. I hope that you will use *The…Journal* in the style most appropriate to you.

How does writing in a journal aid your healing from your cardiac crisis?

In order to heal from any crisis situation, you need to tell your story. Telling and retelling your story is a vital review that helps you understand, accept and finally integrate what happened (the cardiac crisis itself) and what is happening to you — emotionally, mentally, and spiritually. If you don't have a willing ear to listen as you repeat your story again and again, or if you would feel more comfortable with your privacy, the journal is a perfect vehicle. You can repeat as much as you need; you can go back to earlier writing to survey your path and progress. You can change your mind or your story without having to make yourself understood to someone else.

Expressing feelings is an essential task in the healing process. If you don't let yourself know what you're feeling, and don't permit yourself to express those feelings, you will get stuck in the grieving/healing process. Writing in your journal is a safe way to air your feelings. It is also a constructive method because it encourages you to explore and uncover feelings that may be otherwise inaccessible. What you may not feel free to say aloud to someone is safely articulated in your journal. It doesn't seem to matter if you go back to read through what you've written or whether you read it to someone else. What matters is that you have lifted those feelings out of the dark, and brought them to light. Via pen on paper, you can discover and vent (bring into the air).

Letting go of the old and accepting the new is another important component of healing. When you write about your daily activities and your feelings and thoughts about those actions, you can begin to understand what may at first glance seem random. Reading past journal entries can help you track the development and existence of patterns that you might not otherwise notice. This is particularly important in recovery, when you are trying to make changes in your lifestyle and don't understand why change is so difficult. Writing about old and new patterns may increase your understanding, and give you the needed impetus and ability to let go of old habits and establish new ones.

Parts of your personality will struggle with what has happened. Those parts prefer to yearn for your pre-cardiac reality, rather than surrender to what's happened and move into the present. Actually putting the words on paper can help you to accept reality.

Maybe the most important activity in the healing process is searching for meaning. Writing in a journal creates a stable record of your inner journey. A crisis, which certainly heart disease is, makes you vulnerable (open). Because inner thoughts and questions are accessible during recovery, it can be a time of great inner growth, and spiritual healing. Give yourself regular, quiet time to pursue those thoughts and questions undisturbed. Use your journal as a rich record of your reflection. Writing about the serious questions you now face is a method of actively participating in your inner journey.

Often the questions are without answers, but if you practice silence and maintain an open attitude as you write, you may experience insight, inner guidance, or fuller understanding. Insight usually comes in a flash and, like a dream, is quickly forgotten. Write down those flashes immediately so you won't lose them. Then you can return to your journal to think and write further about the meaning of the insight. I often receive a flash of insight or a creative idea when I am alone in my car. If I wait until I reach home, it is always lost. I keep a small tablet and pen in the car so I can jot down key words at least; then I take that scrap with me to my journal writing.

About the actual writing — Find a special place for writing in your journal. Make it a cozy and comfortable place, a place away from the distractions of every day life, like the phone and television. If you can schedule it daily, or every other day, you will find it easier to build the habit of regular journal writing. Knowing that heartmates live very busy lives filled with responsibilities, I specifically made *The...Journal* purse-sized so you can carry it with you, and write in it in the doctor's waiting room, on a park bench, while baby-sitting your napping grandchildren, or whenever you have a "found" moment.

There is no one right way to use this journal. During the first few weeks, you will probably devise your own pattern and style of writing, whether it's early morning or late at night when every one else is asleep. The paper was chosen so you could use your favorite pen, pencil, or even different colored markers. There are faint lines for those who prefer a guide when they write. If you don't like them, ignore them and write any way and in any size that is comfortable for you.

Some people **PRINT**, others *write*; some journals are neat, others are barely legible, some write uphill or down, and others write *around*

Experiment with style, and feel free to change your writing to express who you are and how you feel. I hope you will use this journal creatively to further your personal healing.

Cynthia L. McCurtain, a heartmate, wrote me in the fall of 1989: "After reading Heartmates®, I know that it is not my inability to cope, but a very normal reaction to crisis." She included a page from her journal, written during her husband's hospitalization, and she gave me her permission to share it with you:

the pain comes and washes over me
i walk out in the hall so that you won't see
i leave tears on the walls
on the floors in a private corner
and breathe deeply
come back and smile.
it's not so hard to bring you smiles
for you are my happiness
my heart holds your ache
and your anger
it belongs to me too.
i could tear down a wall with my bare hands right now
but i won't and i don't
i'll just sit quietly for you now
for you always.

i can't change things
i just pray for the courage to accept things the way they are
and my courage comes.
you have always been my strength
let me be yours.
let us be each other's — always.

MEDITATION

When you think of meditation, you may conjure up an image of a lonely monk at the top of a high mountain, a Buddhist sitting in the lotus position, silent for long hours, or a mystic returned to nature, avoiding responsibilities of the world.

Thought is an energy, and through meditation you can focus thought to build or maintain an idea or energize a quality. Meditation is an inner mental action — a conscious, deliberate use of thought for a specific purpose. Meditation is a practical and purposeful discipline, like regular physical exercise. As physical exercise fosters rehabilitation by tuning and strengthening the body, so meditation aids recovery by tuning and using the mind in a purposeful way.

Training your mind to be focused, orderly, reflective, quiet, attentive, open, and receptive will give you skills that have broad applications in your everyday and spiritual life. As recovering heartmates, you'll find that meditation on qualities will increase your awareness of energies you need that can be available to you in your daily life. Meditation can quiet and calm your mind, establishing a stable foundation for decision making. Meditation can attract the energy of qualities to help you cope with and grow from the cardiac crisis. And finally, meditation — when you focus your mind on questions of identity, meaning, and purpose — can help you approach your real Self and deepen your spiritual connection.

MEDITATING ON QUALITIES

Meditation is a practice, a discipline requiring patience and repetition. First you must make the choice to meditate. I suggest that you experiment with the meditation practice described here before you make a long-term commitment. If you decide to continue, be kind to yourself if your expectations don't immediately correspond to the reality of your practice. You can choose to meditate daily, or twice or three times a week. Acquiring any new habit is a challenge; the forces of inertia and lethargy, and the old excuses of not having the time or being too busy will be tough to overcome. Your reluctance may get stronger before you overcome it, but perseverance and commitment will yield marvelous results and will enhance your healing process.

Because meditating on qualities may be an entirely new concept, here is a detailed description of the process. You can follow these instructions as long as you need to, and whenever you're ready, you can make individual changes to suit yourself.

Phase 1: Preparation
Sit comfortably in a quiet place away from distractions where you can have privacy for 10-20 minutes. Reread the weekly entry. Choose the quality in the weekly entry that is most interesting or inviting to you. Close your eyes (if that will help you focus inward and avoid being visually distracted), and take a few deep breaths. Relax your physical body as much as you can, keeping your spine straight and your feet in contact with the floor. Take a few deep breaths, and stay focused on your breathing to help calm your feelings, and empty your mind. The idea is to be relaxed, but not passive; tension-free, but alert, with your full attention on the quality chosen for meditation.

Phase 2: Reflection
This phase of the meditation is the time to think about the quality and its many aspects. You may want to follow all the suggestions in the order here or select one or two on which to focus.

Imagine the quality written inside your mind: notice that it is written in an appropriate color, and in the kind of letters that fits the quality itself. First, think of words, phrases or ideas that you normally associate with this quality. Think of synonyms for the quality; think of opposites of the quality. Think about how you feel about this quality, in yourself and in others. Identify people in your life or people you know of who have this quality. Think about situations when you've needed this quality. Think about times when you have used this quality and how that affected you and the situation. Think about how your cardiac recovery or your family's would be different if you had more of this quality available. Think about how this quality affects your life, your family's life, life in the broader world. Think about questions you may have about this quality: its source; how scarce or abundant it is; what stops its spread throughout the world; what advantageous effect more of this quality might have in your personal life and in the world.

When you have thought about the quality as fully as you can (in 3-5 minutes), staying alert, return your attention to your breathing, and take a few deep breaths.

Phase 3: Reception
This phase of meditation goes beyond our skills of organization and reason. In the western world, we are less familiar with this way of using the mind. The task is to hold your mind open, alert, and receptive, and invite the unconscious mind to join the conscious mind so you can receive deeper understanding or insight. Continue to sit comfortably, and focus on your breathing. It is not necessary to change your breath, just observe it as a way of focusing inward. Now gather all of the ideas, thoughts, and feelings from your reflection about the quality, and imagine putting them into a clear, crystal bowl. Hold the bowl up and imagine the rays of the sun shining into your bowl full of reflections. Now focus your attention on the bowl and its contents. Notice any thoughts or feelings you have as you hold the bowl, and calmly return your attention to the open space you have prepared and are holding for insight.

Stay expectant (for 1-2 minutes or as long as you can remain focused), open to any changes that happen as you observe the bowl, its contents, and the sun's rays. If there is no response, acknowledge your disappointment and the difficulty of maintaining patience and receptivity. You will be open again when you next meditate, and further insight is possible between now and then.

Phase 4: Transforming Vision Into Action
This final phase of the meditation is also called creative meditation, because it combines the information and energy from the reflective and receptive phases, and uses your mind and imagination to bring your awareness into your active life. Transforming awareness so that its energy can be used in the world is the essence of the mind/body connection. The transformation grounds awareness making it both practical and purposeful, helping you cope with the daily struggles and adaptations of living with heart disease.

Focus again on your breath as a technique of holding your attention on the quality. Sit comfortably, and again collect your thoughts, feelings, and insights. Now think about a situation in your life right now that would benefit from you having access to this quality. Imagine that just before you entered into the situation, you would call on the energy of the quality to be with you. Then imagine yourself entering the scene and expressing the new energy as you live the event. Notice how you feel different, how your actions are different, how your view of yourself and the situation change when you have that energy.

Option: Take the time to imagine other scenes that you need to cope with in your life: at home; with your heartmate; at work; with friends. Notice the effect of the quality on the situations — better or worse.

Spend no more than 3-5 minutes on this last phase of the meditation. Before you leave your comfortable chair, take a few more breaths and clear your mind and feelings. You may want to write notes, about your thoughts and your plans for action, in your journal before you return to your daily routine.

You may find it useful to meditate more than once on the same quality. Stay with it as long as you continue to strengthen your understanding of the quality, or find that you benefit from the focus.

Choose the quality in the weekly entry that you are most familiar with, feel most confident about in yourself. Or choose a quality that you think you altogether lack. If none of the qualities provided in the weekly entry fit your needs, look through Appendix D where you will find a full list of qualities and select one.

Variations
1. Instead of meditating on the quality, focus your attention on the affirmation in the weekly entry. Write the affirmation on a three-by-five card, and put it where you will see it and remember to repeat it several times a day. Even if you don't believe you can live the affirmation, given how you feel or where you are in your recovery, repeat it aloud or to yourself in a positive voice. In the same way that the energy of a quality is attracted to you when you pay attention to it by meditating, repetition of the affirmation will also attract energy.

2. Read the weekly entry. Look at the qualities and pick the one you most want to develop, or most need in your situation right now. On a three-by-five card, write the quality in large letters in the color that in your mind fits the quality. Add a design to decorate the quality and attract your eye and the energy of the quality. Put the card in a place where you will see it often. My favorite places are the refrigerator door, and the mirror above the bathroom sink. Look at the word each day to keep its image present in your mind, even when you aren't paying conscious attention.

Imagine how you can express the quality in your recovery. Watch how others in your life express this quality. Write about the quality in your journal. When you stop noticing the card, it may be time to change qualities, or give the quality new life by making another, different colored card with different shaped letters or decoration to hold your attention until you are ready to focus on another quality.

MENTAL IMAGERY

You have already been introduced to mental imagery in the section about meditating on qualities. But the images you already have, especially subconscious ones, are also an important aspect of your healing from the cardiac crisis.

We all create our own world views based on our images of reality, drawn from our perceptions of our experience. Your images are supported and reinforced when your reality is comprised of things you take for granted in your life.

When we are unaware of what our images are, we are controlled by them. For example: If your image of the hospital is a place with a competent and caring staff, you'll feel satisfied with the quality of care your spouse receives. If your image of the hospital is a place of helplessness and isolation, that gives rise to a very different interpretation — that the hospital is an impersonal, untrustworthy place. The truth is probably somewhere in-between, but your image is your reality.

In the adult world, images are rarely discussed or taken seriously. Images are considered to be the product of children's imaginations, or of the senility of the aged, or the delusions of the mentally ill. Imagery doesn't get the respect it deserves in our culture, even though in some arenas — like athletic training, enhancing self-esteem, and trying to influence cancer — imagery is consciously used as a resource.

What are images made of? The imagination is a sophisticated human function that integrates components of the mind and the feelings. Below our awareness, i.e., subconsciously, our minds and emotions interpret and define our reality. Thus our images form the basis of our world view and are the foundation of our actions. We trust our images; they influence what we think and do. We respond to our images as if they were reality. Because we believe in our own images they have a powerful influence over us.

Until the cardiac crisis, you probably trusted your images: the security of your life-style; your relationship with your mate; your expectations of your future. The wound of heart disease shattered your images of reality: you could no longer trust your image of your life, your relationship, your future. Part of your process of healing is repairing your images.

The process of repairing your images includes becoming aware of obsolete images, those that no longer match your reality. You need to grieve for them, let them go, and build new ones that mirror your present reality. In *Heartmates® A Guide for the Spouse and Family of the Heart Patient,* I wrote about the significance of heartmates letting go of obsolete images and "updating" them to help us live in relation to a new reality that includes heart disease:

"Marsh's heart attack changed my image of who my husband really is. I had never given much conscious thought to his

mortality. In the life-threatening crisis that brought Marsh to a bed in the coronary care unit, I
saw what I had not noticed or thought about until then. Marsh is mortal. That means he will die. Maybe not now, but he won't live forever.

That thought came as a great surprise! I knew that I would die; that realization had come with my mother's death ten years earlier. But I had never applied that to Marsh. My image was of an invincible man. Not only was he physically strong and active, his energy for life had always seemed so unfaltering.

If I thought far enough into the future, to our eighties or nineties, I could imagine us aged and dying. But the day my image was shattered I was only forty-three.

Marsh was my first love. I 'fell for him' when we were in high school. My image of him then was of a handsome, blue-eyed blond with an athlete's body, a scholar's mind, an intensity for life, and a powerful moral drive. Had I never looked at him again? Why hadn't I seen the twenty-three years of changes?

The man I saw looking out at me from the tubes, wires, and machinery in the cardiac care unit that night was a half-bald, gray-faced, middle-aged man. Where had my adolescent hero gone? Who was this sick and aging man, his blue eyes flecked with fear and disbelief?

Why had I never noticed time passing? Why had I never brought the image of my mate up to date? My perception of him was unconnected to the real world with its unrelenting passage of time.

As painful as it was to look time in the face, there was no way to avoid it. Little by little, reminded by my own graying hair and the lines in my face, I began to integrate my image of us, making it more accurate and realistically current. We are no longer teen-age lovers, but our lives aren't over by any means. Now my image of us as vital human beings is enriched with the maturity and wisdom that comes with experience."

Your images may need an overhaul too. If you want to work more with your images, see Appendix E for imagery exercises adapted from my first book, *Heartmates®*. They include a Relaxation Exercise, a Guide for Examining Images, The Evening Review Exercise, and An Evening Review on Boundaries.

A MESSAGE FROM THE AUTHOR

I am grateful to so many for their support and cooperation in helping to make this book possible. In particular, I want to acknowledge those heartmates who have contributed so much to the healing of others by appearing in the videoseries, *Portrait of the Heartmate,* and for permitting their heartfelt thoughts to appear here: Sharon Anstett, Dorothy Atkinson, Mary

Charpentier, Ethelyn Cohen, Mitzi Crowley, Ruth Fram, Lavonne Garcia, Yleen Joselyn, Robin Lalor-Schleck, Gretchen Mahigan, Cynthia L. McCurtain, and Ardis Niemann Noonan. Thank you, Gareth Esersky, for your elegant editing, and Bonnie Barland, for your beautiful format and book cover design. Much love and appreciation to my family and friends, who continue to support me through my many stages of growth. A special note to Marsh, my heartmate and my soul mate: thank you for your undying love; I love you. And I thank the teachings of Reform Judaism and psychosynthesis for the spiritual foundation that continues to guide me in my growing relationship with God.

Hope is the thing with feathers
That perches in the soul
And sings the tune without the words
And never stops at all.
—Emily Dickinson

And to every heartmate who will use this book, I want you to know I truly believe in the possibility of recovery. I hope your healing will be complete.

Rhoda F. Levin
Minneapolis, Minnesota
January, 1995

The Heartmates® Meditation Journal

Part I: Early Recovery...

"Help, I Don't Get It!"

I remember telling the staff, even the doctors. He can't come home yet: he's not ready, I'm not ready. I remember thinking: how am I going to know if he's all right? Am I going to wake up and find out he's quit breathing? Would [he] get back every time he went for his walk?

– Mitzie C., Heartmate
Portrait of the Heartmate Videoseries

In the early weeks after a cardiac crisis we sound like classic cases of shock — and we have been shocked! Whether we are quiet or outgoing, organized or scattered, enthusiastic or detached, our nearest, though not dearest, companion is anxiety.

Some of us feel it in our bodies: we're stiff or we ache; we hold our jaws tight and almost wrap our shoulders around our heads for protection; we may be dizzy or shaky or nauseated.

Our feelings toss us like we're riding bucking broncos: we're hopeful then depressed; grateful then scared; relieved then sad; helpless then angry; even guilty.

Our minds feel thick and slow, or empty or scrambled. It's difficult to concentrate, remember, or focus.

Recognizing our shock, we need to take small steps to take care of ourselves: Eat regularly and well; good nutrition is a must for your recovery. Nap and rest frequently; make up for disrupted sleep. Walk daily; exercise is essential to maintain health. Take time to do something you like to do by yourself.

Affirmation:
I will be gentle and kind to myself today.

Related topics to think/write about:
List ways I can take care of myself each day
Write my self-care activities into my daily schedule/calendar

Qualities to meditate on: Calm. Quiet. Simplicity.

Date

This is the _____ week of my recovery.

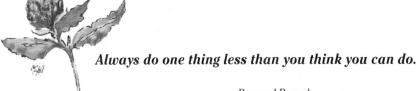

Always do one thing less than you think you can do.

– Bernard Baruch

The idea is to stop "doing" and to assess what's needed ... then use your energy for what really matters. If you just "go, go, go" because that's what you're used to, or you think keeping busy will make this nightmare go away, you're fooling yourself.

Having your partner home from the hospital, no matter how well he's recovering, is exhausting as well as exhilarating. As a heartmate, you need permission to let go of the old routine to take care of yourself and your recovering partner.

Dishes will wait, and laundry too. If you're too uncomfortable leaving things undone, ask someone to help. Conserving energy for what's important is the key to making your way through the early days of recovery when so much is new and uncertain. The idea of reorganizing your daily routine to accommodate a recovering partner is fatiguing too.

As much as you can, incorporate what you know and do automatically. Use it as a base from which you can plan necessary change.

Affirmation:
I will use my energy today on what is truly important.

Related topics to think/write about:
List what I need to do daily during these first weeks of recovery for myself and my partner. Make another list: things that can wait
Plan ways to replenish my energy

Qualities to meditate on: Order. Rest. Surrender.

Date

This is the _____ week of my recovery.

I was scared and I was tired and...and I didn't talk to anyone who told me I should be.

– Ethelyn C.
Portrait of the Heartmate

Heartmates, like healthcare professionals, focus all their attention on the heart patient. We are deeply concerned for the welfare of our loved one whose life is threatened. Add sitting all day at the hospital, awaiting word from the doctor, being unaccustomed to the hospital's rules and regulations, trying to understand a strange technical language, being isolated from our familiar daily routines, and it's no wonder heartmates are tired and anxious.

It is especially important that heartmates take good care of themselves. Acknowledged or not, we too are in a crisis, from which we will need to heal and recover. Beyond healing ourselves and maintaining our health, we want to provide support for our mate's recovery too.

The old Buddhist wisdom, "Eat when you're hungry, drink when you're thirsty, sleep when you're tired" fits what heartmates need to hear. Contemporary wisdom would add, "Get regular exercise, and ask others for support as you need it."

Affirmation:
I accept the need to take care of myself.

Related topics to think/write about:
What kind of care do I need: my body, my feelings, my mind, my spirit?
Balancing my needs, my partner's needs, my family's needs

Qualities to meditate on: Balance. Energy. Renewal.

9

Date _____

This is the _____ week of my recovery:

They were very good at the hospital with the edu-cation, the material they sent home with me, the meal plans, but then I had to execute it. I felt like I was a slave in the kitchen; the meal planning took so much time, there were so many changes, I tried so hard to make meals to please him.

— Gretchen M.
Portrait of the Heartmate

Feeling capable after years of meal planning and cooking, I was especially frightened to feel insecure and incompetent in the kitchen. Diet seemed to have life and death implications.

I thought I had to start over completely, learn to cook in a whole new way. If I didn't throw away everything in my freezer and count every mg. of salt and cholesterol, I believed Marsh would keel over and die.

I was so anxious I tried to change everything all at once. I wish I had been guided with words like "gradual" and "moderate."

If you and your mate can talk about and plan dietary changes together, you can avoid becoming a nag, a punishing parent, or a culinary cop. Total deprivation of favorite foods will almost always backfire — a little planned "cheating" can go a long way!

Remember:

Lasting change is accomplished by building habits...

Habits are formed over time and with practice...

Take small enough steps to succeed...

Share intermediate victories...

Plan special treats to celebrate success...

Affirmation:
I can change, a little bit every day.

Related topics to think/write about:
Make a priority list of lifestyle habits that I want to change

Make a plan: break down my first priority into moderate, "do-able" steps

Qualities to meditate on: Celebration. Creativity. Patience.

13

Date _____

This is the _____ week of my recovery.

If you're like most cardiac spouses, you probably have a slew of unspoken, unaddressed, and un-answered questions. They may torment you when you are trying to sleep or pop up at odd times, catching you unaware. You may find them circling around and around in your head without any landing gear.

— Rhoda Levin, Chapter 4 "Keeping Your Head on Straight"
Heartmates® A Guide for the Spouse & Family

Studies indicate that the cardiac spouse's greatest need is for information. As heartmates we have questions and we want answers. But it isn't that simple.

Medicine doesn't have all the answers, especially the specific ones. There are too many variables that must be taken into account for you to get a specific answer about your mate's progress and prognosis.

Unaware of this, you may think, "If I know, I'll feel less anxious." But when you get a vague answer, your anxiety increases.

Heartmates are recovering from a crisis, and we're grieving. Grief plays havoc with feelings; few of us realize that our minds are also affected. Grievers have reduced ability to remember, concentrate, focus, organize ideas, make decisions.

I remember those early cardiac weeks; a voracious reader since first grade, I couldn't concentrate long enough to read a popular magazine. Worse, I had little patience or humor about my limits.

Affirmation:
I am entitled to have questions and answers.

Related topics to think/write about:
Write my list of questions (Check off when answered; add to the list as you have more; think about who can best answer each)

Qualities to meditate on:
Appreciation. Comprehension. Humor.

Date _____

This is the _____ week of my recovery.

Because people aren't mind readers, and they aren't gonna know you're feeling lousy if you don't tell them....

– Sharon A.
Portrait of the Heartmate

As difficult as you may find it to ask for support, it is selfish not to. Most heartmates are fortunate to have family and friends who sincerely want to be supportive. They are kind and goodhearted, even if they don't understand exactly what you are experiencing. If you turn them away you deprive them of the blessing of doing a good deed for you. If you don't tell them what you need, they're left in limbo, wanting to help but not knowing how to please or help you.

You may have an inner voice that tells you that you "should" handle the situation yourself, you "shouldn't" be a bother to anyone, others have it worse, or you're not deserving. Say "no" to that voice. It's wrong!

What's right is that the cardiac crisis is an extraordinary time in your life, your mate's life, and your family's life. The manners, courtesy, and protocol you've observed in ordinary situations just doesn't apply.

Give others the opportunity to help you, and receive that support as gracefully as you can.

Affirmation:
I deserve support and will ask for it.

Related topics to think/write about:
List things I need from others (from a hug to a hot-dish, camaraderie to a casserole)
My feelings about giving and receiving to and from others

Qualities to meditate on: Generosity. Grace. Openness.

The Heartmates® Meditation Journal

Date

This is the   week of my recovery.

> *How would I support us? Where would we live? Who would shovel the snow? ...once I went through that, I was able to feel inside that, 'Gee, I hope to G-d this doesn't happen — I would be very sad, but I would make it.'*
>
> — Robin L.
> *Portrait of the Heartmate*

When Marsh had his first heart attack, our children were just 13 and 11. Prior to that event I had always been confident that with our talents, hard work, and good luck we would always have enough money to meet our needs.

But the heart attack shook my confidence about everything. A big part of my fear, fueled by a lack of information, was concern about our financial security. What would happen to our family if he were disabled, if he died? Would we have to sell our home? How would I provide the kids with the education we wanted for them? Some days the terror was so bad, the question racing through my head was, "How would we eat?"

One day I stealthily called the Social Security office to find out what our kids would get if Marsh were disabled or died. I was flooded with relief momentarily, and that was followed by powerful guilt feelings. Just saying the words, disabled and dead, might magically cause exactly what I so feared.

Strengthening yourself with information to help you plan for any contingency is a good thing to do! Imagining a variety of situations and how you would cope in each circumstance is a powerful way to ready yourself for your changed life which hereafter will include heart disease.

Affirmation:
I am strong; I will survive and thrive.

Related topics to think/write about:
Questions I have about my internal resources and my external circumstances
My feelings about what I don't know enough about (finances, work, etc.)

Qualities to meditate on:
Goodwill. Imagination. Positiveness.

Date _____

This is the _____ week of my recovery.

_____

_____

_____

_____

_____

_____

_____

_____

_____

_____

_____

_____

_____

_____

_____

_____

_____

_____

_____

_____

_____

_____

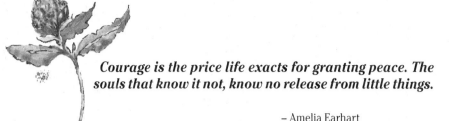

Courage is the price life exacts for granting peace. The souls that know it not, know no release from little things.

– Amelia Earhart

Courage is the most obvious quality in the heartmates I have met all around the world. From the very first moments of a cardiac crisis, we summon our courage:

To face the information we hear, about how ill our partner is, and what we can expect ...

To visit our loved one, and maintain our hope ...

To hold our families intact as each member receives the news and joins those waiting in the hospital or at home ...

To acknowledge our feelings — our fear and pain — through our tears and our words ...

Facing reality, whether there's good or disappointing news, requires courage. But peace will continue to elude us if we resist reality.

Affirmation:
I have many strengths, including the ability to face reality.

Related topics to think/write about:
What is my style, my personal obstacle, of resisting reality?
How can I replenish my spirit which has been severely tested by this crisis?

Qualities to meditate on: Courage. Perseverance. Reality.

Date _____

This is the _____ week of my recovery.

_____
_____
_____
_____
_____
_____
_____
_____
_____
_____
_____
_____
_____
_____
_____
_____
_____
_____
_____
_____
_____
_____

Some days you feel great; other days you can't seem to pull yourself out of the doldrums. Your spouse has returned to work and your family is "back to normal." But what was normal before bears little or no resemblance to life as you know it today.

– Rhoda Levin, Chapter 3 "At the Heart of the Matter"
Heartmates® A Guide for the Spouse & Family

Immediate recovery is over and, from the outside, everything looks stable, except that from the inside everything feels different.

My thoughts were: Why do I feel depressed when he's recovering so well? Is there something wrong with me? Now that everyone is so positive and hopeful, why do I feel I can barely make it through the day? Where is my usual energy and enthusiasm for life? Will I ever feel like me again?

The answers are simple, but not easy to accept: You are in the midst of adapting to a new reality, one that includes your partner's heart disease and all that implies.

Depression is a normal, natural reaction to the changes heartmates experience. Loss and gain are the two components of change. Change demands reaction. Losses demand a physical, emotional, mental, and spiritual response. There are no short cuts — we must experience grief to get through it. That's what healing and recovery are all about!

Affirmation:
> I am capable of dealing with my grief.

Related topics to think/write about:
> Things that are different in my life
> List nourishing activities for my body, feelings, mind, and soul (make this list from your bubble bath!)

Qualities to meditate on: Clarity. Flexibility. Will.

Date

This is the _____ week of my recovery.

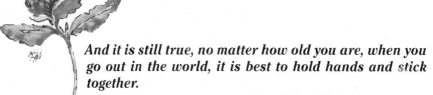

And it is still true, no matter how old you are, when you go out in the world, it is best to hold hands and stick together.

– Robert Fulghum

This may be kindergarten wisdom, but it's information cardiac couples need. Both the heart patient and the heartmate have been through a difficult crisis, only a small part of it physical.

Early separations in a cardiac crisis can spread to include other aspects of being together. From the first night, when the heartmate returns to a dark house and a cold bed, after leaving her partner in the bright, all-night light of the hospital, everything is different. One of you is sick, the other well!

Being fearful, sad, or angry about your mate's situation may be difficult to talk about
with him. But both of you have experienced the surprise, the shock, and the body's betrayal, and both of you face the uncertainty of the future. Suffering the experience in isolation only adds to its difficulty.

So hold hands. Talk to each other about your reactions and realizations. You can face reality better together than alone. The reward for overcoming isolation is intimacy.

Affirmation:
    I do not stand alone; I am brave enough to reach out.

Related topics to think/write about:
    How have the rules and roles shifted since my mate's illness?
    How can I balance my need for privacy and my need to share?

Qualities to meditate on:
    Communication. Intimacy. Partnership. Trust.

Date _____

This is the _____ week of my recovery.

_____
_____
_____
_____
_____
_____
_____
_____
_____
_____
_____
_____
_____
_____
_____
_____
_____
_____
_____
_____
_____
_____
_____
_____
_____

It was very important to explain to [daughter] that it wasn't her [fault], and then let her share my feelings about being sad about P. [so I didn't have] to put on a front, that everything was okay when it wasn't.

– Robin L.
Portrait of the Heartmate

It is common for children of all ages to assume magically that any family tragedy is their fault. "If I hadn't argued with him the night before; if I hadn't disobeyed him; if I hadn't...."

We need to tell our children clearly and remind them often that their parent's heart disease is not their fault! Clarify that heart disease takes a long time to develop. Verbalizing feelings is not a risk factor for a heart attack.

It is impossible to protect your children from reality. If you mask your anxiety and do not talk about Dad's illness, or you treat the situation with a pretense of lightness or detachment, it won't work. Kids instinctively read energy and easily sense when you're not being straight with them.

They also extrapolate from your behavior. If it isn't okay for Mom to express feelings about this, it must mean they shouldn't express or even feel their feelings. If no one lets anyone else know how they feel, there is little opportunity for family members to support each other in this family crisis.

It's normal for everyone in the family to have a whole range of feelings in this situation.

Affirmation:
I protect my children best with my caring and my honesty.

Related topics to think/write about:
What are my children's needs in this situation? Which needs can I support?
Who/where are others who can meet the needs I can't?

Qualities to meditate on:
Community. Harmlessness. Integrity.

Date _____

This is the _____ week of my recovery.

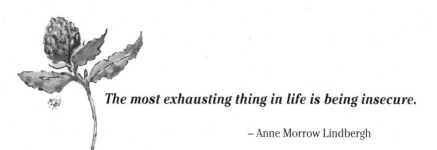

The most exhausting thing in life is being insecure.

– Anne Morrow Lindbergh

Heart disease is not something you or your mate chose — nor is its progress something you or your doctors can predict.

One of the hardest things for me about Marsh's heart disease was that I had to face uncertainty. I like to be able to plan; I feel good when I'm in control. In the early days of recovery, I felt insecure and exhausted. And I kept trying to control and manage whatever and whomever I could.

I remembered Mel Brooks' joke about the existence of God in his *2000 and Thirteen-Year-Old Man* album: Phil, worshipped leader of the tribe, was hit by lightning. In awe, one caveman told another, "There's something bigger than Phil!"

For me, heart disease was a lesson about my relationship to that "something bigger than Phil." Some call that God: others a Higher Power, the Maker, or the Force. Eventually I got the message. Both Marsh and I are vulnerable to a future beyond my planning and my control. We are mortal.

Rest and the Serenity Prayer can help while you await deeper understanding and wisdom.

> God, grant me the Serenity
> To accept the things I cannot change,
> The Courage to change the things I can,
> And the Wisdom to know the difference.

Affirmation:
I accept the reality of uncertainty, the permanence of change.

Related topics to think/write about:
Make a list of those things I can and can't control
Reactions when I repeat the Serenity Prayer
How is it advantageous to know my mate and I are mortal?

Qualities to meditate on: Peace. Serenity. Wisdom.

Date

This is the   week of my recovery.

How could this be happening to us? We're too young for this; our family's too young for this...just angry for how the chips fell the way they did. The other part of me [at] the other extreme...I'm so grateful that he is here.

– Ethelyn C.
Portrait of the Heartmate

Our early, natural reactions to the cardiac crisis protect us until the reality can sink in. First, there is a kind of numbness, shock, and denial, and that desperate wish that we'd wake up and this nightmare would be over. Heartmates describe the discomfort as just going through the motions, not really living their lives. They feel unreal, like their feet aren't connecting them to the earth; their body parts feel unfamiliar or disconnected.

As the days and first weeks pass your frozen state begins to melt. The shock is replaced with a confusing combination of feelings: anger and gratitude; cheerful optimism and deep disappointment; anxiety and serenity; all interwoven. How can you simultaneously feel so furious and grateful, so relieved and so sad, so fearful and yet peaceful because it is beyond your control?

The roller coaster of feelings and the confusion are normal aspects of the early healing process. As much as you can, recognize the feelings and acknowledge that there is nothing wrong with you. You are not crazy!

Affirmation:
My feelings are a normal response to the crisis I am in.

Related topics to think/write about:
Without being concerned with organization, write short entries describing your feelings each time you journal this week.

Qualities to meditate on: Acceptance. Faith. Optimism.

49

Date
_____

This is the   week of my recovery.

I went to a lady for a massage one day. I was struck by what a gentle, loving thing that was. I was so familiar with the feeling of being deprived of somebody's touch....

– Mary C.
Portrait of the Heartmate

There is an historic World War II study from a London orphanage indicating that babies who weren't touched or caressed enough did not thrive. Although we're not babies, the implications for all humans, heartmates included, seems clear. In order for us and for our mates to heal fully, we need to be touched on a regular basis in positive, appreciative ways.

The cardiac crisis which separated us may have erroneously taught us that the patient is too fragile to touch, too ill to touch us. We may even believe that to arouse our mates sexually would be dangerous. No wonder we shy away from touching.

It's important to honor this basic human need. Begin to ask for the touching you need to receive and to give: the touch that says, "I love you," "I'm delighted to be sharing today with you," "I'm glad you survived."

Touching nourishes the spirit and the body of the heartmate. Find a loving massage therapist. Exchange back rubs with your mate. Make a daily practice of holding hands and cuddling, and spooning every night!

Affirmation:
I deserve to be touched in a loving, respectful way.

Related topics to think/write about:
List obstacles to touching and being touched
How I feel about and what it means to me to be touched lovingly

Qualities to meditate on: Celebration. Generosity. Love.

The Heartmates® Meditation Journal

Date
This is the   week of my recovery.

The way we operate is that we use our roles to define ourselves; when parts of our roles are taken away from us, we feel like we're nobody. Men particularly have a problem with that. If masculine functions are taken away they feel diminished....

– David Keith, M.D.
Portrait of the Heartmate

Women feel diminished too when their functions at work and at home are usurped as a result of illness.

Women patients tell me how frustrated they are when their husbands assume housekeeping roles. Home is a long-standing venue of power for women. "How can he botch the laundry, forget items when grocery shopping? Can't he clean right (i.e. my way)? What's my value without my power to decide what we eat, who's invited to the house, how the house looks? Under the anger may lurk the fear of losing self along with the role of housekeeper. Women aren't practiced at being taken care of, so they're awkward receivers.

Heartmates' role changes differ, but the feelings are similar. Much as I loved him, it was difficult to have Marsh around for weeks. I'd go into the kitchen, and there he was — with nothing to do. I'd want to use the bathroom to get ready for work, and there he'd be. Of course, his routine was as new as mine, but I felt confused. I was grateful for his survival and recovery, and simultaneously annoyed having him under foot and in my way.

Role reversals, temporary or permanent, are part of the newness of being a cardiac couple. When change threatens your daily routine, your ability to function, your sense of worth, your very identity, understanding that all change is stressful may help you to cope with it better. Take a deep breath; count to ten. Observe what is happening; acknowledge that change is your reality. Talk about it with your partner. Look for any humor in the situation to shift your perspective.

Affirmation:
I am a worthwhile human being who can accommodate change.

Related topics to think/write about:
What has changed in my life and how I feel about those changes
What has changed in my mate's life as a result of heart disease

Qualities to meditate on: Humor. Power. Resilience.

Date

This is the   week of my recovery.

...he seemed so dependent, and I had never ever seen him that way before. It terrified me.

– Ellen Sue S., Cardiackid
Portrait of the Heartmate

Children's anxiety about the potential loss of a parent is a powerful catalyst for action. Commonly, kids switch roles and become parents to the parent who is ill. Magical thinking suggests: "If I do for Dad or Mom, nothing bad can happen to them."

A year after Mom's heart attack, a 40-year-old cardiackid was still visiting every evening after work — her own social/recreational life totally sacrificed. A 28-year-old cardiackid and her husband, who had a weekly bridge game with her folks, had to stop coming. She couldn't stand watching her dad eat chips or peanuts and her mother fail to control his diet.

The protectors simultaneously express their caring and reduce their own anxiety. The parent, on the other hand, feels watched, nagged, insulted, and condescended to by his overprotective children.

Focusing on your kids isn't meant to increase your burden. It will help you understand how they are experiencing being part of a cardiac family. You can't and shouldn't try to fix everything while you are working on your own recovery, supporting your mate's rehabilitation, and maintaining the family. You are not a bad person simply because you can't do everything!

As you recognize that your kids are in crisis too, you need to seek support for them in the larger community. Ask for and accept help from relatives, friends, coaches, teachers, and clergy, knowing you can't do it all.

Affirmation:
I will express my love by stepping back and letting go.

Related topics to think/write about:
Ways that I am overprotective of my mate and my children

How I can be more comfortable without taking responsibility for everything

Qualities to meditate on:
Cooperation. Dedication. Responsibility.

Date

This is the   week of my recovery.

You gain strength, courage, and confidence by every experience in which you really stop to look fear in the face.

– Eleanor Roosevelt

Women, who before the cardiac crisis may have believed they were of the "weaker sex," find themselves faced with two of humanity's deepest fears: fear of being abandoned, and fear for their own survival.

In confronting those fears, women find that they possess great strengths and powerful qualities: resilience; perseverance; patience; flexibility; clarity; compassion, and forgiveness. Few find themselves weak; most find themselves surprised by their strengths.

Isn't it ironic that we must suffer pain and bear crisis to find and grow our powers?

May we use these newly-found or newly-acknowledged powers for our own healing and well-being, and for our families and others as well.

Affirmation:
I am strong enough to face my fears.

Related topics to think/write about:
My specific fears: what are they, how realistic are they, what can I realistically do so they don't control my life?

My new-found strengths and how I can use them in my life

Qualities to meditate on:
Liberation. Power. Understanding.

Date

This is the   week of my recovery.

And suddenly you stop and have time to think about the future, about where your life is going, and what changes are going to happen because of the heart [disease]. For me it was a sudden dip into depression.

– Sharon A.
Portrait of the Heartmate

Once your early shock and numbness wear off, it is natural and normal to experience depression. Right about this time, your mind may get busy trying to figure out what your new life will be like.

When depression and an innovative mind get together, results can be disastrous. The combination of sadness, disappointment, and catastrophic expectations about heart disease may suggest to you a permanent future that is in reality only temporary or totally inaccurate, even at this early period of recovery.

You are aware now, as never before, of how uncertain and fragile life is. Facing so much reality can be frightening, but crisis also provides opportunity.

Crisis opens people. This can be an important new beginning: a re-evaluation period of your life, its meaning, your values and priorities.

As you turn inward for faith and strength, remember also to reach out for support from those in your community who can honor your healing.

Affirmation:
I am resilient; I can adapt to a life of uncertainty.

Related topics to think/write about:
Write down the scary things my mind says are my future
Write about what makes me sad, disappointed, depressed, powerless

Qualities to meditate on: Determination. Openness. Truth.

The Heartmates® Meditation Journal

Date _____

This is the _____ week of my recovery.

...he went through times when he was suffering with depression, having angry feelings and I guess I thought it was my job to try to control those feelings, and to make him happy, cheer him up, try to make him see the positive side of life. I've come to realize that if he wants to feel those feelings, it's all right.

– Mary C.
Portrait of the Heartmate

Everything I read drove home the point that a positive attitude was the necessary ingredient for full recovery. I thought it was my responsibility to control Marsh's feelings, and I believed I had the power to do so successfully.

But instead of Marsh expressing more positive attitudes, instead of us getting closer, instead of me feeling loved and appreciated for my efforts, I was stonewalled. The harder I worked to "make" him feel grateful and positive about his recovery, the more silent and withdrawn Marsh became.

You can't feel someone else's feelings any more than you can be in his skin and take away his physical pain or spiritual anguish. You can pray for him.

But you can recognize what *you* feel when he feels angry or depressed. You can talk to yourself in a positive way. You can take charge of how you respond and react to your feelings. You have choices about how, if, and when you express or don't express your feelings.

Affirmation:
I am responsible for my own feelings, and no one else's.

Related topics to think/write about:
Differentiate my feelings from my mate's by making an annotated list describing my feelings about: heart disease, my mate's actions and attitudes, the changes in my life, my own recovery

Qualities to meditate on:
Compassion. Detachment. Harmlessness.

Date

This is the   week of my recovery.

Something that has worked well for many cardiac couples is making a pact to share one thing each day that you appreciate about yourselves. In that way a realistic and ongoing assessment of your situation can continue. You will have something worthwhile to talk about with each other every day.

– Rhoda Levin, Chapter 2 "On the Road to Recovery"
Heartmates® A Guide for the Spouse & Family

An important part of your healing involves "re-pair"ing the heartmate connection.

Physically separated at the advent of the crisis, each of you had different experiences. With no privacy in the hospital and unsure of your new roles, your communication became stilted. You probably felt like strangers even if you'd been together for fifty years.

Healing is about getting reacquainted, rebuilding the trust that you are partners. Begin to let each other in; share what happened to you, how you felt, what it meant. These are the tiny but significant steps vital to becoming partners again, and dropping the roles of patient and well spouse.

Set aside a short time each day just to talk: Plan, share thoughts, say what you want and need, appreciate yourself and each other, celebrate progress in recovery and acknowledge the preciousness of life today.

Affirmation:
    I will do my part for our partnership.

Related topics to think/write about:
    Obstacles that make it difficult to trust the partnership
    Things I want to share with my mate

Qualities to meditate on: Friendship. Trust. Will.

Date

This is the   week of my recovery.

The Heartmates® Meditation Journal

Part II: Mid-Recovery...

"...The Long Haul!"

I was definitely D's nurse for months after the heart attack, to the point where he would turn to me and say, 'Well, do you think I should eat that? Do you think this is too much salt? This would be okay, wouldn't it?' At every turn I was losing my identity as his lover and his wife.

– Lavonne G.
Portrait of the Heartmate

Healing the couple relationship is a part of your task together after acute recovery is accomplished.

No relationship is perfectly equal, or perfectly perfect. The ease with which you assimilated the caretaking habits of the well spouse were quickly interwoven with your mate's assumption of the role of the patient. Wanting to reclaim your role of wife and lover is natural. You both may still be afraid and unaware of your new roles of being sick or well.

To work on re-connecting as mates, explore these activities:

Talk with your mate about shifting and equalizing responsibility for lifestyle changes important for continued recovery.

Set aside time to talk about household and family responsibilities you took on when he became ill that the two of you can now share.

Plan times to be separate, for each of you to pursue your individual interests.

Make dates regularly to be physically affectionate with each other.

Affirmation: I will use my power to return my mate's power to him as he is capable of assuming it.

Related topics to think/write about:
   Assess areas of our lives where I am over-responsible, under-responsible
   Ways I can reinvigorate our partner relationship

Qualities to meditate on:
   Cooperation. Creativity. Responsibility.

Date

This is the _____ week of my recovery.

Cardiac spouses share the unique experience of being in a crisis precipitated by someone else's illness. Your mate is in crisis too, but the experience is not the same. You suddenly find yourself in a situation entirely beyond your control that threatens your security and will change your future.

– Rhoda Levin, Chapter 1 "At the Hospital"
Heartmates® A Guide for the Spouse & Family

I've always been most comfortable when I think I'm in control of a situation. As a child I learned to hide my insecure feelings behind a mask of exuberant confidence. I specialized in the things at which I excelled, and rarely tested myself with goals beyond my control. As an adult, my imperiled feelings buried, I masqueraded as a woman without fear. I shone, sometimes brilliantly, and succeeded at almost everything I did.

My automatic response to my mate's heart disease was to act as I always had. Only this time it didn't work! His heart disease was beyond my control and my confidence. I drained my energy cheer leading for him, myself, family and friends. And my efforts failed to stop what was happening. I was subject to outside forces that were changing my whole life, and I couldn't predict what was coming.

Perhaps my biggest lesson from Marsh's heart disease was learning to accept human limitation — my own and his.

Affirmation:
I am human and in God's hands (or) I am being held by the universe.

Related topics to think/write about:
Ways that I can cooperate with what is happening
Recognizing what I can and can't control

Qualities to meditate on: Letting go. Surrender. Trust.

The Heartmates® Meditation Journal

Date _____

This is the _____ *week of my recovery.*

_____
_____
_____
_____
_____
_____
_____
_____
_____
_____
_____
_____
_____
_____
_____
_____
_____
_____
_____
_____
_____
_____

Physicians have always believed in the useful-
ness and, indeed, the necessity of attitudes as
aids in the healing process....Whether this ingre-
dient goes by the name of the patient's own hope-
fulness or determination or faith or confidence or will
to live ...is not as important as the fact that the positive
emotions and attitudes are potent factors in recovery.

– Norman Cousins
The Healing Heart

Your recovery and your partner's can be affected by your optimism or pessimism. Learning to think positively increases your control over your perception of your present situation and points to methods which can positively affect your future. It is something you can train yourself to do, and the rewards are great!

To avoid pessimistic thinking, verify the accuracy of what you tell yourself. Ask yourself, "What is the evidence for my belief about the meaning of what has happened?"

To shift your focus from the most negative causes, look for alternatives that are changeable, specific, and non-personal. Ask yourself, "What else may have contributed to what has happened?"

If your negative belief is correct, ask yourself, "Even if my negative belief is correct, have I exaggerated its implications? What does it really imply?"

It is useless to dwell on a negative belief. Ask yourself, "Is my belief destructive?" "Is this situation changeable?" "How can I change it?" You will achieve a sense of progress by focusing on solutions and resolutions.

Affirmation:
I will learn to think optimistically.

Related topics to think/write about:
Choose a specific and immediate situation in your life. Using the guide to optimistic thinking above, analyze your thinking and plan the changes you can make.

Qualities to meditate on: Control. Enthusiasm. Optimism.

Date _____

This is the _____ week of my recovery.

*We were planning a family train trip to Chicago.
I was upstairs getting packed and D. was down-
stairs making sandwiches and all of a sudden,
he said, 'I'm out of breath.' I came running down
the stairs, my heart pounding, my knees shaking. I
came into the kitchen. He said, 'What am I going to do?
I'm out of bread.' That tells a lot about how I was those
days!*

– Lavonne G.
Portrait of the Heartmate

When the routines we count on for security are broken by the unexpected, or when we mistake something benign for what we fear most, we
respond instantaneously with fear.

The category of symptoms described for "vicarious victims of
trauma" fits heartmates to a T. Your experience with the urgency of a cardiac crisis has made you vulnerable. Your fear doesn't know the difference
between burnt toast and the house going up in flames. So it is nearly impossible for you to discern a harmless cough from one that sounds like your
mate is struggling for his last breath.

At times like this, you need to slow down, take a few deep breaths,
and ask yourself, "What is really happening here?" Other ways to combat
fear include writing about it or talking about it with your mate or a friend.

Affirmation:
    I can master my fear by recognizing it and
assessing real danger.

Related topics to think/write about:
    Make a list of my questions, and where I can get
answers
    Think/write about my strengths — that have
gotten me through the crises of my life

Qualities to meditate on: Calm. Courage. Humor.

Date _____

This is the _____ week of my recovery.

_____
_____
_____
_____
_____
_____
_____
_____
_____
_____
_____
_____
_____
_____
_____
_____
_____
_____
_____
_____
_____
_____
_____
_____
_____
_____
_____

I was being the mother hen with P. and being very intrusive in his life — 'Now don't do this, don't do that' and 'Do you think you should really do this?' Finally he just told me loud and clear that this wasn't going to be an acceptable lifestyle....I'm slowly finding ways to give up being overprotective and accept his responsibility for his own health and life.

– Robin L.
Portrait of the Heartmate

Many cardiac couples are not as verbal as P. and his "mother hen," but may struggle with comparable feelings. When I was writing *Heartmates®*, Marsh's way was to remind me that if I treated him like he was an invalid, it invalidated him. That forced me to stop and think! I didn't want to invalidate him, but there were situations when I rushed in — to carry something I thought was too heavy for him, or to urge him to "do less" because of my fear.

Whether or not you are aware that you have taken on more responsibility since your mate's illness, these new patterns form the foundation of your post-cardiac relationship. Habits establish themselves quickly. Temporary emergency measures quickly crystallize into a permanent change in the division of labor.

Identifying and understanding changes in responsibility indicate that you are recovering.

Affirmation:
I can differentiate between being responsible and being over-responsible.

Related topics to think/write about:
Ways I am more and less dependent on my mate now
Ways my mate is more and less dependent on me now
My feelings about my responsibilities since the cardiac event

Qualities to meditate on: Freedom. Goodwill. Responsibility.

Date _____

This is the _____ week of my recovery.

_____

_____

_____

_____

_____

_____

_____

_____

_____

_____

_____

_____

_____

_____

_____

_____

_____

_____

_____

_____

_____

_____

_____

We've found that the longer we're together and the closer we are, that there are lots of ways of making love and loving each other without actually having intercourse....and both of us feel very satisfied and very, very close.

– Dorothy A.
Portrait of the Heartmate

While day-to-day aging tends to blur issues, a chronic illness focuses us clearly. Most heart patients are physically capable of returning to their normal sexual practices within six weeks of a cardiac event.

But impotence, whether caused by medications, depression, or fear, is a real problem for many cardiac couples. A man's impotence triggers his fears of rejection, depriving his partner, or feeling unloved. Heartmates may struggle too with the fear that intercourse is too dangerous. It's hard to "make love" when you have unvoiced feelings of fear, anger, and resentment.

Your sexual needs may be in flux along with other changing values and priorities. This may be the single most difficult subject to talk about with healthcare professionals, friends, even with your partner. If the long-term physical result of the illness is a lost or reduced sexuality, you need to mourn that loss.

Communication is the key to returning to loving physical intimacy. Express and forgive feelings that form an emotional barrier. Ask for what you want; acknowledge your need for his physical caress to become partners again. Experiment to find satisfying ways to be intimate that fit your specific circumstances.

Affirmation:
I am loving and lovable.

Related topics to think/write about:
Things I want to discuss with my partner
Ways we can celebrate our partnership

Qualities to meditate on:
Friendship. Love. Tenderness. Trust.

The Heartmates® Meditation Journal

Date

This is the   week of my recovery:

The decision to resume your own activities is an individual matter. It's very important to be involved in something besides caring for your recovering mate. Time for yourself... is an important part of this transition. Maintaining interests in other areas of your life is essential for your own needs and to restore a realistic balance to your relationship.

– Rhoda Levin, Chapter 2 "On the Road To Recovery"
Heartmates® A Guide for the Spouse & Family

It seems overwhelming to wean yourself from the all-encompassing role of caregiver and reinvest in your own life. It's frightening to be gone for an hour to buy groceries, let alone leaving your recovering partner for the better part of a day or overnight.

Activities that were a normal part of your life before heart disease may now seem unimportant or frivolous to you. Social engagements may take too much energy, energy you just don't have available. A fascinating book requires too much effort, and you have neither the concentration nor the interest.

Every turn you take is fearful. The old is no longer comforting; the new has its own hazards. You wonder what is wrong — have you gone crazy? Will life ever seem predictable again?

You are normal! You have not gone crazy! It takes many weeks and months to establish a new routine, one that includes heart disease but not to the exclusion of everything else.

Take your time; don't be pressured by others' timetables. Grief is unique to each of us. Let your energy level and interest guide your return to functioning in the larger world.

Affirmation:
I trust my own pace.

Related topics to think/write about:
List things important and unimportant to me now. (You may want to do this every month for some time to recognize your progress)
Make a graduated plan and timetable for returning to outside activities

Qualities to meditate on: Balance. Energy. Reality.

Date

This is the _____ week of my recovery.

Slow down.   There's nothing more precious than now.

– Stephen C. Paul
Inneractions

Must we be in crisis to hear the wisdom in the old adage: "Take time to smell the roses"? Why not walk in the sunlight, hear the birds, appreciate sunrise and sunset?

All we need to do to take in the nurturance available in nature around us is look. It's free and available to us in all its abundance. Rushing through each day, trying to "do it all," we miss what's essential: Being Here. Now.

When we don't like the present or are afraid of what's happening, we try to fix it or avoid it by focusing on the past, yearning for what's lost. Or we concentrate on the future, wishing for something to look forward to; anything but what's happening now.

Coming to terms with a new reality which includes heart disease will be easier if we look for the positive, the precious, and feel grateful for what we do have. In order to have "now," we need only remember a few simple things:

Now is all we really have.
Focus on who and what is available to you now.
Fill yourself full with the abundance in the moment.
Experience gratitude for being alive right now.

Affirmation:
I will give myself the gift of cherishing this moment.

Related topics to think/write about:
What do I find positive and precious in my life?
What and who in my life nurtures me?

Qualities to meditate on:
Acceptance. Appreciation. Positiveness.

Date

This is the   week of my recovery.

You can change the way you cook, and you can adjust to coming home earlier on Saturday night. You can exercise regularly, and you can learn to live with less money, and you will still be you. But the changes that cardiac spouses experience go deeper. They affect the very center of your identity.

– Rhoda Levin, Chapter 2 "On the Road To Recovery"
Heartmates® A Guide for the Spouse & Family

People commonly identify themselves according to their responsibilities, the roles they play in daily life — what they do, not who they are. But the cardiac crisis is an uncommon experience and a powerful invitation to discover a deeper identity.

We tell and retell our story of what's happened, and recall earlier losses, in an attempt to understand the meaning of this cardiac event in our lives. We clarify our values; we hone and refine our priorities.

We peel away our outer layers in search of our core. We find the reality of our own mortality as well as our partner's. In understanding limitation, some of us find or deepen our faith in the immortality of our souls. Others find connection in surrendering to the mystery beyond our mental comprehension.

Your partner's heart disease is a catalyst for your spiritual development as well as his. Spiritual growth is the greatest opportunity of grieving the losses inherent in the cardiac crisis.

Affirmation:
I am more than what I do.

Related topics to think/write about:
Write "my" cardiac story: focus on the changes I recognize in my life
Changes in my values and priorities since heart disease

Qualities to meditate on: Comprehension. Faith. Wonder.

The Heartmates® Meditation Journal

Date _____

This is the _____ week of my recovery.

_____

_____

_____

_____

_____

_____

_____

_____

_____

_____

_____

_____

_____

_____

_____

_____

_____

_____

_____

_____

_____

_____

_____

_____

I went with my daughters to the park. I...watch[ed] them playing; they were so small and such a neat age. I remember ...seeing people riding by on bicycles, whole families — husbands, wives, small children. And suddenly the impact hit me — we may never get to do that again!

– Lavonne G.
Portrait of the Heartmate

Months have passed since your mate's cardiac event, and your new lifestyle is becoming routine. Yet your recovery is slowed because you're still mourning the loss of your "normal" life, life as it was before heart disease. The unexpected often prompts your mourning: a physical activity like family biking, the weekend ritual of your grandkids playing horsy with your mate.

So many heartmates use their energy trying to recreate life as it was before heart disease. But it's not possible: everything is different! Let yourself know and feel what you've lost. Unless you do, you won't be able to construct wholeheartedly "the new normal." Your family's new normal is comparable to other cardiac families' because it includes changes due to heart disease. It's different from other families' because your situation and your family are unique.

Be gentle with yourself as you adapt to the changes. Allow yourself to feel sad, and make space and time for the real sadness in your life. Shed tears if they're there, write about it, tell a friend, and know that, as with all feelings, sadness too shall pass.

Affirmation:
I am strong enough to experience my sadness and my disappointment.

Related topics to think/write about:
The positive and the negative about the changes I am making in my life
My feelings about changes in my family because of heart disease

Qualities to meditate on: Grace. Purification. Release.

Date _____

This is the _____ week of my recovery.

Sometimes the loneliness comes from not having anyone to share pleasure with: a woman ...says that when they went on vacation 'I went with M. and he went with his [disease].'

– Maggie Strong
Mainstay

Whether it is the adventure of a new place, the pleasure of a warm getaway during the cold winter, the relaxation of a weekend fishing and walking in the woods, or the love of a visit with your grandchildren, yours is a lonely dream. Sometimes your mate just won't go. If he does, he seems to have lost his ability to have fun, relax, or be playful.

Safety may be his first priority. He may be afraid to be further than a phone call away from doctor and hospital. His fear may define spending money on "pleasure" as wasteful.

In your loneliness it may feel like you're struggling against a powerful, but invisible mistress. This seductress has taken your mate's attention, your closeness, even your physical intimacy. He is engaged, but not with you. It feels like you've lost your partnership.

You have choices other than continuing to compete with this invisible mistress!

You can talk directly with your mate, bringing the fears lurking in the shadows out into the light. You can risk telling him that you have needs too. Of course his recovery is important, and, although different, so is yours!

You can begin to go places and do things alone. Being by yourself is not being lonely. It's different from the experience of being with someone who isn't with you. You can make plans with friends and find pleasure beyond your heartmate relationship.

Affirmation:
I am entitled to experience the abundance of life.

Related topics to think/write about:
The difference between being alone and being lonely
How comfortable am I with each? How do I handle each in my life?

Qualities to meditate on: Abundance. Adventure. Play.

The Heartmates® Meditation Journal

Date

This is the   week of my recovery.

Now I don't feel anxious that if I'm not there and awake every minute, that he'll die. I used to feel I didn't dare leave to do anything, because then if something happened, I wasn't there to take care of it. And now I know I can't ... I can't keep the inevitable from happening with anybody; none of us can.

– Dorothy A.
Portrait of the Heartmate

The over-responsibility this heartmate conquered is familiar to all of us. I knew her earlier when she was angry, frightened, discouraged, and exhausted. Her serenity makes us wonder: "How did she make the shift, let go, surrender?" "How long will it take me to have the wisdom she possesses?"

I'm reminded of another heartmate, complaining about having to change her cooking style: "I really resented having to cook without salt, not eat beef...but eventually, when you stop fighting things, it gets a lot easier."

There's the key! "When you stop fighting things...." How did she do that?

Over time both heartmates expressed their feelings of fear and rage, sadness and disappointment. Recognizing and expressing feelings, verbally or on paper, always precedes acceptance and integration. Liberated from the stranglehold of those feelings, both heartmates arrived at a new perspective, an appreciation for the preciousness of what they had, individually and with their partners.

Affirmation:
 I will respectfully acknowledge my feelings without judgment.

Related topics to think/write about:
 Write about your strongest feelings, particularly ones you disapprove of
 Think/write about safe and harmless ways to express your feelings

Qualities to meditate on:
 Acceptance. Detachment. Understanding.

The Heartmates® Meditation Journal

Date

This is the _____ *week of my recovery.*

Mourning makes peace with change
Grief does not have to do with despair

– Yakima Indian Nation

In *Fear of Fifty*, Erica Jong argues the right of her friend to grieve: "...everyone wanted her to perk up....But she needed to mourn. Her need was made more painful by the denial of death that pervades our culture. 'Dust yourself off and go on,' said the collective voice of collective wisdom. 'Haven't you been grieving an awfully long time?' ....How they dared to judge another's grief I did not know."

Heartmates everywhere deserve such a forceful supporter and advocate.

Grief will not succumb the instant pressure is brought to bear on it; it will not reduce itself to a 20 second sound byte. It will not be hurried like food rotating in the microwave; it will not yield its lessons or its gifts instantaneously like e-mail spinning around the planet.

Grief takes time, reflection, and experience. Tell your story again and again. Shed tears for your losses. Update your images and accept human limitation, your own and your mate's. Our bodies, feelings, minds, and spirits accommodate the monumental lessons offered by the crisis, then discover and accept what is new — but only over time.

Each person's pace and style is unique; mourning will not be rushed, even when others who love you wish it to be so. Take the time you need. Good grief!

Affirmation:
        I will honor my grief by giving myself the time I need.

Related topics to think/write about:
        My image of who I was, and who my mate was, before the cardiac crisis
        What losses have I mourned, am I mourning, do I have left to mourn?

Qualities to meditate on: Identity. Integrity. Meaning.

Date _____

This is the _____ week of my recovery.

I emphasize finding sources of pleasure. I've had people reject that idea, say 'Are you telling me to have fun at this terrible moment?' But that moment is life....The more you can become unfused and the more outlets and pleasure you can find, the more you have energy and love and emotions to give to the person who is disabled.

– Clara Livsey, M.D.
Mainstay

Rejecting pleasure is often either an attempt to avoid feeling guilty, or concern about how others will see you. How can you think about your own pleasure when your mate is ill? Only a bad and selfish person would take pleasure in such a circumstance!

But let's look logically: does denying yourself pleasure help your mate recover? And since your partner may survive for another thirty years or longer, is it appropriate to avoid pleasure just to protect your image of selflessness?

If you choose to stay wholehartedly in the relationship when your mate becomes ill, it becomes even more important for you to develop your individuality, your wholeness. If you don't, you will become invisible, and actually experience yourself disappearing in his illness.

Starving your heart and soul, denying yourself the beauty and pleasures of life, only feeds your resentment and bitterness. Nourishing your heart and soul normally leads to sharing — and a natural response will be to bring energy and love back into your relationship, in a joyous recycling.

Affirmation:
    I will enjoy this moment.

Related topics to think/write about:
    The activities and things that give me pleasure
    Plans for including small, realistic pleasures in
my day

Qualities to meditate on: Beauty. Joy. Light. Play.

Date _____

This is the _____ week of my recovery.

He still feels more comfortable if I'm the only one who knows whether it's safe for him to eat something or not, 'cause if he doesn't know then he can go ahead and eat it. And I do have difficulty knowing how I can get away from that responsibility. I was perhaps too eager to take on the job at the beginning and now I would like to unload it.

– Gretchen M.
Portrait of the Heartmate

The role of "patient" is emotionally destructive over the long haul, and may even slow your mate's physical recovery. Some people feel safer, more "loved" if they're babied, but they also resent their loss of power. Even when your efforts are motivated by caring and concern, taking on too much responsibility may backfire, trapping you into doing more than you should. Enabling your spouse to remain helpless isn't healthy for either of you or your relationship.

If you try to carry kids once they have learned to walk on their own, they often respond by kicking you. The same letting-go you learned as a parent applies to re-establishing a partner relationship with a mate recovering from a cardiac event.

A combination of rest and responsibility is the best way for your mate to regain strength and confidence. And your recovery depends on shifting the balance of power and responsibility in relation to both of your real strengths and limitations.

Affirmation:
My mate and I are separate: each of us individual and whole.

Related topics to think/write about:
My style of encouraging helplessness and ways I can let go
Think/write about my ideal of sharing responsibility and power in my heartmate relationship

Qualities to meditate on: Liberation. Power. Surrender.

Date _____

This is the _____ week of my recovery.

_____

_____

_____

_____

_____

_____

_____

_____

_____

_____

_____

_____

_____

_____

_____

_____

_____

_____

_____

_____

_____

_____

_____

_____

_____

We all will have illness and illness is a teacher.

– Rabbi Tsvi Blanchard
To Join Heaven and Earth

Rabbi Blanchard notes: "Illness, whether our own or of someone we care for, has a way of focusing our attention on the essential issues by calling into question the conventional beliefs we use to hide from our own vulnerability. Illness punctures our defenses, leaves us wide open and exposed to a welter of emotions; we are prey to our imagination and to our fears; we feel weak and powerless....we find ourselves pondering the seeming imponderables about the meaning of our lives and our relationships. We perceive, however dimly, that we need to be healed; and not just physically, but more profoundly, spiritually as well...."

I felt so alone, so crazy, back in 1981 when Marsh had his first heart attack. There were no resources available to validate my condition or guide my healing. It was by struggling with my personal need that I became committed to creating resources so that future cardiac families would not be left so isolated.

Just a decade later it seems that everyone from rabbis to radicals are aware of the needs of heartmates (anyone whose loved one is ill). If it takes a whole village to raise a child (Old African Proverb), it takes a whole community to heal a family. The first step, recognition, is happening everywhere, hallelujah!

Affirmation:
I will pay attention to what my mate's illness has to teach me.

Related topics to think/write about:
My questions (and new answers) about the meaning of my life and relationships
My ideas about the nature of spiritual healing; what I need now for my own healing

Qualities to meditate on: Meaning. Service. Wisdom.

Date
This is the   week of my recovery:

For there is nothing to guarantee that we will be able to remain long enough or deeply enough in front of the unknown, a psychological state which the traditional paths have always recognized as sacred. In that fleeting state between dreams...[a person] is said to be able to receive the truth, both about nature and his own possible role in the universal order.

– Jacob Needleman
A Sense of the Cosmos

We have lived facing the unknown in a way very specific to heartmates: We didn't know if or how our partner would recover, nor did we know how we would respond to the demands of heart disease minute to minute.

Living with uncertainty is by far the most difficult challenge of the cardiac crisis, and it often requires faith and courage beyond what we believe we possess.

It doesn't feel as if you had a choice about being "in front of the unknown" in relation to your mate's heart disease. But there is a lesson you can take from all your experience: You have not only survived the challenge, but come through the crisis stronger, not weakened by it.

Those qualities strengthened by the cardiac crisis now provide you the ability and skills to confront the unknown in broader context. They are the stepping stones to the sacred, the mystery of life and meaning.

Affirmation:
I commit myself to the spiritual task of opening to the unknown.

Related topics to think/write about:
My thoughts, images, and feelings about not knowing, about uncertainty
My thoughts about the universal order, and my role in it

Qualities to meditate on:
Order. Steadfastness. Universality.

Date _____

This is the _____ week of my recovery.

_____

_____

_____

_____

_____

_____

_____

_____

_____

_____

_____

_____

_____

_____

_____

_____

_____

_____

_____

_____

_____

_____

_____

_____

_____

_____

_____

_____

I am dying inside if I don't take care of myself....
how can I hold on to myself and love her?

– Greg Alch (from a personal story told at
"Finding Our Way" workshop in Minneapolis)

One of the most painful tasks of the well partner is to accept that you are well and live in the well world. This must be balanced with the reality that you love and live with someone whose world is the world of illness.

It does not make your partner well if you deny your wellness, or ignore your own needs. Nor can you bypass your guilt about being well (similar to the guilt expressed by survivors of accidents, fires, wars, or the Holocaust) by avoiding reality, pretending the difference doesn't exist.

Your mate's illness may set you both up to believe that he has all the weakness and you have all the strength. You want to utilize your competence on his behalf, but you also need the freedom to share your limitations: your shrinking patience, your irritation and resentment, your disappointment, your sadness for both him and you. If you express your weakness, it may very well give your partner internal permission to find and express his strengths, his hope, and optimism.

Taking care of yourself, defined differently by every heartmate, is not selfish. It is an absolute necessity in order for you to thrive. Without that foundation, you cannot love or care for your mate as fully.

Affirmation: I will love myself and my mate.

Related topics to think/write about:
What are my strengths? What do I need as I face the reality of my mate's illness?
What do I need to balance internally? And balance between me and my mate?

Qualities to meditate on: Generosity. Harmony. Peace.

Date _____

This is the _____ week of my recovery.

_____
_____
_____
_____
_____
_____
_____
_____
_____
_____
_____
_____
_____
_____
_____
_____
_____
_____
_____
_____
_____
_____
_____
_____
_____
_____
_____

I found myself looking at my life...saying, 'I may be a sole supporter here before long.' I didn't trust him. I didn't trust his health anymore.

– Mary C.
Portrait of the Heartmate

Before his cardiac event, you might have described your spouse as stalwart, rugged, or vigorous even though somewhere in your consciousness you knew he was also human and mortal. It is common to acknowledge strong images and even forget the fragility of life.

But the shock of your mate's heart disease shatters the trust you built over the many years of your relationship. The cardiac event feels like a betrayal. Once you know that his heart, his body, his health, and his life are vulnerable, your image of him as invincible is lost. You may even vow not to get close to him again to avoid the pain of future betrayal.

Can you regain trust? Because trust is based on experience, it can only be rebuilt a little at a time and in keeping with the reality of the present moment.

Define carefully what you can trust as you experience each day. For example, as he continues to recover, you can trust that he will awaken each morning, that his endurance and strength are returning, etc.

Life is ephemeral. To prepare yourself for a variety of possibilities, ask all the questions you have, and seek all the information you need. Plan for all contingencies.

Talk about your experience of trust, both its loss and rediscovery with your mate, or a friend who can understand.

Affirmation:
I will open myself to realistic trust.

Related topics to think/write about:
Things I trust about myself and about my heartmate
My feelings about betrayal and my fear of being abandoned

Qualities to meditate on: Clarity. Faith. Love. Trust.

Date _____

This is the _____ week of my recovery.

I'm angry at his bad genes and I'm angry that he doesn't watch his diet like he should. I have trouble separating out what is his right to do...as an adult, and what is his obligation to me, being married, and what he owe[s] me as a cardiac spouse.

– Yleen J.
Portrait of the Heartmate

Anger is a much criticized emotion, especially when it's women who are expressing it. It's not ladylike, it's unattractive, it turns others off or sends them away.

Anger is usually my first response when something unjust happens. Anger is the energy that leads me to react to the injustice, and permits me to respond rather than feel hopeless in the face of it. Other times my anger is like the superficial layer of a wound, visible and ugly. It covers the hurt that I find difficult to accept, and at those times anger is my defense.

Anger is a normal feeling during the recovery following a cardiac crisis. For heartmates who often feel depressed, lethargic or hopeless, anger can be a blessing. Anger is a hot energy which fires the power to act. You've no choice about whether to feel angry or not. But it is your choice to decide to utilize the energy in a positive, constructive way.

Be as respectful as you can of your anger and the anger of others, even if it doesn't make logical sense to you. If you find yourself angry at the hospital, at God, at your mate's genes, don't dismiss the anger — cull its energy to help you, your mate, and your family with your healing.

Affirmation:
I will use the energy of my anger constructively.

Related topics to think/write about:
Examine my past and present attitudes toward my anger
New ideas for utilizing the energy of my anger

Qualities to meditate on:
Discrimination. Forgiveness. Vitality.

Date _____

This is the _____ week of my recovery.

_____

_____

_____

_____

_____

_____

_____

_____

_____

_____

_____

_____

_____

_____

_____

_____

_____

_____

_____

_____

_____

_____

_____

_____

The Heartmates® Meditation Journal

Part III: Toward Full Recovery...

"I Can See The Light!"

We find that the lesson we learn again and again is that of accepting heroic helplessness.

– Florida Scott-Maxwell
The Measure of My Days

For me, entangled in meaningless activity and distracted by the shiny outside world, the cardiac crisis was a gift, a gift that helped me find myself. I didn't experience the gift early on when I was filled with a sense of responsibility for husband and children, nor while I was terrified and striving to hold everything together all by myself. In those days I was blinded by old visions of heroism, old standards of action, and control, and the illusion of power.

Marsh's heart disease taught me to recognize and accept my helplessness. It was a turning point in my life, and I became a different kind of heroine. I had grown the courage to face what can only be faced alone: the meaning and purpose of my life, the significance of my life, and my death.

Paradoxically, as I confronted those questions alone, a whole community opened. I became more attracted to cooperation and less to worldly competition. More whole within myself, I began to deepen my relationships and connections.

Affirmation:
    I am whole and a part of all life.

Related topics to think/write about:
    The lessons that heart disease has taught me
    Ways my values and priorities have changed
since my mate's heart disease

Qualities to meditate on:
    Cooperation. Harmony. Wholeness.

Date _____

This is the _____ week of my recovery.

When I think about my friends, they think about their parents as permanent people — I think about my parents as temporary!

– Sid L., Cardiackid
Portrait of the Heartmate

Kids must confront the reality that their parents are mortal. A parent with a life-threatening disease teaches children that lesson. Early images of parents usually include superhuman qualities. Heart disease requires kids to rework these images to match reality.

Their needs become apparent as children of every age work through the meaning of this family crisis. Some are eager to talk about it; some never do. Kids' life choices are altered: going away to school or not; marrying early or late; taking over the parent's business; moving to different parts of the country; having their own children early or late, etc.

As you learn the lesson of mortality you help your children indirectly. You affect the family climate in the way you respond to the new reality that heart disease is an important aspect of the family, but it isn't be the family's sole concern.

Another bittersweet but important lesson is that it's impossible to protect children from reality. Perhaps it was my own denial of death that made me say, "They were too young to have to learn that." Marsh's illness caused the family much pain, but it also accounted for much learning and love. I'm writing this on the 13th anniversary of his first heart attack. I still appreciate what I learned and I'm so grateful for his survival.

Affirmation:
I celebrate the love and learning given me in my life.

Related topics to think/write about:
My most important learnings from my mate's heart disease
Things I want to discuss with my children

Qualities to meditate on: Love. Meaning. Wisdom.

Date

This is the   week of my recovery.

Courage is resistance to fear, mastery of fear — not absence of fear.

– Mark Twain

The question I'm asked most often in my work with heartmates is: "When will the fear go away?"

Here's my answer: You have been wounded by the cardiac event. Wounds scar over with time. You have your scars and the wounds buried beneath them with you throughout life. Over time, scars fade, and your fears diminish too.

But when your routine is broken by something unexpected, it's as if the scar bursts open, the wound is new, and you suffer fear as if it were the original event again.

A personal example: I was away at a professional conference, and returned to my hotel room between meetings late one morning. The phone's message light was pulsing! Instantly I was paralyzed with fear. Who would call long distance in the morning? Only someone with terrible news! I reached for the phone, and it seemed to take an eternity for the operator to return with my message. It was from my kids, and it began with the words, "Sorry if we scared you, but there is good news...", and the message continued. I was limp and exhausted as I hung up the phone.

My body and feelings had responded to the unexpected as if it were an emergency not a happy message.

Affirmation:
I am strong enough to master my fears.

Related topics to think/write about:
Describe in detail my five greatest fears
Ways I have dealt with and can deal with the unexpected

Qualities to meditate on: Courage. Reality. Serenity.

Date _____

This is the _____ week of my recovery.

I left the hospital [again] with the feeling of, 'Okay, this is our life and doggone we're really going to enjoy it. I'm going to quit...run[ning] around frantically finding a new doctor, a new drug, a new fixit. I'm just going to relax and enjoy what we have.' And it was just like a weight had left me after all those years.

– Dorothy A.
Portrait of the Heartmate

Major tasks of grieving include acknowledging your feelings and figuring out how to make lifestyle changes.

The work is exhausting. You're engaged in a powerful and lonely struggle, trying to change the realities of heart disease. You're fighting everything and everybody, and the struggle is intensified when you feel isolated and misunderstood. Unlike a bad dream that disappears in the light, you wake every day to the fact that your mate's heart disease is still there.

In many cases, it is absolutely right that you take the responsibility of being your mate's defender. He may be too ill or weak to be his own advocate.

But there comes a time, after many months and sometimes years, when you stop struggling and experience acceptance. His recovery may not be as full as you once had hoped. Your acceptance involves knowing that you can't be responsible for another's life, and that you can't protect your mate from death.

With acceptance comes peace — and forgiveness for your mate and yourself. Surprisingly you now have renewed energy for life and a new perspective embracing gratitude for the precious moments and days you still have to share.

Affirmation:
I accept my power and my limitations.

Related topics to think/write about:
Things I've been frantic about that I can consider letting go of
My sense of compassion, forgiveness and joy

Qualities to meditate on: Calm. Forgiveness. Peace.

Date

This is the _____ week of my recovery.

...the 'good woman' ...doesn't recognize her own feelings...doesn't know she has needs or that in order for her to recover from her crisis she needs to take care of herself. She has been granted no permission to express her resentment about having to care for a mate who may not be caring for himself. Or worse, she may be caring for a mate who is only caring about himself.

– Rhoda Levin, Chapter 5 "Shifting Responsibility"
Heartmates® A Guide for the Spouse & Family

We grew up in an age when we and others measured our worth by how well we cared for our men and our children.

But times have changed, and we have come of age. Today women have more opportunity to develop as full human beings; our lives have purpose and meaning beyond the caretaking role.

We may have given more than half of our lives to caring for others. But at mid-age we are pregnant with ourselves, creative in ways never dreamed of in youth. We have both roots and wings. Being in a relationship always makes the achievment of individual goals more complicated, but it does not invalidate women's need for their own lives.

We must not let our mate's heart disease become a barrier excluding us from the challenge of being and becoming ourselves.

Affirmation:
     I redefine myself as I integrate my worthiness.

Related topics to think/write about:
     What are my individual opportunities at my age and in my situation?
     Ways that I want to express my creativity

Qualities to meditate on:
     Creativity. Goodness. Individuality.

The Heartmates® Meditation Journal

Date _____

This is the _____ week of my recovery.

_____

_____

_____

_____

_____

_____

_____

_____

_____

_____

_____

_____

_____

_____

_____

_____

_____

_____

_____

_____

_____

_____

_____

_____

_____

_____

_____

...one of the things that happened in our family is that suddenly we were all aware of our mortality. M. and I were aware of our own and our children were aware — maybe not so much of their mortality but of ours. And even though it's such a painful thing, there's a special bond in the family. It's a deep appreciation of each other.

– Mary C.
Portrait of the Heartmate

I have heard heartmates describe the cardiac event as the best thing that ever happened — a kind of wake-up call. The awakening was about love and the meaning of relationships, about mortality and the preciousness of life, about making time and space in life to experience the new.

But first you must grieve the loss of the old life and the old dreams. Generally that takes at least a calendar year, so that all family occasions, change of seasons, and holidays will be part of the new reality. Each situation which now includes heart disease is experienced as the "new normal." As that process nears completion, a shift begins, and your attention is less on grieving than on the new opportunities presented to you.

Your energy level tells you when you've grieved enough. You awaken with energy for the day ahead of you. Your humor and sense of perspective return. You once again think about and plan enthusiastically for your future.

Affirmation:
I am preparing myself to live fully in the present by grieving past losses.

Related topics to think/write about:
My thoughts about the significance of the gift of life
How I want to live from this day forward

Qualities to meditate on: Gratitude. Humor. Joy.

181

Date

This is the   week of my recovery.

Teach us to face life with faith and courage that we may see the blessings hidden away, even in its discords and struggles. Life calls us not merely to enjoy the beauties that surround us, but to exult in heights attained after the toil of climbing. Grief is a great teacher, when it sends us back to serve and bless the living.

– Rabbi Max A. Shapiro

Years ago my rabbi told me he had counseled many bereaved in his job as a clergyman, but not until his own beloved wife died did he really understand the losses of his congregants.

As a clinical social worker, I too have guided people in relation to various kinds of life losses, but being a heartmate taught me a depth of compassion and understanding learned only through experience. Thank you, God, for blessing me with gifts enabling me to express my experience to help others heal.

It isn't every heartmate's professional job to counsel others, but grieving the losses inherent in your cardiac crisis has changed you. You can be more compassionate about your own limitations and failings. You can be more tolerant about your mate's struggles as well. And as you touch others in your community, they too will benefit from your experience with grief.

Affirmation:
I will live as a blessing to myself and those around me.

Related topics to think/write about:
The blessings from my struggles with my mate's heart disease
What grief has taught me

Qualities to meditate on: Compassion. Education. Service.

The Heartmates® Meditation Journal

Date _____

This is the _____ week of my recovery.

_____

_____

_____

_____

_____

_____

_____

_____

_____

_____

_____

_____

_____

_____

_____

_____

_____

_____

_____

_____

_____

_____

_____

_____

Many times a day I realize how much my outer and inner life is built upon the labors of so many others, both living and dead, and how earnestly I must exert myself in order to give in return as much as I have received.

– Albert Einstein

We focused on self-care during the early weeks of recovery; it is fitting near the end of the year to indicate again how important self-care is to your long-term recovery. You may hear an inner voice saying, "He survived, and you're still in transition when it's almost a year...you're self-indulgent, decadent, self-serving, selfish." Don't listen. Self-care does not exclude caring for others. But how much of each kind of caring must be a consideration when women who have been so well trained by our society to take care of men and children, barely take an opportunity to care for ourselves.

"Some of us heal ourselves by participating in healing the world, and others...focus on healing ourselves and by doing so participate in healing the world." "Opening Your Heart," Chapter 10 of *Heartmates*® What's important is that we watch and right the balance of caring for others and for ourselves, and that we focus on giving and receiving, so that we are neither depleted nor concerned only for ourselves.

Affirmation:
I am learning to balance giving and receiving.

Related topics to think/write about:
Examine my inner voices and their messages about how I should be
Evaluate my needs: which are and are not being met at this period in my recovery

Qualities to meditate on: Awe. Balance. Perseverance.

Date _____

This is the _____ week of my recovery.

We'd always talked about buying a cabin and I'd completely ruled it out after D.'s heart attack, because I was afraid of being so far away. At a cabin in the woods, I wouldn't be close enough to an ambulance, a hospital, a doctor. What would happen if he had chest pain or...? We bought it! It was a celebration of my freedom to do things again without constantly worrying about the umbilical cord to the hospital.

– Lavonne G.
Portrait of the Heartmate

This celebratory story provides a snapshot from the lengthy process of mourning: loss of dreams, loss of freedom, life dominated by fear and its accompanying limitations and accommodations.

The grief process includes expressing fear, changing priorities, acknowledging a new reality, all over a period of time. After many months, something interior changes.

You wouldn't be a heartmate if you didn't still feel fear sometimes, but having arrived at this new stage of recovery, you can now live more freely. When the fear comes, it is no longer more powerful than you. Its intensity is less; it neither lasts as long nor paralyzes you.

Free of the grip of grief, your reality once again affords energy for and interest in the present and future. Not every heartmate can buy a cabin, or travel to a faraway place, but each heartmate needs to mark this significant passage.

Celebrate the new awareness together. There is only now! You can choose to live today fully, joyously.

Affirmation:
I celebrate life and my life today.

Related topics to think/write about:
Review ways that fear still dominates my decisions and actions
Ways I can express more beauty, joy, love, meaning in my every day life

Qualities to meditate on: Celebration. Freedom. Vitality.

Date _____

This is the _____ week of my recovery.

...each wound we suffer and eventually heal from is a soul-making experience with the potential to awaken our willingness to participate in the healing of the world.

– Joan Borysenko
Fire In The Soul

In the early months it's natural for heartmates, wounded by the cardiac crisis, to experience depression and anger. It's also natural as healing progresses for heartmates' energy to return. As it does, many heartmates and patients too want to help heal others.

Some work with other cardiac families in their communities to show their gratitude. I've received many letters from *Heartmates*® readers describing their experiences and their desire to share with others. Others have interests that take them far from heart disease, but the motivation is the same: to help heal our wounded planet. They serve AIDS victims and families, deprived and abused children, literacy programs, etc.

There is no right way to participate in healing. Not everyone makes dramatic life changes as a result of the cardiac crisis, nor would it be right that they do. Healing from the cardiac crisis presents an opportunity to search your own heart and mind for what is right and loving for you to do, and permission to express the outpourings of your heart.

Affirmation:
In my unique way I am a devoted citizen of this planet.

Related topics to think/write about:
Examine my planetary interests and my plans to act on them
My understanding of myself having had a soul-making experience

Qualities to meditate on:
Integration. Liberation. Spontaneity.

Date _____

This is the _____ week of my recovery.

Let there be peace on earth and let it begin with me.

– Sy Miller & Jill Jackson

No heartmate can take responsibility for the whole world, yet many feel guilty about not doing more when there is so much injustice, war and poverty on earth. No single person can fix the world, but each heartmate can work on inner peace.

Almost a year after the cardiac event you're probably still far from peace with yourself. The drain on your energy has been significant. You've had losses to grieve, and a complex process for you and your family to learn: finding and accepting a new normal that includes heart disease.

Most heartmates need at least one full calendar year to struggle with the feelings about what happened and is happening. Some heartmates are still feeling angry and confused about what's happened to their relationship and how to repair it. Other heartmates are still learning about long-term lifestyle changes and how to think optimistically. Still others continue to cope with days of depression and disappointment.

Inner peace is a wonderful goal to work toward. Perhaps world peace can only come once we've done the individual groundwork of making peace within ourselves.

Affirmation:
Peace on earth and let it begin with me.

Related topics to think/write about:
What peace looks like in my personal, family, and work life
Paths I can take to inner peace throughout the course of my day

Qualities to meditate on: Light. Purpose. Transformation.

Date _____

This is the _____ week of my recovery.

> *Heart disease doesn't have to be an end. It can be a new beginning.*
>
> – Rhoda Levin, Chapter 10 "Opening Your Heart"
> *Heartmates® A Guide for the Spouse & Family*

Happy anniversary! Congratulations! You have completed a year of active work on your recovery. This is the 52nd week in the *Heartmates® Meditation Journal.* You've reached the end of this book, but, it is hoped, not the end of your healing journey.

Our culture is not very proficient at honoring endings, but they are important to acknowledge. It's the same with relationships in your life — saying good-bye, making a clean ending, frees your energy to experience hello and embrace the new. When some of your energy is stuck in the past, you can't fully accept the present.

Observing endings and beginnings, turning points, anniversaries, special occasions and achievements mark the special moments in life. They can be delightful and fun times too, both to plan and to execute. Heartmates' unique celebrations include planting a tree, decorating the house with a banner made on your home computer, a romantic evening together, preparing and eating a special meal.

By now you are skilled at journaling as a method to reflect on your life, and at meditating on qualities to grow and capitalize on your strengths. You'll find additional quotations and qualities in the appendices of this book if you'd like to continue using this format. Or you may want to wing it on your own now. One way to celebrate this end and beginning is to buy yourself a gift: a beautiful new journal to welcome the next period of your recovery.

Affirmation:
     I can say good-bye; I look forward to the next hello.

Related topics to think/write about:
     Consider and plan celebrations to mark milestones in my life
     Things in my life now that I need to say good-bye to

Qualities to meditate on: Clarity. Renewal. Synthesis.

Date

This is the   week of my recovery.

Appendix A: Recommended Reading List

This list is divided by subject for your convenience. I have chosen books that are readable, practical, to invite further exploration in areas that interest you, and to expand on the growth experienced as you used this meditation journal.

Heartmates® A Guide for the Spouse and Family of the Heart Patient. Rhoda F. Levin, New York: Pocket Books, 1994; Minneapolis: MinervaPress, 1994.

On Grief and Loss:

Companion Through the Darkness: Inner Dialogues on Grief. Stephanie Ericsson, New York: HarperCollins, 1993.

Healing After Loss: Daily Meditations for Working Through Grief. Martha Whitmore Hickman, New York: Avon Books, 1994.

Necessary Losses. Judith Viorst, New York: Simon & Schuster, 1986.

Sailing. Susan Kenney, New York: Viking Penguin Inc., 1988. (fiction)

Stones for Ibarra. Harriet Doerr, New York: Penguin Books, 1978. (fiction)

Two-Part Invention, The Story of a Marriage. Madeleine L'Engle, New York: Farrar, Straus & Giroux, 1988. (autobiography)

When Bad Things Happen to Good People. Rabbi Harold S. Kushner, New York: Schocken Books, Inc., 1981.

On Growth:

Fire In the Soul: A New Psychology of Spiritual Optimism. Joan Borysenko, New York: Warner Books, 1993.

Inevitable Grace: Breakthroughs in the Lives of Great Men and Women: Guides to Your Self-Realization. Piero Ferrucci, Los Angeles: Jeremy P. Tarcher, Inc., 1990.

Lighting a Candle: Quotations on the Spiritual Life. Molly Young Brown editor, New York: HarperCollins, 1994.

Soul Mates: Honoring the Mysteries of Love and Relationship. Thomas

Moore, New York: HarperCollins, 1994.

On Healing:

Healing Into Immortality: A New Spiritual Medicine of Healing Stories and Imagery. Gerald Epstein, M.D., New York: Bantam Books, 1994.

Healing Words: The Power of Prayer and The Practice of Medicine. Larry Dossey, M.D., New York: HarperCollins, 1993.

Heart Illness and Intimacy, How Caring Relationships Aid Recovery. Wayne M. Sotile, Ph.D., Baltimore: The Johns Hopkins University Press, 1992.

Mainstay: For the Well Spouse of the Chronically Ill. Maggie Strong, Boston: Little, Brown and Company, 1988.

The Power of the Mind to Heal. Joan Borysenko, Ph.D. & Miroslav Borysenko, Ph.D., Carson, CA: Hay House, Inc., 1994.

On Meditation:

Active Meditation: The Western Tradition. Robert R. Leichtman, M.D. & Carl Japikse, Columbus, OH: Ariel Press, 1982.

How To Meditate. Lawrence LeShan, New York: Bantam Books, 1974.

Healing Into Life and Death. Stephen Levine, New York: Doubleday, 1987.

The Inner Guide Meditation. Edwin C. Steinbrecher, York Beach, Maine: Samuel Weiser, Inc., 1988.

On Journal Writing:

Life's Companion: Journal Writing As a Spiritual Quest. Christina Baldwin, New York: Bantam Books, 1990.

On Mental Imagery and Ritual:

The Art of Ritual: A Guide To Creating and Performing Your Own Rituals for Growth and Change. Renee Beck & Sydney Barbara Metrick, Berkeley: Celestial Arts, 1990.

Guided Meditations, Explorations and Healings. Stephen Levine, New York: Doubleday, 1991.

Imagery in Healing. Jeanne Achterberg, Boulder, Colorado: Shambhala, 1985.

Appendix B: Additional Quotations

For use in Part I: Early Recovery

The myth is that everything will be the same as it was. The truth is that nothing will ever be the same again.

> – Rhoda Levin, Chapter 2 "On the Road To Recovery"
> Heartmates® A Guide for the Spouse & Family

Being in a hospital at a time of serious illness is like living in a foreign country — you don't know the rules, you're always an outsider.

> – David V. Keith, M.D.
> Portrait of the Heartmate

He's had to make substantial changes in his...practice. So layered with the other kinds of concerns is a real change of image, change in status, and a kind of acknowledged grieving.

> – Ardis N.
> Portrait of the Heartmate

Some days you feel great; other days you can't seem to pull yourself out of the doldrums. Your spouse has returned to work and your family is 'back to normal.' But what was normal before bears little or no resemblance to life as you know it today.

> – Rhoda Levin, Chapter 3 "At the Heart of the Matter"
> Heartmates® A Guide for the Spouse & Family

Much of the time I felt very much alone, except when I could pick up the telephone....

> – Gretchen M.
> Portrait of the Heartmate

Everything felt different. Living together was different; sleeping together was different.

> – Ethelyn C.
> Portrait of the Heartmate

It isn't easy to affirm your strengths. Most of us are more comfortable with criticism than with compliments. We find it difficult to appreciate our positive qualities, and we are more aware of our weaknesses than our strengths. But taking credit for doing your best is an important part of the recovery process.

> – Rhoda Levin, Chapter 2 "On the Road To Recovery"
> Heartmates® A Guide for the Spouse & Family

It's normal to be angry...saddened. If you don't grieve over it, then you will carry it around as an invisible weight on your back...the same is true for the spouse! Depression is also quite normal following a heart attack.

> – Robert Eliot, M.D., F.A.C.C.
> Portrait of the Heartmate

The impulse to protect your children from pain and anguish is universal. But the truth is, it's impossible to do so. The cardiac crisis has occurred. You, your mate, and your children have been and will continue to be affected. Even if you could protect your children from hurt, it wouldn't necessarily be doing them a favor. Learning how to cope in a crisis is a valuable part of growing up.

> – Rhoda Levin, Chapter 9 "Heart Disease is a Family Affair"
> Heartmates® A Guide for the Spouse & Family

...we were probably all in a state of shock, because it was such an unexpected thing...and on the other hand, there was something very calming...almost comforting about it, because we all knew that it wasn't in our hands at all.

> – Mary C.
> Portrait of the Heartmate

For use in Part II: Mid-Recovery

Staying in touch with your purpose while you act is difficult, particularly during the acute phase of the cardiac crisis, and even as you reorient your life during recovery....Taking time to think about your decisions can keep you connected to the purpose behind your actions.

> – Rhoda Levin, Chapter 4 "Keeping Your Head On Straight"
> Heartmates® A Guide for the Spouse & Family

A deeper part of you knows that it's not going to go on forever....the 'shoulds' maybe aren't such a big deal anymore.

> – Ethelyn C.
> Portrait of the Heartmate

Fear of the unknown can be fought only with faith and courage. You will never achieve peace of mind unless you come to terms with reality.

> – Rhoda Levin, Chapter 6 "Does Time Heal All Wounds?"
> Heartmates® A Guide for the Spouse & Family

...the fact that I was totally dependent on him financially and I needed to change that in order to feel more secure in my life.

> – Mary C.
> Portrait of the Heartmate

Achieving goals, short or long-range, is less important than having them.

> – Rhoda Levin, Chapter 4 "Keeping Your Head On Straight"
> Heartmates® A Guide for the Spouse & Family

I finally came to the conclusion that I couldn't live like this, because I was so concerned about his life...so now I have developed the philosophy: in order to have life, I must live.

> – Bonnie B.
> Portrait of the Heartmate

Be generous in your expectations of yourself.

> – Rhoda Levin, Chapter 8 "Re-pairing the Heartmate Connection"
> Heartmates® A Guide for the Spouse & Family

...there are areas over which you have little or no authority. You can't make heart disease disappear. You can't change what has already happened to you and your mate because of heart disease. You can't even change how you feel about it. Your power is limited to choosing what your attitude will be about what is happening. You can be in charge of the way you will accept and adapt to a new reality, a new life.

> – Rhoda Levin, Chapter 4 "Keeping Your Head On Straight"
> Heartmates® A Guide for the Spouse & Family

For use in Part III: Toward Full Recovery

As serious and significant as your relationship is, nothing is a more powerful healer than humor. Being able to laugh at yourselves and your situation will help you see things as they truly are and enjoy your togetherness.

> – Rhoda Levin, Chapter 8 "Re-pairing the Heartmate Connection"
> Heartmates® A Guide for the Spouse & Family

Coming close to death, having it almost in the room with us on several occasions, also makes us very aware of how beautiful our life is together and how many wonderful things we share.

> – Ardis N.
> Portrait of the Heartmate

I think that D's heart attack brought me to reality — that D. was mortal and that he was human. It never occurred to me....that he would ever get sick, that he wouldn't be there to be strong, pay the bills, and help everybody who needed help, and mow the lawn and fix the porch. And suddenly he was human....it put us on an equal plane....I felt closer to him and I think he feels closer to me, because I see him as he is and he's okay the way he is.

> – Lavonne G.
> Portrait of the Heartmate

Remembering and caring enable you to integrate and accept the loss....The cardiac spouse's losses are real and important, albeit intangible, invisible to others, neither legitimized by society nor voiced by you. If you don't allow yourself to grieve, you will get stuck ....And you'll be bereft of the seeds born from grieving and necessary to plant a new crop of realistic dreams for the garden of your future.

> – Rhoda Levin, Chapter 6 "Does Time Heal All Wounds?"
> Heartmates® A Guide for the Spouse & Family

The prairie has informed my life: wild, free, open, non-judging, gentle and fierce...I just remember being wildly happy...I would get lost in the space between sky and earth. My memory of this gift seems to include no intellectual things, only glorious, intense, soul-sweet yearning to be connected to it... Winter nights gave the gift of stars and northern lights....I know the prairie still runs in my blood and fuels every creative endeavor and is the place I feel at home on the earth.

> – Kitty Kotchian Smith
> Personal Journal

The cardiac crisis turned you in on yourself. Becoming more introspective and self-centered is a normal and instinctive means of self-protection. Your world got very tiny, as you concentrated on coping with your personal issues....Recovery might be defined as the gradual process of moving back into relationship with the larger world around you....At the height of the cardiac crisis, your attention was necessarily focused on yourself. As you emerge, you may experience dissatisfaction, restlessness, and an urge to search your life for new meaning.

> – Rhoda Levin, Chapter 10 "Opening Your Heart"
> Heartmates® A Guide for the Spouse & Family

Appendix C:

Affirmations for Weeks in Part I - Early Recovery

I will be gentle and kind to myself today.
I will use my energy today on what is truly important.
I accept the need to take care of myself.
I can change, a little bit every day.

I am entitled to have questions and answers.
I deserve support and I will ask for it.
I am strong; I will survive and thrive.
I have many strengths, including the ability to face reality.

I am capable of dealing with my grief.
I do not stand alone; I am brave enough to reach out.
I protect my children best with my caring and my honesty.
I accept the reality of uncertainty, the permanence of change.

My feelings are a normal response to the crisis I am in.
I deserve to be touched in a loving, respectful way.
I am a worthwhile person who can accommodate change.
I will express my love by stepping back and letting go.

I am strong enough to face my fears.
I am resilient; I can adapt to a life of uncertainty.
I am responsible for my feelings, and no one else's.
I will do my part for our partnership.

Affirmations for Weeks in Part II: Mid-Recovery

I will use my power to return my mate's power to him as he is capable of assuming it.
I am human and in God's hands (or) I am being held by the universe.
I will learn to think optimistically.
I am loving and lovable.

I can differentiate between being responsible and being over-responsible.
I can master my fear by recognizing it and assessing real danger.
I trust my own pace.
I will give myself the gift of cherishing this moment.

I am more than what I do.
I am strong enough to experience my sadness and my disappointment.
I am entitled to experience the abundance of life.
I will respectfully acknowledge my feelings without judgment.

I will honor my grief by giving myself the time I need.
I will enjoy this moment.
My mate and I are separate: each of us individual and whole.
I will pay attention to what my mate's illness has to teach me.

I commit myself to the spiritual task of opening to the unknown.
I will love myself and my mate.
I will open myself to realistic trust.
I will use the energy of my anger constructively.

Affirmations for Weeks in Part III: Toward Full Recovery

I am whole and a part of all life.
I celebrate the love and learning given me in my life.
I am strong enough to master my fears.
I accept my power and my limitations.

I redefine myself as I integrate my worthiness.
I am preparing myself to live fully in the present by grieving past losses.
I will live as a blessing to myself and those around me.
I care about myself and I care about others.

I celebrate life and my life today.
In my unique way I am a devoted citizen of this planet.
Peace on earth and let it begin with me.
I can say good-bye; I look forward to the next hello.

Appendix D: Qualities

Qualities for Meditation for Weeks in Part I: Early Recovery

Week 1:   calm - quiet - simplicity
Week 2:   order - rest - surrender
Week 3:   balance - energy - renewal
Week 4:   celebration - creativity - patience

Week 5:   appreciation - comprehension - humor
Week 6:   generosity - grace - openness
Week 7:   goodwill - imagination - positiveness
Week 8:   courage - perseverance - reality

Week 9:   clarity - flexibility - will
Week 10:   communication - intimacy - partnership - trust
Week 11:   community - harmlessness - integrity
Week 12:   peace - serenity - wisdom

Week 13:   acceptance - faith - optimism
Week 14:   celebration - generosity - love
Week 15:   humor - power - resilience
Week 16:   cooperation - dedication - responsibility

Week 17:   liberation - power - understanding
Week 18:   determination - openness - truth
Week 19:   compassion - detachment - harmlessness
Week 20:   friendship - trust - will

Qualities for Meditation for Weeks in Part II: Mid-Recovery

Week 21:   cooperation - creativity - responsibility
Week 22:   letting go - surrender - trust
Week 23:   control - enthusiasm - optimism
Week 24:   friendship - love - tenderness - trust

Week 25:   freedom - goodwill - responsibility
Week 26:   calm - courage - humor
Week 27:   balance - energy - reality
Week 28:   acceptance - appreciation - positiveness

Week 29:   comprehension - faith - wonder
Week 30:   grace - purification - release
Week 31:   abundance - adventure - play
Week 32:   acceptance - detachment - understanding

Week 33:   identity - integrity - meaning
Week 34:   beauty - joy - light - play

Week 35:   liberation - power - surrender
Week 36:   meaning - service - wisdom

Week 37:   order - steadfastness - universality
Week 38:   generosity - harmony - peace
Week 39:   clarity - faith - love - trust
Week 40:   discrimination - forgiveness - vitality

Qualities for Meditation for Weeks in Part III: Toward Full Recovery

Week 1:   cooperation - harmony - wholeness
Week 2:   love - meaning - wisdom
Week 3:   courage - reality - serenity
Week 4:   calm - forgiveness - peace

Week 5:   creativity - goodness - individuality
Week 6:   gratitude - humor - joy
Week 7:   compassion - education - service
Week 8:   awe - balance - perseverance

Week 9:   celebration - freedom - vitality
Week 10:   integration - liberation - spontaneity
Week 11:   light - purpose - transformation
Week 12:   clarity - renewal - synthesis

List of Qualities:

Abundance ♥ Acceptance
Admiration ♥ Appreciation ♥ Awe
Adventure ♥ Balance
♥ Beauty ♥
Being ♥ Belonging ♥ Bliss ♥ Brotherhood
♥ Celebration ♥
Change ♥ Clarity ♥ Communication
Community ♥ Compassion
Comprehension ♥ Control ♥ Cooperation
Courage ♥ Creativity ♥ Dedication ♥ Delight
Detachment ♥ Determination
Ecstasy ♥ Education ♥ Efficiency
♥ Energy ♥
Enthusiasm ♥ Eternity ♥ Expectancy
♥ Faith ♥
Flexibility ♥ Forgiveness
Freedom ♥ Friendship ♥ Generosity
Goodness ♥ Goodwill
Grace ♥ Gratitude ♥ Harmlessness
Harmony ♥ Healing ♥ Honesty
♥ Humor ♥
Imagination ♥ Inclusiveness
Individuality ♥ Inspiration ♥ Integration
Integrity ♥ Intimacy
♥ Joy ♥
Letting Go ♥ Liberation
Light ♥ Love ♥ Loyalty
♥ Meaning ♥
Obedience ♥ Openness
♥ Optimism ♥
Order ♥ Partnership ♥ Patience
Peace ♥ Perseverance ♥ Play
Poise ♥ Positiveness
Power ♥ Purification
Purpose ♥ Quiet
Reality ♥ Release
♥ Renewal ♥
Resilience ♥ Responsibility ♥ Rest
Serenity ♥ Service ♥ Silence ♥ Simplicity ♥ Sisterhood
Spontaneity ♥ Steadfastness
Strength ♥ Surrender
♥ Synthesis ♥
Tenderness ♥ Transformation ♥ Trust
♥ Truth ♥
Understanding ♥ Unity ♥ Universality
♥ Vitality ♥
Wholeness ♥ Will
Willingness ♥ Wisdom ♥ Wonder

Appendix E: Imagery Tools

Here is a simple imagery exercise that requires no more than ten minutes a day. It can be done at the beginning and/or end of the day; taking ten minutes in the middle of the day can be revitalizing as well. To be effective, it should be done daily, preferably at the same time and in the same place. Have someone read the exercise to you the first few times, until you can follow the order without the distraction of having to read it. Or record it for yourself on audio tape leaving enough pause time to follow each direction.

RELAXATION EXERCISE

Sit in a comfortable chair, with your spine straight and your feet flat on the floor. Close your eyes and focus your attention on your breath, following its natural cycle in and out. With each inhalation, be aware that you are taking in clean and clear energy. Experience the release of tension as you exhale. Allow your breathing to remain neutral, don't change it in any way, just notice that with each breath you are more in touch with your depth and you become more relaxed.

Focus now on your body so that it can relax and you can let go of the tension you carry there. Begin with your feet: first your right foot, then your left. Imagine all of the tension flowing out through the bottom of your feet and into the earth below. Now allow the muscles in your calves and thighs to relax as well. First your right leg, then, your left. Your legs feel warm and loose. Now pay attention to your abdomen, where you may feel tightness and stress. Let your breath flow through your abdomen, and let go of the tension. Now focus on your back, with its many muscles, and your shoulders. Breathe energy into your shoulders, and feel the tension let go. Now attend to your arms, first the right, then, the left. Let go, first in your upper arm, then the lower part, and last your hands and each of your fingers. Experience the tightness flowing out of every fingertip. Feel your neck relaxed and free as the tension flows from it. Concentrate now on your jaw, letting it relax, letting your mouth open naturally as you let go of holding it tight. Now focus on your eyes and allow them to let go. Feel the muscles behind your eyes relaxing and expanding. And last, the top and back of your head. Feel your head get light and clear as your mind stops racing. You are alert but not busy. Now that your body is relaxed, focus once again on your breath. Breathe in whatever quality you need at this moment - calm, peace, serenity, patience, freedom, compassion, love - and exhale any remaining tension or tightness.

Imagine yourself in a beautiful green meadow. You are able to rest and be nurtured by the beauty of nature surrounding you. You feel the warm sun on your skin, the solid earth holds you securely. The air is fresh and there is a pleasant cool breeze. You can smell grasses and wildflowers. You hear birds singing and the babble of a nearby brook. Take some time to enjoy the peace and the calm. Allow yourself to be filled and quieted.

Stay in this serene and beautiful place as long as you are comfortable. When you are ready, focus your attention on your breathing again. Breathe as fully and deeply as you naturally can. Notice how you feel as you do. Now, very gently, bring your awareness back to the present and slowly open your eyes. Take a moment to stretch your body as tall as you can when you rise and return to your everyday reality.

Here is a Heartmates® exercise designed to help you examine the images that presently motivate or direct your life. Use each set of questions as a guide. Respond with both your head and your heart. Don't be concerned about writing full sentences, making sense, or being logical. Use these questions to explore your images as fully as you can.

HEARTMATES® GUIDE FOR EXAMINING IMAGES

1. What do you recall about first visiting your mate in the hospital? See your mate and the coronary care unit as a still photo; then add sounds, smells, and movement to your image. What nonverbal message did you receive about your spouse's condition? In your mind's eye, see yourself then. What were you feeling, thinking, doing? Describe your communication, feelings, level of intimacy with your mate.

2. Create an image of your mate's physical heart. As much as you can, visualize the actual damage as well as its symbolic meaning. Then see the healing that has occurred. How is your mate's physical and emotional heart different now from before the onset of heart disease? Based on your image, how do you envision the long-term quality of your mate's life? Imagine yourself five years, ten years, and twenty years into the future. What effects has your mate's heart disease had on your life? How do you expect the picture will continue to change?

3. What image of home and family do you have from the period of active recovery? What concerns did you have then about caring for your mate, your family, yourself? See in your mind's eye the network of communication and feelings that connected your family then. How was the family different during recovery from the way it was before the cardiac crisis? What is your image of your family now? As you see your family at present, note what issues your family is dealing with and what is going well for all of you.

4. Look into a mirror of your past. Who were you before your mate's heart crisis? What was important to you? What was your relationship with your mate like? How was your daily life organized? What were your priorities? How did you define your purpose for living? Gather this past image of you and set it aside.

5. Stand in front of the same mirror right now. Who are you today? What do you know about your strengths and limitations? How do you feel about yourself now? What is important to you today? What is your relationship with your mate like? How do you organize your daily life? What are your priorities? What is your purpose for living? Gather this present image of you and put it alongside your past image.

6. Step back far enough so you can see both images in the mirror. Visualize how being a cardiac spouse has changed you. What have you learned? How have you weathered the changes? How would you assess your acceptance of what's happened to you? Have you forgiven your mate, yourself? Are you taking care of your most important needs? Are you continuing to mourn your losses and heal your wounds?

Purposeful examination of our images allows us to update them continually as time passes and conditions change. One of the advantages of taking stock and comparing past and present images is that you can appreciate new qualities you've developed in yourself as a response to the cardiac crisis.

The Evening Review

The Evening Review is a daily exercise designed to enhance personal growth. It is particularly useful to the cardiac spouse because it provides a structure to establish regular introspection, a quiet time when you can think about your day. It can help you focus on questions about life raised by the cardiac crisis. The process of doing the exercise facilitates acceptance of reality, in regular and small steps.

The Evening Review can be used as a recovery tool, helping the cardiac spouse to focus on self. Reviewing is a mental activity, naturally operating during a crisis, that helps a person to think clearly, see reality, and establish order in the chaos of the crisis.

EVENING REVIEW EXERCISE

The review is best done as the last activity of your day. Before going to sleep, review your day in your mind, "playing" it like a movie, backward, beginning where you are right now, then the time of late evening, then the time of early evening, then the dinner hour, the afternoon, and so on to the morning when you awakened.

This exercise can be used to examine yourself and your life as a whole. It can be modified, as in the example below, to focus on some aspect of yourself, on some inner process or pattern you'd like to know more about. The attitude with which you do the exercise is most important. When you examine your day, do it as much as possible as the detached, objective observer, calmly and clearly registering each phase of what has happened. Then move on to the next phase without excitement, without becoming elated at a success or unhappy about a failure. The aim is to calmly register awareness of the meaning and patterns of the day, rather than to relive it.

Many have found it valuable to write down, perhaps as part of your *Heartmates® Meditation Journal*, observations, insights, or impressions. By reviewing your notes over a period of time, you may discover patterns and trends not otherwise apparent.

REVIEW OF BOUNDARIES

This modification of the Evening Review consists of reviewing your day from the point of view of your boundaries. Psychological boundaries are protective membranes best used to deflect what is detrimental to the system and to attract what nourishes it. (Consider how skillfully a plant protects itself from poisonous or unneeded elements and finds nutrients in the appropriate quantities to sustain growth.)

Before doing this exercise the first time, you might identify activities and relationships that are particularly nourishing or depleting at this point in your life. If you keep a journal, reviewing recent writings may provide insight.

As part of your Evening Review, some of the things that you may want to keep in mind are:

1. What is my experience of my boundaries? Have there been changes in my boundary system since the cardiac crisis began? Are there changes as I become aware of my boundaries and how I use them?

2. How do I evaluate environmental influences? From which can I get nourishment or from which do I need protection?

3. How skillful am I in using and shifting my boundaries? In what situations and with whom is it easy or difficult?

4. What do I allow in? What do I push away? What in myself do I protect (my heart, my mind, my body, my feelings)?

You may consider these questions during the review exercise itself, or, if this gets in your way, you may want to think about them at the end of your review. They are meant to provide a choice of perspective and all need not be covered. Their main purpose is to increase awareness of your boundaries and protection.

Keep the exercise simple, and particularly at the beginning give it no more than fifteen minutes a day (including journal writing).

Heartmates® is an ongoing therapeutic program designed to serve the cardiac spouse and family during and after a cardiac crisis. To be included on our mailing list, please print your name and address below and mail to:

Heartmates, Inc.
P.O. Box 16202
Minneapolis, MN 55416

Or write your questions and concerns to us via e-mail at:

heartmates@aol.com

Your age now: _____ Your spouse's age: _____
Date of onset of heart disease: _____
What has changed most in *your* life since the onset of your mate's heart disease? _____

_____

What concerns you most right now? _____

_____

A completely revised trade paper edition of the acclaimed book, ***Heartmates® A Guide for the Spouse and Family of the Heart Patient***, is now available. This is a handbook beginning with the hospital experience and continuing over time to help you cope with marital and family issues, life-style changes, developing optimism, emotions and self care. US $12.00, including shipping and handling.

A Videoseries, ***Portrait of the Heartmate***; each of five-20 minute programs focuses on a different topic. Titles are: *"After A Heart Attack," "Understanding Cardiac Care," "The Road To Recovery," "Family Concerns," and "Renewing The Relationship."* This series is available for personal use and costs US $59.95, including shipping and handling.

A new interactive and user-friendly resource; ***The Heartmates® Meditation Journal: A Daily Companion for Partners of Heart Patients.*** This yearlong aid focuses on the changes in the heartmate's life when a partner has heart disease. A beautiful edition, *The Heartmates Meditation Journal* makes a wonderful gift and will fit in purse or briefcase...a support companion you will want to use daily. US $15.00, including shipping and handling.

Heartmates® Inc. will accept personal checks, or will bill you.
❏ Heartmates® A Guide for the Spouse & Family $12.00
❏ Portrait of the Heartmate Videoseries $59.95
❏ The Heartmates® Meditation Journal: A Daily Companion $15.00

NAME _____

ADDRESS _____

CITY _____ STATE _____

ZIP CODE _____ PHONE (____) _____

Fax us your order (612) 929-6395 or call (800) 9HM-3331

AWAKENING AMERICA

AWAKENING AMERICA

BACK THROUGH THE GATES OF
MORAL DECENCY

KARI BITZ

TATE PUBLISHING
AND ENTERPRISES, LLC

Published by Tate Publishing & Enterprises, LLC
127 E. Trade Center Terrace | Mustang, Oklahoma 73064 USA
1.888.361.9473 | www.tatepublishing.com

Tate Publishing is committed to excellence in the publishing industry. The company reflects the philosophy established by the founders, based on Psalm 68:11,

"The Lord gave the word and great was the company of those who published it."

Book design copyright © 2013 by Tate Publishing, LLC. All rights reserved.
Cover design by Rtor Maghuyop
Interior design by Jomar Ouano

Published in the United States of America

ISBN: 978-1-62295-064-5
1. Religion / Christian Life / Inspirational
2. Religion / Christian Life / General
13.05.29

Praise for *Awakening America:*

Prayer and fasting is so basic, yet so integral to the spiritual life of an individual or congregation. Through it we discover a level of intimacy and power with God which cannot be found through any other effort. These are critical days for our nation and the church, we must become people who know how to fast and pray.

—Pastor Leon Freitag
Superintendent, North Dakota

Kari Bitz brings a timely and much needed look at the condition of America, masterfully finding a balance between challenge and encouragement, conviction and hope, between God's love and His holiness–the joy of following the King of kings and the responsibility that comes with this privilege. It is time to engage, and Kari brings it all together in a way that any believer can understand–but will challenge even the veteran of the faith.

—Pastor Mic Rhoads
Victory Fellowship Church
International Worship Center
Bismarck/Mandan, North Dakota

TABLE OF CONTENTS

OVERVIEW

We must have revival and spiritual awakening in the nation if we desire for our families and children to live in a nation with freedom of religion as we have had. The moral fiber of the nation is coming apart with immorality. It is becoming anti-Christian rather than post-Christian or Christian. This will cause a problem in days ahead as well as in the next generation. The Christian heritage that once was in our nation and our children would have grown up with, is crumbling before our eyes. What we have taken for granted is being taken away from us. The morality of the nation is crumbling. And our next generation will have the consequence more than we understand.

But we can *all* make a difference. Every time we think it is impossible for there to be spiritual revival, we must look to God instead. With God all things are possible. What occurred in the past before spiritual awakenings? And what were God's people doing? They all have certain characteristics that have preceded them. Prayer and fasting has almost always been a key. There are other things as well but those two were almost always keys.

The reason we have not seen a greater increase in this is because many of us do not understand both the *need to do it and the benefits* of it. This book will focus on why it is worth doing and what the big picture is concerning it. Why do it for ourselves as well as for our nation and families? If we do not get the foundation back, our nation will crumble with immorality and never recover. We will not have God's blessing. And it will never return if we do not have repentance. I am going to give you, in unity with other Christians, a way to go back through the gates to take the land for Christ! What gates? The gates of moral decency.

Most of us want to make a difference in our nation as well as leave a legacy for the generation coming next. Many are concerned about the welfare of our families, marriages, even today's youth. The things they are exposed to are way beyond what we were exposed to as children. Revival. How bad do we want it? Can we do it? *Will* we do it? Will we make the change that God calls us to do in the nation we are in through prayer, fasting and other things (in this book), including greater obedience to Him?

INTRODUCTION

The greatest fulfillment will always be in obedience to God. Whether difficult or easy or in between, our greatest fulfillment will always be in obedience to God.

After I married and had children, I began to sense God's purpose in my life. My family engaged in the process of being uprooted and moving. Even before this began the most difficult year of my life, I was challenged to lay down my hopes and dreams of every kind. Everything of value in my life was taken through the fire. I am reminded of Genesis 47:31: "And Israel worshiped leaning on the top of his staff." He was never the same after wrestling with God. Through this severe time for me, a vision was birthed in my soul, seared through fiery trials. It is a vision of great revival to come in the wake of unprecedented prayer and fasting. What I did not know at that time was that virtually every revival and spiritual awakening throughout history have begun with God's people uniting in prayer and in fasting.

How often do we think it is impossible to have revival and spiritual awakening in both our nation and our own lives? But is it impossible? No, it isn't. We can make a difference for God and leave a legacy for years to come. In obeying God and choosing to move forward in unity, prayer, and fasting, we will begin to turn a tide that seems impossible to turn.

I wrote this book to help you begin to see hope in the midst of darkness, to *realize* that revival is both possible and necessary, and that the lives of our children hang in the balance if we will not push forward and be radical for Christ. We can *all* make a difference. We must have faith and be faithful to what God calls us to do in our spheres of influence, within our communities. And we must unite with others who are asking God to change our nation. We must continue to hope—for the One who gave us life is able to bring revival and awakening to us. But first we must want it, and must be willing to do what's necessary to make it happen. We must do our part and see what God will do.

My vision is to see a nation changed by the power of God through united prayer and fasting and other things. Acts 3:19 says, "Repent and turn to God, so that your sins may be wiped out, that times of refreshing may come." It is through turning to God and making Him our Lord that times of refreshing come in our personal lives as well as in our nation. We must follow God and pray for our nation, our communities, and our own lives. It is never impossible when God is a part of the equation. He is the One who is able to change the heart of a nation and bring its people back to Him.

Each one of us has a call of God in our lives to follow Him. He has a specific plan for our lives. We are all called to make a difference in our time and in our region for God. It is most surely in following God that we find our greatest fulfillment and growth. I have learned to come to the cross to find revival and refreshing in the One who paid it all. What is revival? Is it not to revive the heart and soul and spirit of people? Is it not to impassion people? The question is, will it come? How? And will you be a part of it?

I invite you to be a part of it.

REVIVAL IS COMING

In the past, nearly every revival that took place happened *despite* the pervasive belief that morality and culture was too far gone for it to be possible. The common belief was that man's sins were beyond redemption. But that belief was shattered with both the First Great Awakening and the Second Great Awakening, which emptied jails, changed culture, and brought millions of people to Christ.

Why will revival come? Because we are right at that place again. He is able to bring it again. What is it worth? What is the common sequence of revival? The sequence almost always begins with prayer and fasting and humbling ourselves before God. Nearly every revival and spiritual awakening has begun with unity in prayer and fasting.[1] Often we hear about people praying at the start of a revival, but according to original accounts, almost all of the revivals in the past began with fasting and prayer.[1] And Jesus himself said that some spiritual things don't come about without prayer and fasting (Matt. 17:21 KJV). So, when will revival and awakening come? When we as God's people unite in prayer and fasting will be one key. It will be in our lives as well as our nation and families if we are willing.

In 1946 many Christians in the nation began to fast and pray. Their number soon increased significantly; and the following year, two evangelists came to the scene, one of whom was Billy Graham. Do you see how God often answers prayer? Are we willing to humble ourselves before God in prayer and fasting to seek His grace and His power in our need? Are we willing to discipline our flesh and take the time to pray? In the 1700s, some considered the church, society, and moral depravity to be too far gone to ever have hope for revival *until* Christians began to unite in prayer and fasting. And what began was *the first great* spiritual *revival and awakening*. Pastors of every denomination joined together to call people from the body of Christ to unite in prayer and fasting and millions of people came to Christ.[1]

The next time Christians again did this in united prayer and fasting was the start of the Second Great Awakening. Millions of people came to salvation *again*. Jails were emptied, saloons were emptied, and the churches were filled. It was this spiritual revival that led to major social change in America and set the foundation for the abolition of slavery. It is God who answers the prayers of His people mightily when we unite in earnest, earnest, fasting and prayer. He awakens the heart of mankind to convict of sin and to bring change to a nation.

In more recent years, an example of heroes who affected our nation stretched to Colombia. A city in Colombia was renowned for its cocaine drug lords who supplied more cocaine than anywhere else in the world. They supplied, just to the United States, 1000 tons a year of cocaine. Simply put, that is equivalent to 2 million pounds of cocaine each year, crossing our borders, killing our people. Their monthly income from the sale of cocaine *on average, per month* was $500 million. They built concrete walls around their complexes so high that authorities could find no way through. The walls were fifteen-to-twenty feet high. The authorities and government had not found a way to stop them. They had not been able yet to take them down. But what man cannot do, God is able to. A couple that God called to this city began to pray and fast for six months. From this, prayer meetings began to grow and continued to grow and increase in numbers. The unity in the city between denominations increased. Leaders of all different denominations united together. Then the first city wide *all-night* prayer meeting gathered, bringing

15,000 people together to seek God and pray on behalf of this city. *Within* ten days of this citywide prayer meeting, a door opened. There began to be a noticeable breakthrough. And within *months of the first citywide all-night prayer meeting, six of the seven drug lords were brought down.[2] What man was unable to do, God did by answering the cry, the earnest petition,* and *the uncomfortable perseverance of his people.*

I sincerely believe that the greatest revival in our nation—will come on the hinds' feet of unprecedented unity of God's people in fasting and prayer.

Will we unite together in prayer and fasting? Could we find a couple of friends to pray together weekly and keep each other accountable to fast in a cord of three? We are stronger when we are three. Could the lost souls in our nation be worth it?

Can we really go back through the gates of morality?

How do we pull morality back into place in a nation? It is by the Spirit of God, the Word of God and by prayer and fasting. There must be increased breakthrough. What we have been doing has not done it. What do we desire most? We must pay a price for revival. The price is our comfort. If we never let go of our comfort we will get the same thing we have had. How much are we willing to do to see our families come back to God and unsaved people drawn to Him?

There are cultural sins or strongholds that are broken only with a lot of fasting with prayer. In one weekly prayer meeting, one guy asked the Lord what to do to break some strongholds in the state. And immediately I sensed the Holy Spirit respond: *It will take a lot of prayer and fasting.* Prayer with fasting is a powerful discipline to master. The Bible speaks of it breaking the enemy's power. "Howbeit this kind goeth not out but by prayer and fasting" (Matt. 17:21 KJV).

Prayer is powerful. Prayer in unity adds even more power because we are praying in agreement. But fasting on top of it is the straw that breaks the camel's back. It is a powerhouse for bringing things to pass in the spirit that we cannot get to pass any other way. God hears the earnest cry of his people. It is like throwing a grenade into the enemy's camp, straight into its stronghold. Tell me that does not have an effect. Fasting in unity with others throws more grenades in and gives it less time to recover and rebuild.

In fact, the late Bill Bright, founder for Campus Crusade for Christ, was quoted as calling fasting with prayer the spiritual atomic bomb for bringing spiritual awakening.[3] He was not ill acquainted with long fasts and prayer.

When you combine prayer and fasting, you have one powerful tool to use against the enemy. It brings breakthrough through the power of God. It breaks the strongholds that are more entrenched and difficult to break. The mercy of God comes with it as well. For the mercy of God comes in to crush justice as we fast and pray in earnestness before Him. Humility brings salvation, does it not?

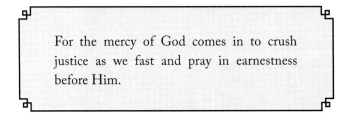

For the mercy of God comes in to crush justice as we fast and pray in earnestness before Him.

We can take this land for Christ, and we can make progress in our country and neighborhoods. You can make a difference in your area by praying and fasting. Do not ever believe the lie that the devil wants you to believe, that your prayers are not effective. They are effective. They are heard by a God who loves us and promises to hear our cries and answer them. Our God is the God who made the universe, the One who holds it in His hands, and He is abundantly able to accomplish what we doubt, if we will only obey Him, fast and pray. Continue to draw near to Him. Follow Him. He is good. Choose His ways for His ways are the best ways. Obey Him, receive his blessings, and *heed* His answers to your prayer. We have a powerful God who is able to do abundantly above and beyond what we can imagine. He is not only the God who is able but He is also the God who is good.

We must each do our part. It is a communal work, whereby each person reaches out, listens to the Holy Spirit and obeys His will. It is not only one thing. It is both. Do you know that obedience brings you something that you want?

How will revival come? It will come through the grace of God, through the power of His Spirit, and as an answer to the earnest prayers of His saints.

How will national repentance come about? We are going to fast and pray for things that we have never prayed for before and see what God does. We will fast and pray in unity because there is increased power in unity and agreement. I have seen God answer the prayers of His people in increasing measure as they gather together in it.

When will revival come? It will come when we unite in a cord of three or small groups, seeking and asking God to change our nation, communities, and families. We need to fast and pray and persevere in it until breakthrough comes. Because it comes as we fast and pray. We need to ask God to continue to unite people across the nation, to convict the hearts of men and women to unite in prayer and fasting. It will come in our lives, in our families, in our neighborhoods- and in our nation if we will continue to seek Him in unity.

Why is it so difficult to unite in prayer and fasting? It is the one thing that the enemy, the devil, fears the most. It is one thing that takes effort to do. Some things are easy to do, especially when they involve the flesh and our natural desires. But it is a blessing to unite in fellowship with other believers.

Praying together solidifies relationships and bends us, empowers us, and changes us. It is His will that we pray together and unite our hearts to ask Him for what we need. As a child comes before their father to ask for help, trusting in the caring of their father, so we come before God as little children, united in our hearts and in reverence before Him to seek, to ask, and to knock. It is through this that we open the floodgates of heaven through which God pours His blessings.

God says in Jeremiah 33:3, "Call to me and I will tell you great and unsearchable things you do not know." Daniel was given revelation and unsearchable things that he did not know on his own. And it was often in fasting before God that he received and found what he was looking for. Revival will come when we as Christians begin again to seek the Lord in unity through prayer and fasting and consistency in it. We must love one another as He loved us. We must help one another as He showed us. We must serve and work to bring unity in the body of Christ. We do this through prayer. It is the beginning point. If we want change in our lives and in the church, nation, communities, and region, we must begin to take time to pray. Carve out the time from our busy schedules to unite in prayer and in fasting together for the sake of our nation. Our next generation is on the line. If we do not step up to the plate as Christians to seek God for a mighty revival and spiritual awakening in our day, we will have consequences that are not God's best for us. Many lives are at stake. We have endured freedoms at times that have not always resulted in the best for us. One is the way we use our time. If we do not make the time, and carve it out, to spend it together in unity and in prayer and fasting, we will miss out on the greatest revival.

For Times of Refreshing

Acts 3:19 says, "Repent, then, and turn to God, so that your sins may be wiped out, that times of refreshing may come from the Lord."

In the days of the Bible, the people wrote on papyrus instead of paper like we have today. It was not porous and the ink was not acidic like ours is today. So when they would write on the papyrus, the ink would sit on the top of it and they would literally take a wet rag and wipe it off completely, as if nothing had been written on it. Acts says that when we repent and turn to God, our sins "may be wiped out". God wipes the sins off much like the papyrus paper. There is no trace of our sin left. And we receive a clean slate to start with.

What are the directives that come before the "times of refreshing"? First and foremost, we "repent and turn to God." We confess sin and turn away from it. We turn toward God. Whenever we remove something that has been there in the past, we must replace it with something new. "Above all else, guard your heart, for it is the wellspring of life" (Prov. 4:23). The heart is the issue. We must guard it above all else. If we remove something from our lives, we must find something better to replace it with. Replace it with time for righteousness. Remove and replace. Reject evil, and cling to what is good.

We must remove sin and replace it with time spent with others who love God, with reading the Word, praying, and seeking God. Replace sin with time spent doing what God calls us to do. Change your habits. Choose to change them. Carve out the time, and you will be refreshed in doing so. "Repent, then, and turn to God, so that your sins may be wiped out, that times of refreshing may come from the Lord" (Acts 3:19).

If we watch programs on TV that are not beneficial or support sin, stop. Replace them with something that is beneficial, that accomplishes something for God, and that is prioritizing righteousness instead. Obey the Word of God. What does it say? "Confess your sins." God is faithful and will forgive you and cleanse you from all unrighteousness. "Therefore, confess your sins to each other, and pray for each other so that you may be healed. The prayer of a righteous man is powerful and effective"

(James 5:16). The verses go on to talk about Elijah and how God answered his earnest prayers.

But first, let's look at this verse. It tells us to confess our sins to each other. We are to be honest and up front about issues in our lives. We are to have a couple people that we can share anything with. We must confess our sins, the sins of our families, and the sins of our nation. With confession of sins comes honesty and humility. Without confession, is there healing and forgiveness?

Do we have the time? We all have the time. The question lies in what our priorities are. Is it our priority to unite together in prayer and fasting for the sake of our communities and nation and families, or are other things more important? It is laxity or apathy that stands in the way of many people uniting together. It is complacency or unbelief that keeps others from seeking God. Are you willing to take the time to do what needs to be done to renew your life and the life of others? Move it up on your calendar on your list of events. Make God your first priority. When Jesus was asked by the religious leaders what the greatest commandment was, His response was very simple. He said, "Love the Lord your God with all your heart and with all your soul and with all your mind." (Mt. 22:37) This is the first and greatest commandment. If we love God above all, then we must place prayer and even fasting at the top of our list of priorities. And if we love God, then we will obey God. Obedience is surely the proof.

> I tell you the truth, anyone who has faith in me will do what I have been doing. He will do even greater things than these, because I am going to the Father. And I will do whatever you ask in my name, so that the Son may bring glory to the Father. You may ask me for anything in my name, and I will do it.
>
> If you love me, you will obey what I command.
>
> John 14:12-15

Why should prayer be a priority for us if God is first in our lives? We are Jesus' disciples, and as such, we are to walk like Him, talk like Him, and live like Him. We are His followers. And Jesus tells us that prayer should be our priority. He quoted the Father's will when He said, "My house will be a house of prayer" (Matt. 21:13). It is God's will that His people and His church be concerned and committed to prayer. If we are not, we are missing out on a huge blessing that God has for us. Jesus taught us to ask. "Ask and you will receive, and your joy will be complete" (John 16:24). We are to communion with the Lord in prayer. Jesus did, and so should we.

If we love God, we will make Him our top priority when it comes to our time, our resources, and our choices. We must make time to seek God in unity for our family, our community, and our nation. *It is high time to rearrange your priorities. When you have God at the top of your list, then you are ready for revival.*

PRAYER

It Is That Important

Our nation needs breakthrough. It is not slightly off course in morality. When God's people needed breakthrough in the Bible, they would unite in prayer and fasting in sackcloth and ashes. And God answered. He answered when the whole nation of Israel sought Him in prayer and fasting because they were going to be destroyed (Esther). They united in a three-day fast, seeking God for breakthrough and intervention or favor in the situation. There were Jews fasting even before these three days. Also notice that it was a fast not only from food. It was actually a fast from water as well.

> Then Esther sent this reply to Mordecai: "Go, gather together all the Jews who are in Susa, and fast for me. Do not eat or drink for three days, night or day. I and my maids will fast as you do. When this is done, I will go to the king, even though it is against the law. And if I perish, I perish."
>
> Esther 4:15-16

How many Christians are in your city? All the Jews in the city gathered together to fast. They needed breakthrough—the mighty hand of God to change the situation. What they could not do on their own they sought the Lord in fasting to do for them. Can we change the course of this nation? God can. Do not ever think that your prayer is too small to make a difference. Likewise, do not ever think that your fasting will not make a difference. There are others praying and fasting in the nation. You are *not* the only one.

Do you remember the story of Elijah? After a success and the Israelites turning back to God, after God working a miracle, he was chased by Jezebel who threatened to take his life. He thought he was alone in his difficulties. "I am the only one left, and now they are trying to kill me too" (1 Kings 19:14). God answered and told him that there were seven thousand others who were likewise committed to Him. Pray and ask God to bring awakening and conviction of sin in the nation. You are combining your prayers with others. And God is hearing and answering. He is storing up those prayers for the right time. Prayer is powerful and effective. It accomplishes. It reaches the ears of God.

Our nation must have a breakthrough. "The god of this age has blinded the eyes of unbelievers, so that they cannot see the light of the gospel of the glory of Christ…" (2 Corinthians 4:4). The love of God is pure and righteous and true. But without the blinders coming off people's eyes, they will never see truth. I remember being in a pastor's prayer group on a weekday morning. I specifically prayed for the unsaved to have their eyes opened spiritually and the blinders be removed. When I finished my prayer I distinctly noticed my own spiritual eyes seemed to be more able to see and understand as well. How often prayer for others springs back to bless us as well. God often returns the blessing that we pray for others. We must pray for our families and nation. Fasting with prayer is the breakthrough cursor to change the course of a nation.

There are difficulties coming if we do not prioritize prayer and fasting, imploring God to change the heart of America. It is leadership that is often judged first and at times can actually bring judgment upon a nation. Without the hand of God, there can be no revival. Government will not be able to fix the hearts of men and women across the nation. People cannot fix it. Only the hand of God can bring the change that is needed. Do not believe a lie. When you pray, God answers. Do not believe a lie. When you pray, God hears. And if we pray the will of God in a situation, we know that He is at work answering what we have prayed for. God promises these things. We must pray.

If the strongholds are too big, begin fasting as well. If your children have not turned back to God yet, add fasting a day a week and persevere for the long haul. I recently talked to a pastor who had been praying for their son who had turned away from Christ. When he and his wife added fasting weekly to their prayers and continued to do it, they began seeing a softening of their son's heart toward God. There has been noticeable change beginning that was not there before adding fasting. Praise God!

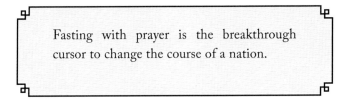

Fasting with prayer is the breakthrough cursor to change the course of a nation.

It is important to have unity in prayer when it is a big request. Ask in unity with other believers. It is powerful. This is something I have learned. There is power in agreement. God promises in His Word that the agreement of two or more who make their request before God will result in receiving. Matthew 18:19 says, "Again, I tell you that if two of you on earth agree about anything you ask for, it will be done for you by my Father in heaven." God begins to work when you ask Him. Get agreement with others on what you pray, if you can; if not, pray on your own.

Are you praying the will of God? Is it according to the heart of God? We know that these requests below are the will of God and that if we pray them, God is at work answering in the hearts of men, women and children.

Begin to pray by:

1. Praising God for who He is and what He has done.

2. Then, confess specific sins of our nation, churches, and personal.

3. Ask for God's forgiveness and mercy.

4. *Confession of sin results in cleansing and forgiveness (1 Jn. 1:8-10). It results in mercy.*

Then bring your requests before God. Ask God for these things:

1. Repentance. Ask God to turn our hearts and the hearts of people across the nation to Him to make Him the first priority in our lives, communities, and nation (Mt. 22:37).

2. All men to turn to Him and come to salvation (Mk 6:12).

3. Christians to "therefore go and make disciples of all nations" (Matt. 28:19). Unbelievers to be convicted of sin and righteousness and judgment (Jn. 16:8).

4. Unity of faith in the Son of God, that Christians will be united in faith and in a common goal. (Jn. 17) Christians to stand united for the glory of God and rise up by faith in God (Jn. 17).

5. Salvation for the lost, that God will open the eyes of understanding of those who do not know Christ, and supply workers into their lives (Matt. 9:37-38; 2 Cor. 4:3-4).

6. God's Spirit to be poured out, that God will manifest and reveal His presence in a very real way in our communities, state, and nation.

7. Times of refreshing to come from the Lord (Acts 3:19; Acts 2:17-18).

8. Salvation. In the face of crisis of all kinds cry out for God's salvation.

9. Healing. Ask God to heal us that we may be truly healed; Save us that we may be truly saved (Jer. 17:14).

10. Ministry. Ask God to open doors of ministry that no man can shut, to do His will.

11. Open doors of opportunity for you to reach out to love your neighbor as yourself (Matt. 22:39).

12. Israel. Ask God to strengthen and protect Israel and bring people to Christ.

These prayer requests are the will of God. They involve some of the more important things of our Christian walk. We must pray for them and that people will come to repentance. We know these are God's will.

Ask and you will receive. Continue to pray for these regularly and watch God bless you as well.

How Do We Pray?

A daily discipline of prayer is important. Many times in the Word of God, we see that Jesus spent time in prayer. He carved out the time to spend in prayer. In fact, He would get up early at times, and His disciples would not know where He was. Other times He would go up on the mountain by Himself to pray. He made the time when He could have done other things instead. Discipline yourself to carve out the time to pray and you will have blessings from it.

Here are a few basics on the subject. Being led by the Spirit with prayer is important. But here are a few basics to apply.

1 Start with a prayer guide. If you have specific requests to pray for, you can unite with many other Christians to pray in agreement for the big things in the Christian walk. Then allow yourself to be led by the Spirit in how to pray them. The more you do it, the better you get at it. Experience is a blessing. Invest in prayer and you will be blessed. It will pay off. And watch how the rest of your day goes when you spend more time in prayer.

2 You can pray out loud or silently. God hears both. Some people kneel to pray. Some sit or rock in a chair. Some sit where they have just read the Bible, and others get up and walk around the house or outside as they pray. God hears

and understands. Begin to do it, and you will find rewards. If you have a hard time staying awake or focusing on prayer, begin praying aloud. And keep a prayer guide in front of you.

3   Set a daily time to pray. A well-established habit can be a blessing for years to come. I find that if you place God first and carve out time to pray and make it a priority, you will get it done. God will reward you for your faithfulness (Matt. 6:6). Make it one of the first things in the day (works the best for many people). The main thing is to set a daily time to do it.

Once you've started with a decision, go ahead and do it. As you continue, you will begin to enjoy it and even look forward to the time. Ask God to guide you in prayer and to continue to teach you to pray

It is to be a priority. If we love God with all our heart and mind and soul, will we not make it a priority to spend the time with God to pray and seek Him daily? Jesus did. He is our example. Pray, and allow God to bless it.

4   Pray with your mind and with your spirit (1 Corinthians 14:15). Pray with both.

Be led by the Spirit and use a prayer guide which is helpful as well. Then pray with your mind and with your spirit. Read the Word of God. Then pray up and pray for power. Ask God daily for counsel, sound judgment, understanding, and power (Proverbs 8:14).

Prayer is powerful and effective, and prayer in unity and agreement is even better. God ordains it to be the way that He works and brings about His will. Pray often, and pray in unity and agreement. Find others to agree with and the blessings of God will fall upon you. Make it the central point for your church and your own life.

We must love God enough to begin to pray and fast together. God's way is the highway. Every time we try to do it our way we have failure. Every time we do it God's way it is success that comes through it. Fasting tends to open up our hearts to correctly hear the voice of God accurately and on time.

Praying with Others

Praying with others. Call each other on the phone, and pray together on the phone. Ask in agreement with others. How do you pray together? Do it from the heart. Do not worry so much about public appearance—to be seen by men for your perfect or good sounding prayers. But rather pray from the heart, and believe that God hears and answers. As it is with many things, the more you do it, the more comfortable you will become with it. You must take the first few steps. So it is when you pray with others. You must start and then grow into it. The main thing is to pray from the heart to God. Jesus told us, Ask and you shall receive (John 16:24).

Some people are so concerned with how they sound that they will not pray with others. When you begin to pray with others, there are several ways to do it. You may begin with short prayers, even one-sentence prayers, until you become more comfortable and the words flow better. These are sometimes called popcorn prayers. Do not worry about what you sound like. Just start praying. God knows our heart in it.

The people who can freely pray in public are usually people who have been doing it longer. Begin and persevere. God hears the heart.

When you ask, ask with faith (Mark 11:24 NIV). How do we do this? Raise your faith before you pray. Focus on God and who He is. A simple way to do this is to start or begin your prayer time with praise and thanksgiving. For example,

> "I thank You, God, for who You are and for all that You have done. You are the Author and Finisher of our faith. You are the beginning and the end. You are the One who is sovereign over all the affairs of men. And yet you tell us to ask for what we desire. You say 'Ask and you will receive and your joy will be complete.' You say, 'The prayer of faith will save the sick' (James 5:15). We come before You in faith and ask that You heal our wounds, that You unite the body of Christ and that forgiveness would be poured into our relationships. We ask that love would abound more and more in all knowledge and depth of insight (Philippians 1:9)."

Don't ask small for things. Ask large, and allow God to work in and through it. Then obey what you sense God's leading is after you pray. Obedience is key as well.

"If you believe, you will receive whatever you ask for in prayer" (Matthew 21:22). Lift your faith before you ask by focusing on who God is and how great He is. What has He done in the past and how has He worked? Thank Him for it. Then, when you ask, ask with faith. Remind Him of His Word as it applies to your requests. Believe that God is going to work when you pray. If it is out of the will of God such as asking for a car that is out of your budget or prompted by greed, why would you want it? Ask God to give you His heart for things. The more that you have His heart for something, the more authority He can give you because you will act in accordance with His will.

James 5:15 says, "The prayer of faith will save the sick" (NKJV). Immediately after that, it speaks of confessing our sins one to another. We are to pray for each other that we may be healed. *Then* comes the verse that says the earnest prayer of a righteous man availeth much (James 5:16). Have faith in asking. Confess our sins, and pray for one another. Then we have the reminder that if we are in right standing before God, our earnest prayer will avail much. It accomplishes. It is powerful. Trust that God hears.

Ask and you shall receive. The first principle is to ask. Seek and you shall find. Knock and the door shall be opened. If you ask, God will not give you a stone. He is a good God who desires to give His children the good things that they ask for (Matt. 7:9-11).

God knows the intent of the heart. Address your heart as well while you pray. I remember hearing of a Christian pastor who had many people's lives changed as he spoke to them. He would often repent of his sins before speaking and seek the mercy of God to not hold his sin against the people that he was speaking to.

Do not be concerned with what you look like when you pray. Pray from your heart.

How Do We Get Our Prayers Answered?

First, we have to pray. If we do not ask, will we receive? "Ask and you will receive, that your joy may be full" (Jn. 16:25 NKJV).

Second, pray the will of God. What do you know is the will of God? What does Scripture speak on? So, pray that in. Then, listen to the leading of the Holy Spirit. What do you sense the Lord impressing on your heart to pray? When God desires to do something, He often impresses His people to pray for it before He acts on it. Among the known will of God is repentance.

It is God's will that we turn to Him and make Him the first priority in our lives. What is the verse that Jesus gave when asked what the greatest commandments are? He replied, "Love the Lord your God with all your heart and with all your soul and with all your mind and with all your strength" (Mark 12:30 NIV). This is the first and greatest commandment.

Pray for it with: *"Lord, help us love You with all our heart, with all our soul, and with all our mind and with all our strength."*

Next, Jesus followed it up with "Love your neighbor as yourself" (Mark 12:31). First, we are to love God. Then we are to act it out by loving our neighbor. Love breaks off the binders and lies that the enemy would attempt to put on us. Agape is an unconditional love for one another. Do you remember the story about the Samaritan man? Luke 10:30 is where the story begins. He got his hands dirty. He reached in to help a man that others—including the religious respected leaders—would not spend the time to help. Who was the Samaritan man? He was a disrespected Samaritan. The Jews did not respect him or even want to associate with him. Samaritans were the rejected people. Yet he was the only one who stopped to help the man in need. He was also the one that Jesus said was fulfilling the law of loving your neighbor. What would our neighborhoods look like if we acted as this man did? Love the unlovely. Get your hands dirty, and find ways to help people. If you want to obey God, begin by loving your neighbor. Reach out to those in need, and get your hands dirty!

Pray it in with *"help us love our neighbor as ourselves."*

Confessing Our Sins As Well

It is God who governs over all the affairs of men. It is God who is sovereign. It is God who works miracles on the behalf of his people as they fast and pray and seek Him. It is also God who directs sovereignly and stands in the way of evil men. Yet it is the prayers of God's people that will shape a nation, for God has ordained the prayers of His people to be the incense and the way that He intervenes. It is the earnestness of His children in prayer and fasting before Him that will bring revival.

Do the same things as you have done, and you will find the same result. But if we desire a different result, we must commit ourselves to a different plan. The plan is first to pray and fast. All revivals have come first as God's people petitioned him seriously on behalf of their needs and of the land that they lived. It is God who answers prayers. He answers and sees the need and directs the course of a nation *as His people pray and fast and earnestly seek Him.* Do not think it is hopeless, for it is the hand of God that changes a nation.

When we look at past revivals, it seems there are times that **when confession of sin** stops, so does the revival. Pride is sin. Arrogance stops the flow of God from working in our lives. Also, sin that is covered over and not dealt with pulls us away from the presence of Almighty God who is holy and just. God hates sin. He loves people but hates the sin. Un-confessed sin is a breeding ground for more sin.

"He who conceals his sins does not prosper, but whoever confesses and renounces them finds mercy" (Prov. 28:13).

The first step is confession of sin. A person who confesses his sins will find mercy. How often does sin result in the desire to cover oneself up? As far back as Adam and Eve, we see that the initial consequence of sin is to hide oneself. Sin can result in shame. But when we bring our sin out to the surface and allow it to be exposed, God is willing and able to cast it away and restore us. Think about it this way: When a wound is not cleansed and then covered up, what happens? It begins to infect the area around it and causes more pain and discomfort. But the quicker we *treat* the wound, the quicker we will be healed and restored. So it is with our failings and our mistakes. He who hides his sin does not find healing. We must open up and allow light to be shed upon our sin and mistakes, shame, condemnation, or guilt in order for God's healing to occur.

"Confess your sins one to another that you may be healed" (James 5:16). It is the first step to healing. Allow someone to love you unconditionally and help you heal instead of covering your sins over and not allowing other people in to your life.

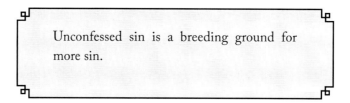

> Unconfessed sin is a breeding ground for more sin.

I had this vision once while I was at an outdoor service. It was held on the grounds of the court house. As the leaders prayed and confessed the sins of people in our nation, I saw a giant crushing ball begin to destroy the courthouse behind them. It was crushing the justice of the courthouse. It continued as long as the people prayed and confessed sins. Instead of having to force people to see and be disciplined for their sin, they choose instead to face it, confess it, and turn on their own. When the confession quit, which was short, there was much more time spent asking for God's blessing. As this time continued, I saw the courthouse being built back up. How many sins we have in our nation. We must confess our sins. "He who conceals his sins does not prosper, but whoever confesses and renounces them finds mercy" (Prov. 28:13). Confession of sin and admission of wrongdoing before God is the first step toward healing and mercy from God. Mercy *crushes* justice all over the nation when people confess sin. We must confess the sins of the nation before God and ask for His mercy and forgiveness.

More Powerful Prayer

Adding fasting with prayer is the large way. If we want a big change in our nation, in our families, in the generation of our children, in our communities, our education system, and so on, we must make a radical difference in what we are doing. The time is now. It is not tomorrow or next year. We will have an eternity to remember the difference that we make for God in the nation now. "Humble yourself before God, and He will lift you up in due time" (1 Peter 5:5-6).

What is it to fear God? It is to have a loving respect for Him. "Blessed is the man who fears the Lord, but he who hardens his heart falls into trouble" (Prov. 28:14). We love God and choose to obey Him in our personal life as well as our corporate life. What is it that God calls us to do? Pray, fast, and obey. Obedience is king, but prayer and fasting give power to our spiritual life as well as the increased ability to hear, ask, and plea to God for help. It is God who helps. It is we who must ask and seek and knock.

We knock in unity as we gather together in groups of three or more to seek God on behalf of this nation, our families, and communities. We need the mighty hand of God. We are helpless on our own, and when we realize this, we become mighty in God and stronger in spirit to do His will and pull down strongholds that must be pulled down. Come before God as a child. To enter the kingdom of heaven, you must have the faith of a child.

When Peter was put in prison by King Herod, the believers were fearful for his life. James had already been put to death. Now Peter was held in prison for public trial. Acts 12:5 says, "So Peter was kept in prison, but the church was earnestly praying to God for him." There was earnest prayer for Peter. God sent an angel and delivered Peter from prison and brought him out. What were the people doing at the time Peter was delivered? They were gathered and were praying (Acts 12:12). God stepped in when His people gathered in prayer for His servant. There were many gathered together, praying. Time and time again throughout history we see God answer in amazing ways when His people are faithful to His call to pray.

As what happened in 1946, God answered with evangelists when His people cried out to Him in prayer and fasting.

When you look at history, the Bible and the history books, you will see that it is the nation that humbles itself that finds mercy. Even blind Bartimaeus cried out for healing (Mk 10:46-52). He cried out for mercy even more when people told him to stop. They thought Jesus was too important to help him. But it was Jesus who, when asked for mercy, stopped and called the man to himself and healed him. He gave him his sight. What was it that Bartimaeus cried out at first? "Son of David, have mercy on me!" He had earnestness, and he persevered. The crowds told him to stop and be quiet. But he did not listen. He continued anyway and he received mercy and healing.

Continue In Prayer

"Praying always with all prayer and supplication in the Spirit" (Eph. 6:18).

Pray in the Spirit on all occasions. Pray with the leading of the Holy Spirit and in unity with others. Pray in tongues. As God has gifted you, pray.

Pray with faith for the unity of the body that they may exercise faith in their lives as well as obedience in what they do. If we will be willing to lay down our flesh needs to seek God and to pursue him, the lives of our children and grandchildren will be changed for good. I say it again: believe. Jesus said, if you have faith as a little child, you will enter the kingdom of heaven (Matt. 18:1-4). We pull down strongholds by believing. We will never act unless we believe, will we? If we do not believe that God answers prayer, will we pray or expend the time to do it? Believe. Receive and obey.

How do we pray with faith? First, we come before God with a clean conscience. We put our eyes on God. He is the *I am*. Begin to pray the names of God. Adore Him for who He is. Thank Him for what He has done. Then begin to ask Him to bring revival.

We need the Holy Spirit to empower and enable us. We need more of His spirit and His power to enable us. When the Holy Spirit came with power upon the disciples who were waiting in Jerusalem, He did it in ways that they did not expect.

Have you ever experienced the power of prayer? When was it? Even Elijah prayed over and over for rain after God had already promised it. God promised it, but Elijah persevered until his servant reported a small cloud "as small as a man's hand is rising from the sea" (1 Kings 18:44). He did not pray once. He prayed numerous times until the answer became apparent. And even then the answer that began was as small as a man's hand. What began small became a heavy rain with clouds that covered the sky.

Do not give up on prayer. Our nation needs it. So do our leaders, our churches and our families. We must have the mighty hand of God to instruct us to obey Him better.

"Righteousness exalts a nation, but sin is a disgrace to any people" (Proverbs 14:34 NIV).

"For lack of guidance a nation falls, but many advisers make victory sure" (Proverbs 11:14 NIV).

"The eyes of the Lord are everywhere, keeping watch on the wicked and the good" (Proverbs 15:3 NIV).

"The Lord detests the way of the wicked but he loves those who pursue righteousness" (Proverbs 15:9 NIV).

"The Lord tears down the proud man's house but he keeps the widow's boundaries intact" (Proverbs 15:25 NIV).

FASTING

Prayer and fasting adds to our arsenal of spiritual
weapons against the devil and helps to make
God our stronghold in times of trouble.

Fasting draws us into the presence of God,
which is the beginning of revival.

If you have never fasted, you are missing out on a mighty spiritual
discipline the Bible talks about more than once. It can bring great
blessings when we do it. It crushes the devil and brings us closer
to God. It is also a means of receiving God's grace increasingly
in our lives, families, neighborhoods and the land we live in. We
need it more than we know because it is earnest seeking of God
and greater humility. Let's look at a few passages from the bible
on prayer and fasting. We do not have a whole book to spend on
it but we will look at a few.

There is power through prayer and fasting to break the
enemy's tactics. Jesus said it. "And he said unto them, 'This
kind can come forth by nothing, but by prayer and fasting"
(Mark 9:29 KJV). When the disciples were unable to cast a
demonic spirit out of a boy, this was Jesus' answer to them. He
was able to cast it out.

Jesus had spent time in fasting before the story above. "Then
Jesus was led by the Spirit into the desert to be tempted by the
devil. After fasting forty days and forty nights, he was hungry."

(Matthew 4:2) After this is when he cast the devil out of the boy but his disciples were unable.

When Jesus was tempted by the devil with food, while fasting, His answer was, "It is written: 'Man does not live on bread alone, but on every word that comes from the mouth of God.'" (Matthew 4:3) If you are tempted by food during fasting, remember that is the first thing the devil tempted Jesus with as well. We must stand our ground and defy evil. Remember when you have hunger pains, that it is seeking God more earnestly and we are overcoming the devil through it.

Fasting appears to give us greater authority over the devil when we look at Jesus' response. There are some spiritual strongholds that are not broken without prayer and fasting. And my belief is that it is these stronger strongholds that make more of a difference once they are broken.

Nearly every revival throughout history, in original accounts, began with God's people praying *and* fasting. Virtually every time it was a combination of both in unity. Often it was small groups, even down to one or two people that began.

There are many times God answered in powerful ways through the Bible.

Ezra sought the Lord for protection. He wanted to be a witness to God's ability to protect (Ezra 8:21). The Israelites needed protection when they were going to travel through dangerous territory with valuable items. They needed God's hand of protection. And Ezra didn't want to take the king's offer to protect them with his horsemen but rather he wanted to be a testimony that their God was the true God and able to protect.

> There, by the Ahava Canal, I [Ezra] proclaimed a fast, so that we might humble ourselves before our God and ask

him for a safe journey for us and our children, with all our possessions… So we fasted and petitioned our God about this, and he answered our prayer.

Ezra 8:21-23

They were traveling through an area that was known for having bandits attack. They sought the Lord in fasting and prayer and God answered. He protected them supernaturally from bandits on their journey through enemy territory even with many valuables such as silver and gold and bronze being carried for the temple along with them.

So we can seek Him for protection in prayer and fasting for our families and churches. We certainly need God's hand of protection in the nation as well.

It weakens the flesh. The flesh fears fasting. The spirit is strengthened by it. Fast and pray, and you will find revival come in your heart and in your spirit. You will be drawn close to God through it and will find the presence of God as you seek Him. Is it hard? It can be. If it is a stronghold, it can be harder at first than if it is not. The flesh fears fasting. The spirit is strengthened by it. The flesh is weakened from controlling us. The spirit is strengthened and increased in ability to hear God's voice. This is generally the case. **When you fast, your heart tends to become more tenderized toward God and obedience often becomes easier.** It helped me allow God to lead me to not go backward in my job choice some years ago. It can also make it easier for you to obey God.

I had fasted when a senior in high school. Then in college and vocation school I fasted some as well, though some of the fasts were shorter. I had quit fasting for a while due to a physical issue. But years later as I was praying with a young woman who called me about serious marriage problems, I felt impressed by the Holy

Spirit to fast for two days. So I told her about it and she agreed to join. We began to fast for two days. I used a couple crackers on the side if needed (since it had been years since I had fasted for long and had quit due to a blood sugar problem). I also used some juice during it.

The first day passed, and I sensed something being held back in the spiritual realm. I remember noticing it and being impressed about the power in fasting. That same day this young woman called me in a very excited voice. She said she had understanding of what the problem was. It was a breakthrough. Of course, Jesus spoke of the demonic being weakened by fasting as well. It is not the only thing, but it is one thing. There is also revelation that comes through it. One man in a serious relationship did a three-day fast after he had received counsel he was not sure was from God. He placed himself in an apartment for the three days and just sought the Lord without food. By the end of the three days, he had much needed revelation. And it saved him from a lot of pain. He had the answer he needed concerning the relationships he was in.

How often we desire there would be a balloon in the sky that would give us a certain yes or no from God? But that is not very common. Nevertheless, taking a day to fast and pray has enabled many people to overcome their indecision and more clearly discern God's leading. Again, abstaining from food helps us move our flesh out of the way and follow God into decisions that have better results and more blessings. For His ways bring joy and peace and provision. Look at the book of Acts. We see that the disciples heard God's leading during fasting.

> While they were worshiping the Lord and fasting, the Holy Spirit said, "Set apart for me Barnabas and Saul for the work to which I have called them." So after they had

fasted and prayed, they placed their hands on them and sent them off.

Acts 13:2-3

The Holy Spirit chose to speak while they were fasting. Many people have heard God's voice better after beginning to fast than otherwise. Take the flesh out and the Holy Spirit comes in to destroy the devil. It is the Holy Spirit who empowers and enables us to follow the ways of God. Get close to God through the power of the Holy Spirit and you will be able to conquer storms that you couldn't otherwise. Do you know that the Holy Spirit speaks? He spoke in the New Testament, and He speaks now. Fast and pray, I say. Fast and pray for our country needs awakening. There are people without Christ who will go to hell for years to come without the power of the Holy Spirit to enable us to share and care and break through strongholds that hold them back from coming to Christ. It is the power of God that is coming in fasting and prayer. It is the power of God to break through things that would otherwise be impossible to break through!

When you need help, fast and pray. Seek God and His Word while you fast and make it impossible for the enemy to drag you into things that are not God's will and not His plan. For it is the power and the blessing of God that comes through fasting, and it is better than even the discomfort of abstaining from food.

The flesh drives sin while the Spirit brings freedom. The Spirit is godly whereas the flesh is ungodly. There are times to fast and pray until you know what to do.

One church declared a fast for every lunch for forty-nine days and had ten people come to Christ. One pastor fasted forty days and had miraculous peace come into a meeting in a church he was negotiating between two parties in. One pastor fasted forty days and after the Lord impressed on his heart that He was moving his ministry ahead ten years because of it.

Fasting is a powerful weapon against some of the stronger spiritual warfare and strongholds that a person encounters. There are some spiritual battles that require fasting with the prayer to overcome (Mark 9:17-29 KJV; Luke 4). I have noticed dramatic changes when I have fasted. Add it to other disciplines.

Another man struggled to overcome pornography but was unable until he added fasting to it. One husband was impressed to fast for his wife for one day and things turned around.

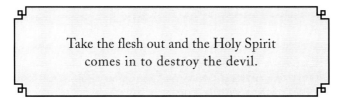

Take the flesh out and the Holy Spirit comes in to destroy the devil.

A storm quieted. After I had fasted for three years regularly, God stepped in and fixed something that I had not been able to fix.

Jeremiah fasted for forty days, it appears, before the infamous time that God spoke to him on the mountain (1 Kings 19:8-9). Strengthened by that food, he traveled forty days and forty nights until he reached Horeb, the mountain of God. There he went into a cave and spent the night. Then God spoke to him giving clear direction and encouragement.

If you look at the book of Daniel, four out of twelve chapters (Daniel 9-12) have to do with Daniel seeking God in fasting and God's response or intervention because of it. Look at Daniel chapter 10. Daniel was concerned about a revelation he received. "At that time I, Daniel, mourned for three weeks. I ate no choice food." He fasted for three weeks. Then an angel appeared to him and what did the angel say?

"Do not be afraid, Daniel. Since the first day that you set your mind to gain understanding and *to humble yourself* before your God, your words were heard, and I have come in response to them" (from Daniel 10). Daniel humbled himself in fasting. He sought the Lord and an angel appeared to him and gave him understanding that he sought.

We Can All Do It

Fasting is not for a chosen few. Rather, it is for everyone. Everyone who is a disciple of Christ needs to fast at some point or during some season of their lives. It is a blessing to fast. And it is a blessing to obey. If we do not obey but only fast we will encounter difficulties. But if we will obey and fast and pray then we will have success. And as we fast and pray in unity revival comes and brings the downpour of heaven upon us.

If you are not fasting regularly, you are missing out on one of the most basic disciplines of the Christian walk. It brings the presence of God, which is the beginning of revival in our lives, our families, our churches, and communities. It is in fasting and prayer that we often find breakthrough that has not come any other way. Continue the habit and discipline, and you will find success and blessings flow through it that you do not expect. Many people become more effective for God through a discipline of prayer and fasting. There are many examples of Christians, through history, fasting, praying, and being blessed with open doors.

Many have found their ministry or usefulness to God increased by this discipline. Look at Jesus. He engaged in a long fast right before His public ministry began. And the people were amazed or astonished at His teaching because He taught as one having authority (Luke 4:1-32).

The apostle Paul prayed and fasted often (2 Corinthians 11:27 KJV). And he was greatly used by God, for the kingdom.

We do not only pray at some point or some season. So with fasting, if we desire the blessings of God and desire to grow in our Christian walk, the power of prayer, and fasting is needed in our lives. It overcomes obstacles that are not overcome without it. Some people have overcome addictions even to pornography by adding fasting. There is power in fasting that we do not recognize in our culture. If we did, there would be many, many people who would eagerly pursue God with it for their families, communities, and loved ones. There are so many people that need extra intervention in their lives. The power of God through prayer and fasting, and doing it in unity and with accountability is extremely valuable to our success as Christians. The average Christian is offered many more temptations than they used to be. Look at television and all the blatant opportunities for lust, for supporting sin or becoming "used" to it. It can desensitize the Christian to God's call to be holy.

We must seek God with earnestness. It is when we seek Him with all our heart that we find Him, is it not? And is it not in the presence of God that we find our wounds healed?

There are people who may believe we do not need to unite in prayer and fasting. My first comment would be they probably haven't fasted and prayed much. They believe that fasting is a thing of the past. But it does not say that anywhere in the Bible. Nowhere in the Bible does it say that "these things," referring to fasting, "have passed away." Jesus's response when asked why his disciples were not fasting while He was with them was that they *would* fast when He was gone. Jesus said "in those days they *will* fast" (Luke 5:35). Jesus told them that the time will come, after He was taken from them, His disciples would fast. And as we look through history at the early church we see that the disciples did fast.

In fact, it was common to fast once or twice a week. There is power in fasting with prayer. It brings breakthrough that is not easily attained without it, in our lives as well as in the lives of those we fast for. It is interesting that Jesus didn't respond to the question about fasting with "they may fast" or "they might fast" or even "they occasionally could fast" but rather "they will fast." The disciples still practiced this discipline even after the gift of the Holy Spirit and even after Jesus was resurrected from the grave. It is a New Testament discipline, which means that it still applies to us today—if we want the breakthrough and power that is with it. The disciples fasted (2 Co. 6:5; 11:27 KJV; Acts 13:2, 3; 14:23).

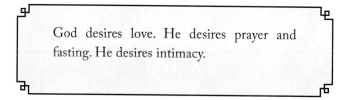

> God desires love. He desires prayer and fasting. He desires intimacy.

What other disciplines does our enemy, the devil, come against more than prayer and fasting? It knows that if we do not ask, or make the time to ask God for things, we miss out on experiencing the power of God in our lives, in our churches, and in our evangelism to the lost. It does not want people to come to Christ. Neither does it want our families and relationships in the church to be examples to unbelievers of the goodness and greatness of God. God desires peace and harmony. Our spiritual enemy, wants *anything* but our lives and those in the Christian community to be examples of the power and love of God. It knows that if we have these things in our lives and communities that people will be drawn to God, that they will seek God, and that more people will be brought to salvation.

God desires love. He desires prayer and fasting. He desires intimacy.

Removing food from the day to fast and pray strengthens us in spirit and weakens our flesh. What does it mean to weaken the flesh? It means that we weaken our natural desires that are antagonistic to God's ways. The flesh is our desire for overeating, for example. It could include the sin of lust, of pleasing ourselves with what feels good rather than what is spiritually beneficial. To please the flesh is to please what feels good to us. "Put to death, therefore, whatever belongs to your earthly nature: sexual immorality, impurity, lust, evil desires and greed, which is idolatry" (Colossians 3:5). It would also include the following "anger, rage, malice, slander, and filthy language from your lips. Do not lie to each other, since you have taken off your old self with its practices and have put on the new self, which is being renewed in knowledge in the image of its Creator" (Colossians 3:8-10).

We discipline our body to make it subject to the things of God. So we discipline our natural desires, and bring them into subjection to what is God's will and what is best. Just because we see something does not mean that we have to focus or dwell on it. Rather, we discipline our minds and our hearts to not be tempted or attached to sin. We focus on the things of God, and it is in fasting and prayer that we can gain the edge to overcome. The Word of God is important, too, of course. Do not ever forget that. We must pray, fast and obey.

Fasting is powerful against the enemy. In fact, it is powerful when united with others in prayer as well.

Fasting in unity with others is powerful. It gives us accountability and strengthening. Where we are weak others are able to strengthen us. How do you fast? First you must decide to do it. Make the commitment in mind and heart to fast. Then, in order to follow through on it, discipline yourself.

If you start with the initial commitment in will, it becomes easier to follow through on. The apostle Paul said this, "But I discipline my body and bring it into subjection" (1 Corinthians 9:27 NKJV). So also the Word of God says in 1 Corinthians 6:19-20: "Do you not know that your body is a temple of the Holy Spirit, who is in you, whom you have received from God? You are not your own; you were bought at a price. Therefore honor God with your body."

We are not our own. All we have is God's. We have been bought and paid for with a price, the price of Jesus His Son's life on the cross. It is God who has given us life. It is we who are to follow and obey. Obedience is key. If we desire greater fruitfulness we must commit our lives to God more fully. The greater our obedience to God, the greater the blessing from God.

Obedience brings blessing. So also does radical obedience bring radical blessing.

It is the blessing of God that adds the most fulfillment to our lives. When we obey God, He blesses us. He adds to our lives the fruit of the Spirit.

Our body is the temple of the Holy Spirit. As such, we need to discipline it and bring it under subjection. We must take care of our body and care for ourselves in a proper and healthy way. Fasting is actually cleansing to the body and allows it to rid itself of toxins as well as take a rest when we do it once a week. The discipline and commitment to do it weekly instills within us a discipline over our flesh that spreads into other areas of our life as well. Because food is a basic need that we all have, our ability to fast from food for a spiritual purpose, to restrain from it temporarily, strengthens our ability to resist our flesh and submit to God. Fasting puts the flesh under our feet and strengthens us in spirit.

There are also times, such as in the story of Manasseh, where God intervenes in our lives with mercy because of our earnest plea with great humility (in fasting and prayer).

But Manasseh led Judah and the people of Jerusalem astray, so that they did more evil than the nations the Lord had destroyed before the Israelites.

> The Lord spoke to Manasseh and his people, but they paid no attention. So the Lord brought against them the army commanders of the king of Assyria, who took Manasseh prisoner, put a hook in his nose, bound him with bronze shackles and took him to Babylon.
>
> In his distress he sought the favor of the Lord his God and humbled himself greatly before the God of his fathers.
>
> And when he prayed to him, the Lord was moved by his entreaty and listened to his plea; so he brought him back to Jerusalem and to his kingdom. Then Manasseh knew that the Lord is God.
>
> 2 Chronicles 33:10-13

Manasseh was king of Judah and led them astray to the point that they did more evil than the nation that the Lord destroyed before the Israelites. He was in sin.

The discipline of the Lord came upon them and they were taken by a foreign army. Manasseh was taken from the position of king to a prisoner. Then he turned to God and humbled himself greatly, most likely in forty days of fasting and prayer because it was great humility. That was a way to humble themselves greatly. And God answered. The Lord was compassionate and answered his plea even though he had done so much evil. And he brought

Manasseh back to Jerusalem and to his kingdom. Humility brought answers from God.

David also humbled himself in fasting and prayer. Look at the reason he did it in Psalm 35:13: "Yet when they were ill, I put on sackcloth and humbled myself with fasting…" He humbled himself before God on behalf of his enemies, those who repaid him evil for good. He sought the Lord in fasting and prayer for their healing. So must we also seek God earnestly for those in the land that we live. There are people who will never know Christ if we do not seek the Lord on their behalf, if we do not reach out to them and pray and fast. It is all eternity to come for those who do not know God. We must have the compassion of God for them for they are blinded by the god of this age (2 Cor.4:4).

When we love God, we must seek and be concerned about the things that are on His heart. The lost, the unsaved, is one. He does not desire that anyone live at enmity with Him, that anyone goes to hell or is separated from Him. (Matthew 18:14: "In the same way your Father in heaven is not willing that any of these little ones should be lost.") It is God's will for those He created to love Him and to live with His presence. He loves people. We must have the heart of God for the lost. We must ask Him for it and seek Him in prayer and fasting.

God intervenes when His people unite in prayer and fasting. It is humility to fast. It is also humbling to fast. In other words, we are humbling ourselves to fast and to depend on Him. We also tend to become more humble as we fast. And empowered, yes.

Look at Esther 4:3. The Jews were going to be annihilated by their enemies. In fact, it was the entire Jewish nation that faced annihilation without any recourse or way to defend themselves from it. They were subject to the man who was second in power who hated them. So what did they do? They fell before the Lord.

"In every province to which the edit and order of the king came, there was great mourning among the Jews, with fasting, weeping and wailing. Many lay in sackcloth and ashes" (Esther 4:3).

They knew that it was the hand of God that would save. So they went to Him. Then Esther also went before the king and risked her life which was at the mercy of the king at the time. Or so we say. It was really at the mercy of the God who they seek. Then after many had already humbled themselves before God in fasting and earnestness, Queen Esther also asked the people to gather together and fast for her to go before the king and request protection for her people.

"Go, gather together all the Jews who are in Susa, and fast for me. Do not eat or drink for three days, night or day" (Esther 4:16). What would happen if God's people would take it seriously and fast and unite and humble themselves before God?

Breakthrough

Fasting tends to soften our hearts to God's will and to the things that He loves. It also helps us be more willing to obey Christ. I remember a time when our family had just moved, and we were in a season of change. I had the desire to start working at an old job, which was comfortable. I remember sensing the Holy Spirit guide me to not do it. But I was finding it hard to obey. I was impressed to fast supper. So I did. And after fasting, I could say no to the old job easier. My heart and will were more willing to obey. Obedience brings blessing. There was blessing that came through being willing to obey God.

We must come before God in greater humility. Humble yourself before the mighty hand of God that He may lift you up in due time. Humility is the opposite of pride or arrogance.

It is the opposite of saying that we can do all things by ourselves. We need His mighty hand to deliver us, lead us, and enable us.

Fasting is a more complete way of humbling ourselves. Fasting in the Bible is a way of coming before God with greater humility. It is asking, seeking, and knocking. Asking can refer to praying. We ask the Father for our needs. Then we come before Him with fasting as well and seek. Finally, with prayer and fasting we also come before God with obedience that follows these. We could look at this as knocking. We ask, seek, and knock with prayer, fasting, and obedience that follows.

Isaiah 58 spoke of what God desires true prayer and fasting to include and result in. It speaks of the many blessings that come through it, but here the people were not obeying as well. They did the act but did not really seek God. Prayer and fasting can pull out depression in some cases. I had a period of depression after going through very difficult things. At times it was actually severe. I had thought that I would hold back from fasting because I felt depressed when I would do it. But the day came after being around others that I became so low I didn't know what else to do. I finally reached a point where I decided if fasting really works, then I am going to do it until this struggle is done. So I began a fast, thinking I would possibly fast up to three weeks. I began the fast. After three days, I stopped due to a problem that came up that week. But what I found after I stopped was that my lows did not reach as low. They had actually improved some—even 25 percent! So from there I continued to fast weekly. I began fasting two days a week for a number of weeks and continued for a time. Is that too much? It began pulling those things out as I continued. After several weeks of fasting two days a week and with the help of other people, my depression *significantly* lessened.

If you have serious depression or are on medication I recommend being advised by others familiar with your situation or medical doctors as well. In my case fasting added the extra punch to pull the bouts of depression out and lessen them. It weakened the enemy's tactics because the devil always wants to steal, kill, and destroy. What man could not do fasting did because it was humility before God, and it was obedience.

It's like dealing with weeds with deep roots. Similar to our nation, there are roots in the nation that are deeper than they should be. These roots need to be pulled out and disempowered by fasting and prayer. Pride is one. We have a serious issue of pride in the nation. To counter pride there must be greater humility. And it must be the people of God. Who else will do it?

Pride goes before a fall and how great that fall can be. Humility protects us from some things. In fact, when we are walking in God's ways, He often blesses our food supply, our financial supply and our families. There is great power in fasting and prayer to pull out some things because God blesses it. God says, "Humble yourselves, therefore, under God's mighty hand, that He may lift you up in due time." Humble yourselves before the mighty hand of God. Humility before God has brought more blessings than pride or self-dependence. Independence from God is sin. Do you notice that humility is around more than one passage that talks about resisting our enemy, the devil (1 Peter 5:5-9; James 4:6-10)? We must pray and fast to remove demonic stuff from our lives, from our families, and from this nation.

Fasting is a discipline given by God to root out evil principalities. Some, I believe, is the power of fasting and prayer itself and some is actually the way God responds to His people humbling themselves. It is greater submission to God.

I remember a man who was addicted to pornography, and, try as he might, he could not break his addiction. He did not try one thing only. But when he added fasting, it finally broke the addiction. Fasting is humility before God. We must fast and pray, humbling ourselves greatly before God. Humility is a key, and it comes in fasting and prayer.

Why do I speak of fasting by itself? It is never by itself but always combined with a relationship with God that is humbling ourselves before Him and seeking His aid. We need to start fasting for our own lives, our nation, our communities, the lost, and the children. It is an old art that needs to be torn apart and redone. We must take it out of the old and build on it anew. It is part of the new, the need to humble ourselves until the mighty hand of God steps in (2 Chron. 7:14).

It is healthy for the body. In fact, years ago I read that if you fast one day a week, you will live several years longer. That is a health reason. It gives your organs a rest and is healthy for the body. Fasting usually also helps keep our weight down. It has increased my ability to discipline myself in many areas, and it decreased my dependency on food. I have become more dependent on humility before God than other things to fill up my needs. I have found as I have developed the consistent, weekly habit of fasting that my discipline in many other areas has increased. Or should I use the word *victory*. I have found increased victory in other areas of my life.

Fasting, prayer and increased obedience is essential to bring national revival. Without it, we will not have revival like we should.

Fasting also opens us up to the things of God. When I was young, I sensed the Holy Spirit ask if I wanted to receive the gift of tongues. I said, Yes, if You fit into my box and do it only this way. I put limits on it. So God responded with, *Then I will not give it to you*. I repented and asked Him a number of times for the gift. Then one day I sensed the Holy Spirit impress on my heart to fast supper and He would give me the gift of tongues. Sure enough, after I obeyed He gave me the gift of tongues. How often He involves our faith as well. He calls us to do something and then brings His promise to pass.

When Jesus healed the blind man, he spit on his eyes. There was spit and mud in the miracle. Yet was it the spit and mud that healed him or was it the faith behind it (Mk 8:22)? It was faith with action wasn't it?

Although there are many physical benefits that often come from fasting as well, our purpose for doing it is primarily spiritual. It is to attain to the flesh to eat and drink and be merry. It is to attain to God to lay it all down for Him. What deprives the flesh will weaken it. If we lust, we strengthen the flesh. When we resist it, we weaken it.

Do not fear it. It is not uncommon for people who have never fasted to be a little scared of trying it. Do not fear it. Food is selfishness if we will not give it to God. It is selfish to need to have something that God has told us we can abstain from or do without if we have the power of God to do it. If you are afraid to begin, my suggestion would be to start with a single meal and fast that to begin with. Once you figure out you are okay with that, then fast from when you wake up in the morning until 3:00 p.m. Or just go ahead and do a two meal fast until supper. You can even do this twice a week as a spiritual fast before God. If you have medical issues, you need to seek medical counsel from your doctor before you fast.

Jesus fasted for forty days when led by the Spirit into the wilderness. It was after this that he entered public ministry. And people were astonished at his teaching. He gave us the example to fast. Some people say, "If there had been an easier way for Him to prepare for public ministry, He would have probably done it." There was something that was accomplished in the time of fasting that needed to be done. It is an example to us. My belief is that it was put in the Bible for a reason: for us to see how Jesus did it and that He did spend time in prayer and in fasting. And when temptation came, he overcame (Matt. 4).

Fasting enables us to be stronger in spirit and overcome the impulses of the flesh, to overcome strongholds and to overcome temptation that the enemy brings.

Many times in the Word of God we see also that Jesus spent time in prayer. He carved out the time to spend in prayer. In fact, he would get up early at times and his disciples would not know where he was (Mk 1:35-37) or he would go by himself so he could commune with God at other times. Most people that are more effective than most, for God, commonly fast and pray regularly. It is known to be powerful and effective for breaking strongholds and overcoming the devil. Look at the story of Jesus' disciples attempting to cast out a devil from a young boy (Matt. 17:21 KJV). It was fasting and prayer and faith.

Increases Our Faith & More

Fasting disempowers the devil and increases our faith. The two go together. Faith is our shield as Christians with which we "quench all the fiery darts" of the evil one. Notice what the enemy goes for? Our faith. Doubts and unbelief are something that it attempts to convince us of so we question God and His ways. It did it with Adam and Eve in the very beginning. The first thing was to cause Eve to doubt whether God really said what He did and whether what He said would come to pass. From the very beginning the enemy has been targeting the faith of the faithful. It wants doubts and unbelief in the Creator of all things who is able and willing to draw you to salvation. It is God's ways that are best. They are the ways that lead us into life and peace, love, and joy. Fasting helps to overcome the devil and increase our faith.

When we earnestly come before God to seek Him, He answers:

For I know the plans I have for you,' declares the Lord, 'plans to prosper you and not to harm you, plans to give you hope and a future. Then you will call upon me and come and pray to me, and I will listen to you. You will seek me and find me when you seek me with all your heart.

Jeremiah 29:11-14

God has good plans for us. They are plans to give us a future and a hope. They involve fasting as well. There are promises of God that come through fasting. This verse above explains that when we call upon God and come and pray to Him, He listens.

2 Chronicles 7:14 says this: "If my people, who are called by my name, will humble themselves and pray and seek my face and turn from their wicked ways, then will I hear from heaven and will forgive their sin and will heal their land." The greatest fulfillment of this verse includes fasting, prayer, and obedience. Fasting in the Bible is a more complete way of humbling ourselves and earnestly seeking God. Isaiah 58 goes on and describes people that were fasting but were not obeying. God said He desires a fasting that includes obedience and mercy for the poor.

If you look at the New Testament Jesus spoke: "When you pray…God will reward you" and "When you fast…God will reward you" (Matt. 6). The verses immediately before these begin by calling these "acts of righteousness." It also tells us "when you give to the needy…God will reward you" (Matt. 6). Giving to the needy is actually included with prayer and fasting as an "act of righteousness." God assumes that we will do all three of these. Jesus said "when" you do these rather than "if." And with all three of these, He promises that the Father in heaven will reward us.

It appears that Jesus fasted when He spoke to the Samaritan woman by the well. His disciples went to town to buy food. When they returned, after Jesus was sharing truth with the Samaritan woman, the Bible says, "Meanwhile his disciples urged him, "Rabbi, eat something." But He said to them, "I have food to eat that you know nothing about." Then his disciples said to each other, "Could someone have brought him food?" "My food," said Jesus, "is to do the will of him who sent me and to finish his work. Do you not say, 'Four months more and then the harvest'? I tell you, open your eyes and look at the fields! They are ripe for harvest" (John 4:34-35). Interestingly, He was apparently fasting here, and He was not waiting until tomorrow to do God's will.

Fasting tends to give you God's heart and compassion for people and situations. Fasting and prayer is a more earnest seeking of God. And it is in prayer and fasting that we both humble ourselves to do it and it brings humility into our lives in increasing measure. Consider this: As you go up with God in power, authority, dominion, and rule, you will also go down before God in humility. We must increase in humility and in our obedience to God in order to go up with God in authority and the like. As the servant with the talent, we must be faithful with what God gives us, for Him to give us more (Matthew 25).

I have watched people who have fasted regularly—such as once a week—be given God's heart for people, the needy, and the unsaved around them more than without fasting. If we have God's heart for people, we will tend to have more authority in their lives as well. The closer we are to God, the more we will be able to pray with His heart for situations. If we have His heart for someone, we will also be entrusted with more from God. Fasting tends to tenderize our hearts to the things of God. It brings our heart closer to His. This brings revival. People who have otherwise felt emotionally stale have found their emotions change and tenderized with God's heart for people and situations through regular fasting and prayer. It changes the inside of us with God's love.

What do you fast for? Breakthrough is one. Look through history, and read the ways that God has answered the prayers of

His people and the humble cry of their heart when they unite in prayer and fasting (i.e., Esther 4-9). Do not believe that you cannot make a difference. We need people like you to come before the Father in heaven in unity and seek His face to bring a miracle. Do not think that your family and grandchildren or loved ones are not affected when His people fast and pray. It is a powerful Christian discipline.

Fasting in the Bible actually refers to covering the mouth. So a spiritual fast is a restraint from food.

If you look at Moses in the Old Testament, he did two forty-day fasts. The first one he did when he received the Ten Commandments. The second forty-day fast was right after the first when God said that He would destroy the entire nation of Israel and make a nation from Moses instead. Moses came before God in earnest plea on behalf of the nation of Israel that God would give mercy and relent. He did not eat or drink for those forty days, and he lay himself prostrate before the Lord. He humbled himself greatly. The result was mercy and salvation of the Israelites. How many were there? There were probably around 1 million Israelites. The entire nation of Israelites turned back to God.

While Moses was up on the mountain, the Israelites turned themselves to worshiping idols, specifically a golden calf that they made. That sounds a little like America. People place things above God. Then the Lord said to Moses, "Write down these words, for in accordance with these words I have made a covenant with you and with Israel." Moses was there with the Lord forty days and forty nights without eating bread and drinking water. And He wrote on the tablets the words of the covenant—the Ten Commandments (Exodus 34:27-28). Now there was a difference in those days that allowed Moses to abstain from water for forty days. Either the atmosphere was different or God stepped in miraculously to allow Moses to do it. We know that now a human cannot go without water for any longer than three days. Moses speaks of his experience in Deuteronomy 9:

> I stayed on the mountain forty days and forty nights; I ate no bread and drank no water... [after which] the Lord gave me the two stone tablets, the tablets of the covenant. Then the Lord told me, "Go down from here at once, because your people whom you brought out of Egypt have become corrupt. They have turned away quickly from what I commanded them and have made a cast idol for themselves."

> And the Lord said to me, "I have seen this people, and they are stiff-necked people indeed! Let me alone, so that I may destroy them and blot out their name from under heaven. And I will make you into a nation stronger and more numerous than they..."

> So I took the two tablets and threw them out of my hands, breaking them to pieces before your eyes.

> Then once again, I fell prostrate before the Lord for forty days and forty nights; I ate no bread and drank no water, because of all the sin you had committed, doing what was evil in the Lord's sight and so provoking Him to anger... (Deut. 9:9,11-14,17-18)

But listen to what he said next: "But again the Lord listened to me." (Deut. 9:19) God honored his request. After Moses humbled himself before God in forty days of fasting and prayer, God turned the heart of the nation of Israel back to Him. *It is God who turns the heart of a nation.* It is we who seek Him for it in prayer and fasting and obedience.

One promise in Isaiah 58:9 is that when we fast, God will say, "Here I am." "Then you shall call, and the Lord will answer; You shall cry, and He will say, 'Here I am'" (Isaiah 58:9 NKJV). Have you ever had the experience that God has answered your cry with "Here I am"? I once was going through difficulties and cried out to the Lord for help. I remember a day that He responded so clearly with "Here I am." It was after I had been fasting a day a week for a time. What does fasting look like according to Isaiah 58? It looks like Christians rising up to do the will of God and strengthening themselves with fasting as well. And it looks like the faithfulness of God appearing on the scene in many ways. The presence of God comes in fasting and obedience.

Jesus spoke against the fasting of the religious leaders (Matthew 6), and yet He Himself fasted (with proper motives). "And when He [Jesus] had fasted forty days and forty nights, afterward He was hungry" (Matt. 4:2 NKJV).

He also told us in the New King James that some spiritual battles are not won without fasting (Matt. 17:21 NKJV). It is closely tied to the passage on faith and commanding a mountain to move. One of the things that is common in fasting is that our faith is increased. That is a common thing. "Faith is the substance of things hoped for, the evidence of things not seen" (Hebrews 11:1 NKJV). "Now faith is being sure of what we hope for and certain of what we do not see" (Hebrews 11:1). Jesus asked the blind men that came to him for healing, "Do you believe that I am able to do this?" They did. So he healed them (Matthew 9:28-31).

Fasting, as a general rule, increases our faith. It opens our eyes to spiritual things and increases our dependency upon God to do things for us that we couldn't do for ourselves. I remember in specific, after a period of fasting a day a week for three years, I felt impressed by the Holy Spirit that He was going to do something for me that I could not do for myself. And He did. It was a miracle by the power of the Holy Spirit and the provision of His people. Remove food from the equation, and we can become more sensitive to the Holy Spirit, to His voice, to His leading, and His presence. Prayer and fasting will bring change in your life and in the lives of those you seek God for. We need times of refreshing in our nation and in our families. Fasting with prayer is an effective tool for changing a nation.

People think it is culturally irrelevant. It is never culturally irrelevant. It is biblical. It is a means of receiving God's grace.

Fasting with prayer is considered by some to be the powerhouse of all spiritual disciplines. It is increased fuel on the fire of prayer. David fasted, too. He said, "My knees give way from fasting" (Ps. 109:24).

It tends to conquer spiritual strongholds in our lives. It is a powerful spiritual discipline, most effective at some things. One lady said she gets excited when she feels hunger pains because she knows that strongholds are being weakened. It is often harder to do *at first*. In a culture that is filled with gluttony and comforts, this is a major milestone. We are temporarily laying down the most basic of our human needs to seek God. We are placing Him first and placing our flesh in submission. Fasting breaks strongholds off our lives and those we fast for. Jesus fasted. He said when He was gone, His disciples would fast (Luke 5:35). His disciples fasted. The early Christians fasted. The apostle Paul fasted. The early church fasted often. Most Christian leaders recognize the importance of fasting and prayer. Most well-known Christian leaders recognize its importance and use it regularly.

It is a powerhouse of spiritual disciplines. Fasting adds the extra fuel to the fire to empower prayer. It tends to increase the breakthrough of prayer. Jesus said there are some things that require prayer and fasting to bring break through (Mt. 17:21; Mk 9:29 KJV). Fasting, in the Bible, is a restraint from food.

It can repair relationships. God answers and gives grace to the humble as well as provision.

Fasting often makes it easier to obey God in other areas as well. If your heart is wrong before you fast, try fasting and watch God work through it. It softens the heart and makes us more sensitive and able to hear God's voice. It decreases our appetite and aids in self-control of our flesh. And when we win the victory over food, many other strongholds and struggles typically lessen, decrease, and even break off. It breaks strongholds of overeating or overindulgence.

Greater obedience results in greater blessing.

Fasting is placing ourselves in a position of obedience that can result in a greater measure of God's grace in our lives.

Fasting with prayer is one of the least practiced, and yet most needed disciplines of the Christian walk. It has been shown to have enormous impact on our personal lives as well as on our nation.

There are things that God has stepped in to do with prayer and fasting that are miraculous. He has intervened when his people humble themselves before Him in it. Jesus gave us an example of fasting. He fasted forty days in the wilderness before His public ministry began (Matt. 4:2). Some commentators believe that He fasted more than that in the gospels. Jesus said "when you fast" not "if you fast" (Matt. 6:17). He assumed we would fast and said God will reward you.

Fasting and prayer tends to bring spiritual awakening and revival in our own lives as well as breakdown spiritual strongholds and deceptions. It makes God first in our lives—over food.

"Heal us that we may be truly healed; Save us that we may be truly saved" (from Jer. 17:14).

What will God do if we will unite in fasting, confession of sin and prayer on behalf of this nation, our families and our communities? Nearly every spiritual awakening that has occurred throughout history began with united prayer and fasting. It is believed by some commentators that when the Day of Pentecost came in Acts 2, the early disciples were united in prayer and fasting. Prayer and fasting seems to bring God's blessings and victory into our lives as we do it.

Why fast? Because God said to do it and out of our love for God (Mt. 6:17). Our nation, families, and communities need the mighty hand of God!

Fasting is placing ourselves in a position of obedience that can result in a greater measure of God's grace in our lives.

Then your light will break forth like the dawn, and your healing will quickly appear; then your righteousness will go before you, and the glory of the Lord will be your rear guard. Isaiah 58:8

I sensed the Holy Spirit speak this to my heart for a church I shared at. I have shared it at some others since:

Pray and fast and obey and I will give you authority in this region you do not have yet. There is power and authority in the Kingdom that you have not experienced that I will give if you will pray, fast and obey.

FASTING MADE SIMPLE

How Do We Fast?

Pick a day of the week and fast weekly. Fasting is a blessing when we do it regularly. A lot of people find that fasting becomes easier to do as they continue in it. Many people use Monday as their day to fast. Then, sometime during the day or night, commit to call a friend (or Cord of 3), and pray together either on the phone through a three-way call or through a conference call. If your phone is able to conference call, you can use your phone to do it. There are also places that you can find that offer free conference calls. You can sign up with them, and they will give you a specific number to call with a password. Then each person that you add to your prayer group can call in to that number and you can pray together over the phone. Three way calling is very easy for most people once you find out how to do it. Decide on a day and time.

If you have never had a prayer partner or cord of three group, you are missing out on a blessing of God. Pray with a guideline, but follow the leading of the Holy Spirit as well. There are blessings that God has promised to us that come through uniting in prayer.

Where Do We Fast?

You can fast anywhere: in the privacy of your own home or at work during the work week. You may fast at home on your day off or fast during your work day. You can fast and go through your regular activities and work through the day. Take the normal mealtimes or other time(s) during the day to spend with God in prayer for the nation, our families, and our communities.

Do it weekly, and it will change your life. You will begin to have authority and victory in areas that you have not had it.

Practical Advice on Fasting

Practical advice: When you drink water while fasting, it is better to drink a glass or two at a time than a half-gallon all at once. It will help to flush your body, but water also gives you energy. This may actually be the case when you aren't fasting as well.

Take a day a week to fast and pray and seek God. Take extra time during the day to be sensitive to the Holy Spirit and to ask God for what you are fasting for. Breakthrough? But the more often or regularly (such as weekly) that you do it, it actually tends to become easier and easier to do. If you develop a habit, it becomes easier. So it is with fasting. You figure out ways to do it, when to start and when to finish, and work it out until you are more comfortable with it.

Here are a few practical tips on fasting:

1. Decide to do it. Make the decision or commitment and begin. Start where you are and grow into it. If we wait to be perfect or do it "just right" we tend to never get it done.

2. Schedule it. Decide which day you will fast. If you forget at first, do not quit. Find a different time and keep going. You can fast and go through your regular activities and work. Set aside time to pray during your usual meal time. A biblical fast is a restraint from food. Liquids help you to not be dehydrated.

A one-day fast is easier to do than a longer fast. It's only a few meals, but one benefit of fasting three meals in a row is that your stomach shrinks. So when you begin to eat again, you feel fuller quicker. Most people will have an easier time maintaining a lower weight when fasting one day a week. The more you become accustomed to fasting, the easier it tends to become.

3. Commit yourself to a liquid fast. What is a liquid fast? It is committing yourself to restrain from food that is solid. I personally don't tend to drink shakes when I fast. Instead, I drink liquids such as water, juice, vegetable juice, fruit juice, orange juice, coffee, or tea, etc. If you desire, you can even use chicken broth for liquid. This type of liquid is essential on a longer liquid fast. It helps your sodium levels to maintain a healthier balance. I actually had a point when I did a three-week fast and found myself feeling better when I began to drink chicken broth once a day. It maintained a healthier balance in my body. Be sure, though, to come off a longer fast gradually. If you run out and eat a large meal or greasy food immediately, you may endure a very sick period after it. Allow your body to gradually adjust to food intake. There is more on this later on. But I want to clear the air and say that a one-day fast or a two-meal fast is not something that you have to concern yourself with as much. There are not as many things to be aware of.

A liquid fast is one of the easier ways to fast. If you feel compelled to use only water, you may. Some people feel better if they use juice lightly. Others feel better without it. You can try it for yourself. Drink plenty of liquids.

People sometimes ask, "What about milkshakes or things like that?" Usually a liquid fast consists more of runnier liquids such as juice, chicken broth, teas, water, coffee, etc. One lady talked to me about her desire to fast. She had done it in the past but just did not want to go without her morning coffee. She had only done a water fast in the past. That meant that she abstained from everything but water while she fasted. But now she was having difficulty getting herself to fast that way. So I suggested that she try a cup of coffee in the morning anyway.

Some people will get a headache during a fast because of the toxins that are released. You can do a few things. One is to drink more water or fluids. The other is to try a little juice and see if it helps. If you are used to drinking a lot of caffeine in coffee or tea and abstain completely, you can end up with a headache from that in itself. But do not feel like you have to completely drop it when you fast. If you feel led by the Holy Spirit to do so, you may. If you do a liquid fast, then liquids are allowed. But please do try to drink extra water. It will help your energy and clarity as well. Not everyone has these types of symptoms. If you do, try a few things and see what helps.

4. Decide on a determined length for the fast. You can fast from 3:00 p.m. Monday to 3:00 p.m. the next day. This is one example. Or you can start your fast in the morning before breakfast. Some people like to start their twenty-four-hour fast by fasting supper first.

If you have never fasted before and are afraid to start with three meals or a whole day, you can start with one or two meals at a time. Start with one or two meals for the first few weeks. It is common for people who are not used to fasting to feel afraid of it.

In some Asian countries, they eat less anyway, actually two meals a day. A day a week is only fasting three out of twenty one meals.

Fasting typically becomes easier as you continue to do it. Work it out for yourself if you use no juice or only a little. The Bible tells us to "work out your salvation with fear and trembling" (Phil. 2:12). So also work out your fasting and prayer. Personalize it a bit, and work it out for yourself. Figure out how much juice to have. Figure out how much water to have. Some people stay away from milk during it. What works for you well may be slightly different from what works for the next person. As you continue to do it, follow guidelines and stay within them, and you will be blessed.

Some of us as Christians are missing out on a powerful discipline in their spiritual walk. It is the discipline of prayer and fasting.

Fasting and prayer is something everyone can participate in. It is not only for the chosen few. It has many things that are blessings from it. It is harder than eating until you become accustomed to it and train yourself to do it. Then for many people it becomes something that they enjoy doing, similar to exercise. It takes discipline to put ourselves into the commitment to fast. Once we make the commitment to do it, we must direct ourselves or discipline our flesh to do it. Compare it other things that we may start. Many people find that exercise is difficult at first. But if you discipline yourself to do it and continue, then it becomes easier. Discipline is the key. Discipline is the key to obey. Obey and God will bless you. Then decide what to do with it. When you fast somewhat regularly, such as once a week, it typically becomes easier to do and part of your schedule. It also brings an increase in your spiritual growth and in your ability to hear and discern God's voice. There are other benefits of fasting as well. It brings revival in those who fast and often those who are prayed for during it.

Pray and spend time with God during your normal meal time. Passages to pray for our communities, families, and nation are: Ephesians 1:15-20; Ephesians 3:16-21, and Psalm 143:8-12.

At the beginning of the fast, tell God what or who you are fasting for. Agree with us in prayer for God to move in and breakdown spiritual strongholds in our families, communities, and nation. Find friends to call, if you are able, to pray with over the phone. But take the time to fast and pray.

It is a restraint from food for a specific period of time and a spiritual purpose.

Fasting with prayer is powerful and effective. It might be a misunderstood thing. Many people do not know what to do with fasting. I find it interesting that our culture is one that does not speak about fasting as much, but it sure speaks about immorality. It speaks of self-gratification that is immediate. But when it comes to the process of growth that lasts, it condones sin rather than actual healing. If we focus on the temporary, we are sure to lose the eternal.

Have you ever fasted more than two days? How long have you fasted? I had a time when I fasted for twenty days, but I did not have the Lord tell me to do it until a day or two before the fast started. It usually helps to have more time to mentally prepare. You can etch on your mind the decision ahead of time, and it will help you prepare mentally. But if it is a long fast you need to come off of it slowly. Do not eat heavy or greasy foods. If it was a water fast then it would be good to start liquids, juice or soup broth first.

The Time Is Now

No servant is above his master. If Jesus united in prayer, we must also. If He said that there is blessing in unity and the Spirit of the Lord is there, we must take it into account (Mt. 18:19-20). We will have more of the blessing and presence of the Lord when we obey and unite with one another than by ourselves. Serious times require serious actions. If you like the course that our neighborhoods, cities, and nation is taking, then don't worry about it. Otherwise, turn to Joel 2:15 that says "Blow the trumpet in Zion, declare a holy fast, call a sacred assembly. Gather the people, consecrate the assembly."

The prophet was calling God's people to get serious about seeking Him. It was a serious time that God wanted His people to gather together and seek Him about. They declared a holy fast, a time that was set apart for God, to humble themselves before God and earnestly seek Him. It was a call to gather an army of people together to fast and cry out to God for intervention. So we also must unite and cry out in fasting and prayer for God to intervene. After this call to earnest prayer and fasting and turning to Him comes this verse:

> And afterward, I will pour out my Spirit on all people. Your sons and daughters will prophesy, your old men will dream dreams, your young men will see visions. Even on my servants, both men and women, I will pour out my Spirit in those days…
>
> Joel 2:28-29

What did the prophet say God would do after they humbled themselves in fasting and unity before God? He said that the Holy Spirit would be poured out and there would be prophecy and dreams and visions. In fact, then it also says: "And everyone who calls on the name of the Lord will be saved; for on Mount Zion and in Jerusalem, there will be deliverance, as the Lord has said, among the survivors, whom the Lord calls" Joel 2:32. The greater Presence of God came after their earnest calling upon God.

We must unite ourselves together. Join the army of God to assemble ourselves together to fast and to pray and to seek the Lord. There is power in unity.

The question is how do we assemble ourselves together? One of the ways is in a cord of 3.

Prayer Requests:

Take time to pray through these prayer requests as well. Ask God to work in your heart during the fasting and open the eyes of your understanding. Pray through Eph.1:15-20.

1. Repentance: that love for God will return and that we will make God first in every area.

2. Salvation for the lost: that God will pour out His Spirit and bring them to repentance and salvation. Pray for the Spirit of God to be poured out upon many and open eyes to salvation and draw people to Christ.

3. Unity in the body of Christ: that we will be one as Jesus prayed and shine to the world that Jesus is real. And for the Love of God to increase in believers that we will see as God sees and love as God loves and win unbelievers to salvation.

4. Healing and salvation: in our nation and families and communities! Pray for healing to come quickly to the body of Christ, to our families and nation.

Heal us that we may be truly healed. Save us that we may be truly saved (from Jer. 17:14).

5. Leaders of the nation: that God will lead them and guide them into righteousness (Jn. 16:8).

6. Ask God to change the nation from the inside out.

What will God do if we will unite in fasting, confession of sin, and prayer on behalf of this nation, our families, and our communities? Persevere in fasting, and you will see blessings of God upon your family.

How do we assemble ourselves together in a way that will work long term? An easy way to assemble across the country and into neighboring tribes and nations is in Cord of 3's. Imagine a thousand people praying and fasting for the same things consistently in your regions.

IN CORDS OF 3

Though one may be overpowered, two can defend themselves. A cord of three strands is not quickly broken (Ecc. 4:12).

We need each other. We need each other. We need each other. No one is stronger by oneself. God made us to be a part of the body of Christ, not to be an island on our own. We need each other.

> Two are better than one, because they have a good return for their work: If one falls down, his friend can help him up. But pity the man who falls and has no one to help him up! Also, if two lie down together, they will keep warm. But how can one keep warm alone?
>
> Ecclesiastes 4:9-11

No one goes it alone. Do not think that you have to go alone. We encourage and strengthen each other, loving each other along the way with our imperfections and quirks. Why do we need one another? That is how God has made us. We are human. We are imperfect, and we need each other. There is a spiritual battle against us, and we need to be united to stand strong. We are more effective when we are united than when we are separated and alone.

To assemble means to unite together in a fitted way. We assemble a puzzle by fitting the pieces together. And the whole of the picture is more than the pieces by themselves. We also assemble and fit together in unity, being strengthened by one another. When you look at the body of Christ, there is an assembling together of the parts to make the whole. We work in harmony and unity, filling in the gaps where the other parts are not able to fill. We all have our strengths and weaknesses but we would all accomplish less without unity. We must assemble and unite together to be more effective for Christ.

How do we unite together? Unite together in prayer groups. You can plan, participate and/or lead groups with a focus to pray together. Unite together in cords of three. Agree to assemble and become stronger together.

Then, sometime during the day or night, on the same day that you're fasting or a different day commit to call a friend (or Cord of 3), and pray together. You can pray in person or on the phone. You can also three-way call or conference call. If your phone is able to conference call, you can use your phone to do it. There are also places that you can find that offer free conference calls. You can sign up with them, and they will give you a specific number to call with a password. Then each person that you add to your prayer group can call in to that number and you can pray together over the phone. Three way calling is very easy for most people once you find out how to do it. Decide on a day and time. Select it and begin.

If you have never had a prayer partner or cord of three group, you are missing out on a blessing of God. Pray with a guideline, but follow the leading of the Holy Spirit as well. There are blessings that God has promised to us that come through uniting in prayer.

When it is hard to make it work, ask God to open doors and ways to pray with people weekly. Set a time and day every week that works for everyone. Establish a way that works for your group. Begin with a day of the week and a time that you will either engage in a three-way call, meet in person, or gather together in some other way. You can call each person separately and pray together, or you can use a freeconferencecall.com type of site to sign up for free conference calls. If a person in your group cannot make it, gather anyway if possible. Mentor those who are not as familiar with prayer. Ask them to be a part of the group and help them grow in prayer. We can all use it and we need it more than ever.

Principle of a Cord of 3

Where is the biblical basis for a cord of three? David had three mighty men (2 Samuel 23:8). Jesus had three of His disciples who were closest to Him. To have others you are closer and accountable to is a godly example that Jesus set (Mt 17:1; Mk 5:37; Mk 14:33). We are not to be loners. The devil will take out the loners easier than those who are united, especially when we are united in prayer.

Even Ecclesiastes 4 tells us, "Two are better than one…a cord of three strands is not quickly broken." Yes this verse has been applied numerous times to a husband and wife and God. But if you look at Jesus, He had an inner group of three disciples who seemed to be closer to Him than others. So, in our prayers for the nation, for our lives and our families, we also strategically organize groups of three or more to pray together and agree together. Jesus said, "Again, I tell you that if two of you on earth agree about anything you ask for, it will be done for you by My Father in heaven. For where two or three come together in My name, there am I with them" (Matthew 18:12-20).

This is a promise from God. His Presence is with us when we unite with other Christians in His name. Unite together in prayer and pray the will of God and we will make a mess for the devil repeatedly.

This is the confidence we have in approaching God: that if we ask anything according to his will, he hears us. And if we know that he hears us—whatever we ask—we know that we have what we asked of him.

1 John 5:14-15

Establish a day of the week to do it. Then do it. Remember that what matters is that we pray, not how we sound. When you make the decision to do it, decide on a day and begin to pray together. Get it established, and you will experience the benefits and the blessings of God through it. Also, fast that day and tell God what the reason for your fasting is. If you are not able for some reason to use that day as your fasting day, then use a different one. But unite together with others to prayer and fast and obey. Set a routine. The successful are more persistent or frequent. Make a simple routine, and follow it.

Do we want a revival in our nation? We must be willing to do what it takes. We obey and we pray. Then pray in unity with others if possible as well. How can you pray in unity if you are out of town or far from your friends or relatives? All you have to do is pick up a phone and call one another. Pray over the phone if need be. Begin with prayer and chat after so you do not run out of time to pray. There are blessings in obedience if we will pray. There are great blessings in obedience. There has never been a time in history when there has been such revival as when God's people have sought God's face in earnestness, confessed sins and prayed and fasted. It has always been in this that the hand of God has revealed itself time and time again. Look through the Bible. Look at examples. God even answers the prayer of a few.

We seek God in unity. Through the Bible we see that in unity God answers. There are verses such as "every matter may be established by the testimony of two or three witnesses" (Matthew

18:16). This one speaks of winning a brother over or dealing with someone who has sinned against you and will not respond to you.

As you look through history, you see many revivals begin with a small group that gathers together in prayer and usually in fasting as well. The principle is: unite and be blessed. Carve out the time to pray on your own and to pray together. It is the building block to change the nation, our communities, and families for God. There is a strength that comes in a cord of three that strangles the enemy's tactics and strengthens us to be able to make a difference in our families, neighborhoods, and nation. There is a blessing of God that comes upon us in united prayer.

Do you have to have only three in your group? No. But it is a principle that works well. I have had times of having more or less in a group to pray. But it is a principle that has worked well.

A cord of three is a way to unite together to bring revival in your area, your families, and your life. God often begins in our lives, but do not underestimate the power of your prayers. God works on the inside of hearts and minds. Do not think that it is useless. We know that God hears and answers. And we must remember that even if our prayers do not appear to revolutionize the nation in a day, God is at work through them. We must remember that the nation would be in worse shape than it is without the prayers of God's people faithfully and regularly praying. Add fasting to it and we will break strongholds more than otherwise.

Do our prayers change everything immediately? Not always in the way that we want to see, but God's hand is at work in and through people's lives and hearts. We see an impassioning of God's people in different areas. There are fires of revival that burn in different areas through the nation. And God is bringing people to Him. So do not think that God does not answer your prayers. Rather, keep the faith and realize that God is working and the nation would be in worse shape without them.

We are accountable to God to pray. Find people to pray with. List people who you could mentor or unite with. Do not think you are the only one. Ask others as well if they are interested. They will be blessed. And if you don't have one (a Cord of 3), do it anyway. Will we pray, fast and obey more than we have?

UNITY IS STRONGER

"Holy Father, protect them by the power of your name—
the name you gave me—so that they may be one as we are
one" (John 17:11).

How did Jesus pray? In John 17, He prayed for unity amongst
believers and protection from the evil one. "My prayer is not that
you take them out of the world but that you protect them from the
evil one" (John 17:15). One of the tactics of the devil is to bring
disunity in the body. It stops God's people from being as effective
and hurts the testimony or witness of Christians through it. This
is not the only place that Jesus gave us the example of praying for
protection from the evil one.

A few verses down, Jesus prayed this:

My prayer is not for them alone. I pray also for those who
will believe in Me through their message, that all of them
may be one, Father, just as You are in Me and I am in You.
May they also be in Us so that the world may believe that
You have sent Me (John 17:20-21).

Jesus continues to pray for unity in the verses following:
"May they be brought to complete unity to let the world know
that you sent me and have loved them even as you have loved me"
(John 17:23). Notice that Jesus is praying for complete unity not

just partial unity. We are stronger when we are united. Discord is disunity and brings problems.

How do we unite? Praying together is a powerful way. There is nothing that will connect and strengthen your friendships more than praying together. I have had unction, ability, and heard the voice of God more clearly after I have prayed with others.

Accountability is another powerful way. It is the place that we arrest some of the most difficult schemes of the enemy. We must have accountability. Get everything out in the open on the table if you need to and deal with it one by one. Find someone who is trustworthy and open up. James tells us, "Confess your sins to each other and pray for each other so that you may be healed" (James 5:16 NLT). Uncover it and pray for one another. The devil always wants to shame, condemn, or silence and intimidate you into covering up sin and struggles. Get them out into the open. Bring someone else in. There is strength in unity. Do not fear evil. Fear God and the process that He gives to get free from sin. Uncover it and admit your need for Him. Allow other people in to help. And pray, fast and obey.

> Accountability is another powerful way. It is the place that we arrest some of the most difficult schemes of the enemy.

Even the apostle Paul wrote and shared about his difficulties. Some people say that he ignored the past, but he put down on paper the many trials he had been through. He asked for prayer. He asked for help, even for someone to come and stay with him. He thanked and expounded on the fact that Timothy stayed with him. He was not a man alone, but rather, he was supported and helped by others.

Jesus also was not alone. He had others with and around Him even though He was fully God and fully human. Even though He was without sin, He was not a loner. He had disciples around Him of which three were closest to Him. He also had personal, specific times that he spent with God alone (Mt. 26:40-41). One of these times was to prepare ahead and avoid temptation. He cried out to God to strengthen Him for enduring the cross. In fact, He actually sweat drops of blood. He needed God's strength and determination to go through what He knew was coming. He also pleaded for God to take that specific thing away, if it was the Father's will. Yet, He submitted to God and "endured the cross, scorning its shame" and was rewarded for it. He suffered for us that we might live with Him. He looked at the long term picture rather than the immediate. He saw the tapestry that God was weaving through it rather than just the immediate thread that was being put in place according to the will of the Father God.

> He saw the tapestry that God was weaving through it rather than just the immediate thread that was being put in place according to the will of the Father God.

There is power in unity. God calls the body of Christ to walk in unity and in love for one another to have the grace of God upon our actions and lives. There is power when united in prayer. There is also increased favor when God's people unite across churches and denominations. Unite and be strong. Unite together in prayer. Get your sins out on the table and begin to build again a unity between us in the body of Christ that is stronger than the tactics of the devil. Rise up in prayer and accountability.

One of the requirements of unity is forgiveness of one another. We must forgive seventy times seven. We must love one another rather than holding a grudge. Peter asked Jesus how many times he must forgive his brother and Jesus's answer to him was seventy times seven (Mt. 18:22 NLT). In other words, it meant an uncountable number of times. Forgive or we lose a battle the devil wants us to lose.

One of the chief ways the enemy will come against us as the body of Christ is through silence, secrecy and unforgiveness or bitterness. We must rise up in the face of challenges and unite together with hands held high to uphold one another in prayer. We must also not put one another down but rather come to each other's aid. And when a brother or sister falls, please pray for them.

OBEDIENCE IS KING

"But seek first the kingdom of God and His righteousness, and all these things shall be added to you" (Matt. 6:33 NKJV).

When we seek Him first, we receive the provision and blessing of God in miraculous ways that we do not expect or foresee. If you want to see miracles in your life, begin to focus on what God's heart is for. What does He care about ? What is it that the heart of God breaks over? Begin to make those things your focus, and the blessing and provision of God will be in your life. Seek *first* His kingdom and His righteousness and all these things will be provided for you as well.

"Abide in Me, and I in you." (John 15:4 NKJV). We are the branches. God is the vine. We must make up our mind to stay and abide with God. Then we will bear fruit. For we can do nothing without Him (vs.5). Allow Him to fill us up in supernatural and powerful ways through the Spirit of the living God.

What is God's heart for? What does He care about? Did you know that people are priceless? No amount of money will redeem someone's soul. We cannot pay enough money to send someone to heaven. We can tithe and supply money for workers to be sent into the harvest fields to reach people for Christ but we must also do our part and reach the people around us.

People are invaluable. No amount of money can send someone to heaven. But God loved us so much that He did the one thing that would bring eternal life. He sent His Son to die and pay for all of our sins that we may live for Him and live for eternity. We are not to live only for this life here and now but for the life to come and for God who sent His Son for us. The exchange is this: if we give our life to help others, they will in turn grow closer to God and come to God. The fact is that we exchange temporary things for eternal things. We exchange the things here and now for what will last forever. Our life is not our own. We are to rise up and live for Him who gave everything for us. What do we have to give? Our all.

"For the love of Christ compels us, because we judge thus: that if One died for all, then all died; and He died for all, that those who live should live no longer for themselves, but for Him who died for them and rose again" (2 Corinthians 5:14-15 NKJV).

Our life is not our own. The greatest excitement in life is living for God. It is the way of adventure and growth and stretching, but it is also the way that brings the greatest fulfillment. I remember hearing a story of a group of pastors overseas who were "hiding out" for their lives in the woods. They were picking gnats off one another, but in the midst of it, they were overcome with great joy. Even in dire circumstances, the Holy Spirit filled them with joy. Even in difficulties the Holy Spirit helps.

> We are to rise up and live for Him who gave everything for us.

Remember when we were little and we put rocks in our pockets? They were our treasured possessions. We must place the cares of our Father in heaven in our pockets, rather than the things of this world.

What kind of cars we drive or how big of houses we have is not the main concern of our Father in heaven. Jesus said, "I tell you that in the same way there will be more rejoicing in heaven over one sinner who repents than over ninety-nine righteous persons who do not need to repent." (Luke 15:7) The heart of

God rejoices over people coming to repentance, to Christ. That is the heart of God.

Then Jesus shares the story of a woman who has ten silver coins and loses one. "Does she not light a lamp, sweep the house and search carefully until she finds it? And when she finds it, she calls her friends and neighbors together and says, 'Rejoice with me; I have found my lost coin.' In the same way, I tell you, there is rejoicing in the presence of the angels of God over one sinner who repents." (Luke 15:8-10).

The heart of God breaks for those who do not know Him because it is all eternity to come. It matters if we put God's cares in our pockets. To put His cares in our pockets means we treasure them and spend time on them. We carry those cares with us.

Do you know how to share your faith with those who do not know Christ? The first step is to be ready in season and out of season. Start with this, the Romans Road to salvation. Do you know it well enough to share it? The Romans Road to Salvation is a road paved through verses in Romans to lead a person to salvation.

The Romans Road to Salvation

The Romans Road of salvation is a series of verses from the book of Romans that are easily used to share the way to salvation. It explains the following points.

1   Who needs salvation.

2   Why we all need it.

3   How God provides our salvation.

4   How we receive salvation.

5   The results of salvation.

The following verses can be written out or listed on a 3x5 note card and taped in the front flap of your bible so you have them handy. You could also put them on a note card and memorize them. They are a valuable tool.

Who needs salvation? All of us.

We have all sinned and fallen short of what is right, so we all need God's saving help, which is salvation.

Romans 3:23 says, "For all have sinned, and fall short of the glory of God." It says that all people have sinned. We have all fallen short of being perfect.

Why do we all need salvation?

The result of sin is death. For every action there is a consequence. Sin brings death. God's desire is to lead us to Christ to receive His gift of eternal life.

Romans 6:23a says, "For the wages of sin is death but the gift of God is eternal life through Christ Jesus our Lord."

The punishment that comes from sin is death. It is not just physical death but spiritual death. But the gift offered to us by God through Jesus Christ is eternal life. It is a new life here and a life spent in eternity with God.

How does God provides our salvation?

Romans 5:8 says, "But God demonstrates His own love toward us, in that while we were still sinners, Christ died for us" (NKJV).

God revealed His love by sending Christ to pay the price for our sins, even while we were still sinners. Before we changed our ways, God sent His Son to pay the price for our sins if we accept Him.

How we receive salvation:

Romans 10:9 says, "that if you confess with your mouth Jesus as Lord, and believe in your heart that God raised Him from the dead, you will be saved."

We must confess Jesus as our Lord. And we believe in our heart. We believe that Christ's death on the cross paid for our sins. We accept it.

Romans 10:13 says, "for everyone who calls on the name of the Lord will be saved."

Salvation is available to anyone who personally places their trust in Christ and makes Him their Lord and Savior.

The results of salvation:

Romans 5:1 says, "Therefore, since we have been justified through faith, we have peace with God through our Lord Jesus Christ."

This brings peace with God into our life.

Romans 8:1 says, "Therefore, there is now no condemnation for those who are in Christ Jesus."

We are forgiven for our sins and are not condemned because we have trusted Christ as our Savior and Lord.

Tell God that you believe He sent Jesus to die on the cross for your sins and that you accept Him as your Savior.

Romans 8:38-39 says, "For I am convinced that neither death nor life, neither angels nor demons, neither the present nor the future, nor any powers, neither height nor depth, nor anything else in all creation, will be able to separate us from the love of God that is in Christ Jesus our Lord."

Read through this Romans Road to Salvation every day for three weeks. You will benefit by having it at your fingertips when needed. If we are able to share God may open more opportunities for us.

These Prayer Requests are important as well:

1   Ask God to enable you to share the gospel concisely.

2   Ask Him to give you boldness and courage to do it.

3   Ask Him to open doors of opportunity to share the gospel with people.

Then read through these verses and the road it paves for the next three weeks and practice it. It doesn't have to be perfect. But do your best.

Be ready for the opportunities that come. If you are not, you are not faithful to God, are you?

God's desire is that we *abound*. "God is able to make all grace abound to you, so that in all things at all times, having all that you need, you will *abound* in every good work" (2 Corinthians 9:8). God is able to make all grace abound to you.

When we are obedient, we can overcome easier. The authority we have is through the shed blood of Jesus Christ, but obedience is a key. As children of God, we grow in our ability to understand and obey God. It is a process. Will we ever be perfect in obedience? No. Paul said, "through whom [Christ] we have gained access by faith into this grace in which we now stand" (Romans 5:2). It is by the grace of God that we stand—the undeserved mercy and power of God. Love the Lord. Follow the Lord and do as He says. The more obedient we are the more success we tend to have.

Love. Love. Love.

Love is godly. It is ordained of God that we love one another and be His disciples. In so doing we prove that we are of God. We prove our Christ-likeness by our love for both God and others.

It includes our love for the lost—those who do not know Christ and have never seen what Christ can do for them. He is the God who is able to transform lives, even the ones that we do not think could be transformed. Look at the apostle Paul. He was a least likely person expected to turn to Christ. We must not give up on reaching out to the lost with the love of God. Find ways and times that you can pray for them with others. Then reach out to your neighbors, coworkers, and family. With truth, love, and the power of God through the unction of the Holy Spirit we can share Christ. It is the Spirit of God who leads us to reach out and emboldens our witness so that others are touched by His hand and changed. Love one another and love the lost.

Jesus did it. The disciples did it. The Apostle Paul did it flagrantly. We are to do it as well.

"Therefore whoever confesses Me before men, him I will also confess before my Father who is in heaven. But whoever denies Me before men, him I will also deny before my Father who is in heaven" (Matthew 10:32-33 NKJV).

Jesus was not ashamed of the Father in heaven but rather confessed the Father before men and His relationship with Him. He was not ashamed of the Father. So we are also not to be ashamed or secret about our love and relationship with God. Jesus is not ashamed of us. We must not be ashamed of Him. Be bold. Be courageous and love one another. Do not hide your faith because you fear rejection. Rather, speak the truth in love. The disciples did. They shared their faith. The apostle Paul, the missionary man, did as well. And look at how many lives God has used his letters to bless. God worked through Paul, imperfect as he was. So also God is able to work through us if we are willing to take our faith to the marketplace. Do not leave it at home, but rather begin to pray that God will bring opportunities and courageous moments for you to reach out and touch the heart of others with the truth of God's word in action.

Let the Spirit lead you. Do not wait for tomorrow to share and witness. There are people dying every day and going to hell for eternity.

Friendship Evangelism

There are different ways to share our faith with others. One is through friendship evangelism. Friendship evangelism includes more than making friends. It is leading them to Christ as well. Do you have friends who are non-Christians? Have you taken the time to reach out to them? If not, why not? Within seven years of coming to Christ, most Christians do not have any non-Christian friends. Yet some of the most fulfilling times in our Christian walk are developing friendships with non-Christians with a goal of leading them to Christ and helping them grow in their new relationship with God.

Leading people to Christ is one of the most rewarding experiences that you will have as a Christian. It is one of the greatest joys of a Christian's life. If you talk to people who have been involved in bringing others to Christ, you will find they had great fulfillment and joy from it. Who doesn't want to lead their friends to Christ? Everyone can do friendship evangelism.

Ask God to place two people on your heart who need Christ. Then begin praying for them daily and developing your friendships with them. What can you do with them, and what do they enjoy talking about? If we will each reach two people for Christ, they will also reach others for Christ. People will come to know true hope, have eternal salvation, and the body of Christ will grow. Not everyone will greet you in evangelism, but remember that it is a seed sown. Some of us sow, and some of us reap. God is the giver of success.

Principles of Friendship Evangelism

Principle #1: Develop friendships. You must be around people who need Christ. You must spend time with them to develop relationships. Ways to be around people who need Christ include asking them over for supper. Invite them out for coffee and develop a relationship with them.

Genuinely care about the person more than how you look to others. Jesus did. He spent time with sinners, the non-religious folks. He ate with them and at times was criticized by those who were more concerned about appearances than people's salvation (Luke 19).

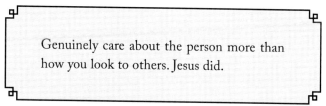

Genuinely care about the person more than how you look to others. Jesus did.

Principle #2: Love people. If you love people, would you not genuinely want to lead them to Christ? Have the goal in mind of eventually leading them to Christ. Be patient. Love them where they are. Be salt and light, seeding their lives with your friendship. People will receive more from you if they know that you genuinely care about them. Take an interest in their lives and welfare. Be their friend. Take time and love people.

Principle #3: Communicate. Then seed your conversation with flags. A "flag" is an indirect approach to sharing your faith. Slip in things about God that give the person bits about your relationship with God to let them know you are a Christian. A couple ideas are:

Tell them you will pray for them and then do it.

Pray for them daily and consistently.

Ask them about it later.

Be persistent, with gentleness. Communicate, communicate, and communicate.

Sprinkle, Spray, And Drench

Which of these do you do when sharing your faith, and why?

"Sprinkle" refers to a mild approach to sharing our faith. We are gentle and consistent in it. We can be an example first. We must let our actions speak.

"Spray" refers to an indirect approach to sharing our faith. This could be done through stories or talking normally and bringing up our Christian faith at times. Stories are effective. It can be an indirect way to share the power of prayer or other ways that God works. You can share stories of how God has worked in your life or other's lives. It has spiritual salt to it. Then you can go on to the next subject or continue with it. For example, I heard a story of a miracle that happened with a man who ended up with a knife to his throat by a criminal and spoke, "Stop in Jesus's name." The guy stopped! (That is a shortened version.) Stories are less threatening but interesting.

People usually like to talk about themselves. Spend the time to get to know people, and ask them questions about themselves. There is a time and a season for everything under the sun. Listen to them. Get to know them. Be a witness and pray for them. God will use it.

"Drench" refers to a direct approach. It may take time to get to this, but you can talk directly on spiritual issues and why you believe what you do. This could include leading the person to salvation.

Trust the Lord as you share. No one is perfect. But God is able to take what we share and use it. Pray that the Holy Spirit will bring understanding to their hearts. And speak the truth in love. Ephesians 4:15 says, "Speaking the truth in love…"

Let your conversation be always full of grace, seasoned with salt, so that you may know how to answer everyone (Col. 4:6).

God commands us to share our faith with others. Jesus said, Go ye into all the world and preach the good news to all creatures (Mk. 16:15). We are to share our faith with the rich and the poor alike.

"For God so loved the world that He gave His only begotten Son that whoever believes in Him should not perish but have everlasting life" (John 3:16 NKJV).

Make the most of every opportunity. The seeds that you sow, God is able to bring back to people's remembrance for years to come. Ask Him to do this each time. Also ask if it is time to plant or time to harvest. To plant or seed is to be more gentle or indirect. To harvest is to be very direct. Pray for God's guidance, and then use your head as well. "Be very careful, then, how you live—not as unwise but as wise, making the most of every opportunity, because the days are evil" (Ephesians 5:15).

I remember a man saying that he was in a coffee shop. He looked over and saw a man that he knew was an atheist. This man asked God if it was time to plant or time to harvest. He sensed the Lord say "Time to harvest," so he walked over to the atheist sitting at the table with his friends.

The man said, "Did you know that the Bible talks about you?"

The atheist said, "No."

The man said, "Proverbs says, 'The fool says in his heart there is no God.'" The atheist started to get offended. The man said, "Those aren't my words. That's what the Bible says. Give me two minutes, and I will prove to you there is a God. Because of the peer pressure of the atheist's friends around him, he said, "Fine". Then the Christian man said, "Pray this: God, I ask you to forgive my sins and accept Jesus as my Lord and Savior." The atheist balked, but the Christian man said, "What does it matter if you pray if there is no God?"

Finally the atheist said the words and suddenly shouted: "I feel it. I feel it. There is a God!" He was won to Christ that day.

Must we share our faith? Yes. It is a command of God. Jesus did. And He commanded His disciples to go ye into all the world and preach the good news (Mark 16:15). We are all responsible to share our faith with others. If we don't, we are disobedient.

How will people hear if we will not share? We are to be the salt and light of Christ to them. We have the duty to share. God is the one who is responsible to bring them to Himself. It may take time for the seeds that are sown to take root and grow. But if we are disobedient and do not share, how will they hear? God has placed you where you are for a reason. Make the most of every opportunity. Be salt and light and do it with love. Speaking the "truth in love" is key.

"Be wise in the way you act toward outsiders; make the most of every opportunity" (Col. 4:5).

As Christians we are to bear fruit. If it is uncomfortable to share your faith, continue to do it with gentleness and love. You will tend to become more comfortable and better at it. You may even grow to enjoy it! Our goal is to bring people to Christ and then *also* to disciple them to grow in Him.

Jesus and the Samaritan woman

Look at the story of Jesus talking with the Samaritan woman, and you'll see several things. (See John 4 for the full story.)

> Jacob's well was there, and Jesus, tired as he was from the journey, sat down by the well. It was about the sixth hour.

When a Samaritan woman came to draw water, Jesus said to her, "Will you give me a drink?"

(His disciples had gone into the town to buy food.) The Samaritan woman said to him, "You are a Jew, and I am a Samaritan woman. How can you ask me for a drink?" for Jews do not associate with Samaritans (John 4:6-9).

Application #1—Jesus was tired and asked for help. You can ask people for help. People love to help you with things they know. Be interested in them. Jesus took time to reach out even though He was tired. Reach out when it's uncomfortable for you, too.

Application #2—He did the "wrong" thing. It was the culturally inappropriate thing to talk to a Samaritan woman. In fact, most Jews would not even travel through the area but rather tiptoe around it instead just to avoid the Samaritans. They were not acceptable to them.

Application #3—He took the initiative to turn the conversation to the spiritual. Jesus took the normal conversation and turned it to a spiritual reality. He took the initiative. He spoke the truth in love. He did not judge her for her sin but loved her where she was and had patience with her.

John 4:16 says, "He told her, 'Go, call your husband and come back.' 'I have no husband,' she replied. Jesus said to her, 'You are right when you say you have no husband.'" He told her about her past that was sinful, but He neither condemned nor rejected her for it. He loved her where she was and at the same time spoke truth to her. Take the initiative, but do it with love and gentleness. The conversation may never turn to spiritual things otherwise, and eternity is a long time to spend without

God. Read the passage again, and see what else you find. The whole story is in John 4.

Do not be afraid to share. Remember to pray. Prayer is invaluable. We need to be prayers and workers. God has called us to be both. Pray after you share. Paul asked for prayer for sharing the gospel.

> Devote yourselves to prayer, being watchful and thankful. And pray for us, too, that God may open a door for our message, so that we may proclaim the mystery of Christ, for which I am in chains. Pray that I may proclaim it clearly, as I should.
>
> Colossians 4:2-4

> Pray also for me, that whenever I open my mouth, words may be given me so that I will fearlessly make known the mystery of the gospel, for which I am an ambassador in chains. Pray that I may declare it fearlessly, as I should.
>
> Ephesians 6:19-20

Pray for God to open a door for the message and then to proclaim it clearly and fearlessly.

One idea for your local neighborhood that is used by some people is to go in prayer teams of two or three to houses in their neighborhoods and ask people if they could pray for them. Then they would continue to pray for them during the week or two after. Then go back and see them again and ask about their prayer request. This type of witnessing has been used by God to draw people to Him. Most people do not mind being prayed for.

Share Your Faith in Word and Deed

We are to share our faith in word and in deed. Love in word and deed. "Jesus of Nazareth… He was a prophet, powerful in word and deed before God and all the people" (Luke 24:19b). He was known for being powerful in His words and in His deeds. That is a testimony. Jesus loved people who were lost (non-Christian). Jesus hung around the lost at times. He even received criticism from other Christians and leaders for it. But He loved people who were lost and He gave us an example to love our neighbor as ourselves (Matt. 22:39). Loving our neighbor is a commandment of God.

Sharing our faith is a commandment of God: "Therefore go and make disciples of all nations, baptizing them in the name of the Father and of the Son and of the Holy Spirit and teaching them to obey everything I have commanded you" (Matt. 28:19-20). This is a commandment for all Christians. We call it the "great commission." We, as Christians, are to *go* out of our comfort zone and make disciples. Disciples are people who are God followers. Jesus said:

> Love the Lord your God with all your heart and with all your soul and with all your mind. This is the first and greatest commandment. And the second is like it: Love your neighbor as yourself. All the Law and the Prophets hang on these two commandments.
>
> Matthew 22:37-40

A man asked Jesus "who is my neighbor?" and Jesus answered with this story of the good Samaritan:

A man was going down from Jerusalem to Jericho when he fell into the hands of robbers. They stripped him of his clothes, beat him, and went away, leaving him half dead. [A priest and a Levite [both religious people] came by him and ignored him. They passed on by. Then a Samaritan came and took pity of him]. He went to him and bandaged his wounds, pouring on oil and wine. Then he put the man on his own donkey, took him to an inn, and took care of him.

Luke 10:30, 37

Application #1: He saw a need and took initiative. The Samaritan saw the need and "went to the man."

Application #2: Meet the needs of people around you in physical and tangible ways. Let them know you care.

Application #3: Stick with people. The Samaritan man stuck with the man. He didn't leave quickly. Take time with people and stick with them. Develop relationships with them. He even gave of his financial wealth to care for him. Have mercy on the people around you.

This is the example that Jesus gave us to fulfill the second greatest commandment: to love our neighbor as ourselves. We are to have love for our neighbor. Meet the needs of the people around you in practical ways. Jesus did. He healed and taught and took time with people. Do unto others as you would have them do unto you. Love your neighbor as yourself.

Not everyone will accept right away. Not everyone will believe. Even Jesus was persecuted for His obedience. But if we do not share, who will?

If we love God, we will obey Him and do what He says. If He says to share our faith with others, or "make disciples," then we need to care about the things that He cares about. I remember a time of hearing a missionary on an airplane speak principles and truth from the Bible but not actually mention that it was Scripture. The secular person they were talking to was amazed and thought they should be a speaker for their business. God can work through it.

How do we stay "different" from culture so we can make a difference? Look at Matthew 5:13. It says, "You are the salt of the earth. But if the salt loses its saltiness, how can it be made salty again? It is no longer good for anything, except to be thrown out and trampled by men." Jesus said we are the salt of the earth. But we can actually lose our distinct flavor, our saltiness if we are not careful. Be obedient. Are we different from the world around us? Do we lose our flavor when we mush with outsiders or do we keep it?

As I sat with a couple over supper at a restaurant recently, the pastor's wife shared her story of her coworker coming to Christ and attending their church now. She has been fasting a day a week and praying as well. She very sincerely believes that it is due to her fasting as well that this coworker came to Christ. Praise God for that. For it is all eternity to come. He opens doors as we are sensitive to Him and fast and pray.

Be Sensitive to God's Leading

How can we make a difference in our communities? Reach out to your neighbors. There are many ways to do it. Be led by the Spirit. Allow the Holy Spirit to lead you. Pray for opportunities to share daily and the courage and open eyes to use them. They will know we are Christians by our love.

Principle 1. Follow the leading of the Holy Spirit. Do you remember the story of Philip?

Now an angel of the Lord said to Philip, "Go south to the road—the desert road—that goes down from Jerusalem to Gaza." So he started out, and on his way he met and Ethiopian eunuch, an important official in charge of all the treasury of Candace, queen of the Ethiopians. This man had gone to Jerusalem to worship and on his way home was sitting in his chariot reading the book of Isaiah the prophet. The Spirit told Philip, "Go to that chariot, and stay near it" (Acts 8:26-29).

God is able to lead you. Stay sensitive to the leading of the Holy Spirit. Also be open to the ways that He guides. Here an angel of the Lord spoke to Philip. He would have had no knowledge of this man's whereabouts or need without being sensitive to the Holy Spirit. It is the Holy Spirit that opens doors that are effective to share through. We can give principles to sharing our faith. And that is good, but the first one is to be led by the Spirit. Principles are a blessing, but apply them as God leads.

Do you notice that Philip was courageous to obey God? He went where the Holy Spirit guided him and from it came an open door. It was the timing that was essential, and it was by obedience to the Holy Spirit that he was able to lead the man to Christ and be baptized. He was not afraid to share his faith even with a sinner and with a stranger.

Philip made the most of the opportunity by obeying God quickly.

Then Philip ran up to the chariot and heard the man reading Isaiah the prophet. "Do you understand what you are reading?" Philip asked. (Acts 8:30)

He initiated the conversation.

"How can I," he said, "unless someone explains it to me?" So he invited Philip to come up and sit with him. (Acts 8:31)

He was at the right time at the right place because the Holy Spirit led him. And Philip explained the Scripture and "told him the good news about Jesus." (Acts 8:35)

They came to some water, and the eunuch said, "Look, here is water. Why shouldn't I be baptized?" (Acts 8:36) The eunuch (someone who served in the presence of the king) wanted to know the truth, but he did not know or understand without someone to help him.

Jesus Was A Friend Of Sinners

Be a friend of sinners. How often are we available to be a friend to them?

"Jesus entered Jericho and was passing through. A man was there by the name of Zacchaeus; he was a chief tax collector and was wealthy. He wanted to see who Jesus was, but being a short man he could not, because of the crowd. So he ran ahead and climbed a sycamore-fig tree to see him, since Jesus was coming that way. When Jesus reached the spot, he looked up and said to him, "Zacchaeus, come down immediately. I must stay at your house today." (Luke 19:1-5). Jesus saw Zacchaeus and told him that he would stay at his house. Jesus initiated. He made himself a friend of sinners. Jesus was muttered about and actually looked down on by "all the people" for befriending Zacchaeus. The people muttered, "He has gone to be the guest of a sinner." But the timing was right. Zacchaeus changed his life and followed Jesus.

For the Son of Man came to seek and to save what was lost (Luke 19:10). We could say it this way as well: Jesus came to seek and to save sinners. He sought them. He initiated the conversations and led them to God. We must follow His example.

What is the result of obedience? It is blessing. And it is life.

Did you know that some of the greatest fulfillment in life comes through sharing our faith with others or winning people to Christ? It is a very, very rewarding experience. That is an understatement. If you have never been able to lead someone to Christ, to walk them into life abundant and new, then begin to pray and seek the Lord to give you the opportunity.

We all share in different ways, but truth is the truth. The truth is that Jesus said, "Whoever confesses Me before men, him I will also confess before My Father who is in heaven" (Matt. 10:32 NKJV). We are not to hold out on our love for God in public. We are to be visible and witnesses of God to the people and generation around us. We are to stand out from the crowd. Otherwise why would we have been told by Jesus to not hide our light under a bowl (Matt. 5:15)? Rather we are to "put it on its stand." Jesus said "Let your light shine before men, that they may see your good deeds and praise your Father in heaven" (Matt. 5:16).

We are the hands and feet of Christ in this generation to do the will of God and to be witnesses to Him. God calls us to witness—to be reflections of who He is in the world. If we will not shine our light, how will God bring people to Christ? We are the body of Christ. Let His light shine through our lives. How has God changed your life? How can you tell someone in a simple way what becoming a Christian has done for you? Has He filtered in joy, love, and peace? What other ways has He worked that you can share with others?

Think through these things. We are to be ready always in season and out of season to give an answer to everyone who asks us for the reason for the hope that we have. We must make the most of every opportunity. We may not get another one. Reach out to those around you.

> We are the hands and feet of Christ in this generation to do the will of God and to be witnesses to Him.

How did people come to believe in Jesus in the gospels?

They saw: They saw what Jesus did. His example was
a testimony.
They felt: They personally felt the difference Jesus made and
the miracles and helps He gave to them.
They heard: They heard His words of truth as well.
They saw His example, felt His touch upon them, and heard
His testimony of who He was.

And this gospel of the kingdom will be preached in the
whole world *as a testimony* (Matt. 24:14).

Prep and share your testimony. God can use it! Who needs
Christ around you? List three people that you will pray for and
reach out to.

Love God Enough To Do It Anyway

For God so loved the whole world that He gave His only begotten
Son that whosoever believes in Him should not perish but have
eternal life (John 3:16).

We must care enough to do it anyway. Invite people to
church. Invite them to a bible study or small group. Invite them
to be around other Christians as well.

Concerning church invitations, here are a few statistics in
the nation:

73% of people who don't attend church were never invited. –
Barna Group [4]
82% of the unchurched are at least somewhat likely to attend
church if invited. – Dr. Thom Rainer [4]
Only 2 percent of church members invite an unchurched
person to church. 98% of church-goers never extend an
invitation in a given year. – Dr. Thom Rainer [4]

Research has showed that out of the millions of people in the nation who do not attend church, many of them would be much more likely if invited by someone they knew. Why not invite people to church? Why not let them know that it is a great place to be and meet others? Why not tell them what Christ has done for you and allow them to go to a place to grow in Christ with friends? Most people do not want to go to church alone.

> You are the light of the world. A city on a hill cannot be hidden. Neither do people light a lamp and put it under a bowl. Instead they put it on its stand, and it gives light to everyone in the house. In the same way, let your light shine before men, that they may see your good deeds and praise your Father in heaven.
>
> Matthew 5:14-16

We are to be Christ's ambassadors in this generation that we live in. We are placed here for a time and for a season. We are here for a reason. We are not to be alone and hidden under the covers as Christians, but rather we are to let our light shine. We are His light to the generation that we are in. We are chosen by God to be here at this time. God will use you right where you are if you will ask Him to.

If you do not have a heart for the lost, ask God for one. Ask Him to give you a heart of compassion for those around you, for those that are in your circle of influence. Begin to pray for them regularly, even daily. Pray that God will do "whatever it takes" to bring the people around you to Christ.

Pray and fast. And then obey.

Do you notice this passage from Matthew 5:16 says "Let your light shine before men, that they may see your good deeds and praise your Father in heaven." It says "that they may see" what?

Your good deeds. You are to *do* good deeds. Ask God for ideas and opportunities to do good deeds.

"If you want to enter life, obey the commandments" (Matthew 19:17). What did Jesus say was the greatest commandment? "Love the Lord your God with all your heart and with all your soul and with all your mind." This is the first and greatest commandment. And the second is like it: "Love your neighbor as yourself. All the Law and the prophets hang on these two commandments" (Mt. 22:37-40). Jesus did not come to abolish the law and the prophets. He came to fulfill them.

The first part of our obedience to God is to love the Lord our God with all our heart, all our soul, and with all our mind. So this requires first that we place God as the number one priority in our lives. He must be first. We follow Him and obey Him. Seek His will, His face, and His direction in our lives. Even our speech and conversations must represent this as well.

If we love God, we obey God. We follow Him and allow Him to guide and direct us, shield and protect us. We must remember that obedience to God is a blessing. Where He guides and directs, He also provides. There is no greater place to be than in obedience to God. We must follow Him. We must follow Him. We must follow Him.

There are times that our feelings are not there when we obey. But we make the choice to do it and act on it because we love God with our heart, our mind, and our soul. We make the choice to obey. We remember and know that God is the Father God who sees what is best, who knows what is best, and who works accordingly in our lives. He is the One who has ordained times and seasons, and we are to follow in it.

Ecclesiastes 3:1-4 says this:

> There is a time for everything, and a *season* for every activity under heaven: a time to be born and a time to die, a time to plant and a time to uproot, time to kill and a

time to heal, a time to tear down and a time to build, a
time to weep and a time to laugh, a time to mourn …

And the list goes on.

There are seasons for us to walk in and live in. There are
times that our obedience to God will work out differently. But
in every season, obedience is to love the Lord our God with our
all. It is to place Him first and decidedly choose to make Him
the first priority. He is King. And we are His landlords over the
things that He has given us to manage, care for, and watch over.
We must decidedly make Him first and place our time, and our
resources on the altar.

Jesus said this, "Seek first the kingdom of God." Place your
money after your love for God. Give and it shall be given to you.
The generous man will himself be blessed (Prov. 22:9). Do not
place money first. Do not hoard wealth.

I challenge you in this: Allow yourself to be in the center of
God's will by first placing Him first in the day through devotions,
reading of His Word, and praying. Then fast and pray with others
sometime during the week. Also, make a way and priority to share
your faith with others and to pray and witness to them. There is
such delight in the heart of God when we witness and share Him
with others. There are needy people—the down and out. There
are coworkers as well. The devil's lies are to stop us from sharing
our faith. They are lethargy. They are complacency—a lack of
concern for the welfare of others.

The principle is to place God first in everything. What
priority is first in our lives? Do we show it in our time, planning,
finances, and conversation with others? Do we reach out to our
neighbors to bring them to Christ? If we love God, we will be
concerned about the things that He loves. This means that we
will place Him as the priority and obey. What is God concerned
about? He is concerned about our welfare for one. And He is
concerned about people coming to Christ and spending eternity

in heaven rather than hell. If we place God first, we will be willing to share our faith. Sometimes it is the people that we least think will ever come to Christ that God will use us to reach out to and minister to. One of the things I see in Scripture is that God loves the sinner. We will never be perfect, but we can "grow up" in Christ. We begin where we are and choose to make changes that are necessary to place God first and commit our lives to Him. Decidedly choose to obey God, and He will bless you. Allow God to use you where you are. Be concerned about what God is concerned about such as unity in the body of Christ and the salvation of the lost. How will we ever take the time to witness when we have so much to do? My answer is to make it. Carve out the time to do it—a few minutes here, a few minutes there. We must make it a priority to pray, to fast, and to reach out to the people around us with the Word of God, His truth, and His love. Pray first. Ask God to open your eyes to opportunities around you to share with others. Every day is made up of twenty-four hours. We all have the same amount of time. Don't worry about everything being perfect at home. How many people are going to hell because we do not make the time to reach out to our neighbors, our friends, our relatives, or our coworkers? We are responsible to reach out, to care, and to share the love of Christ. God is responsible to, by His Spirit of truth and grace, cause the seeds that we sow to grow and mature and come to fruit or salvation. It is God who takes care of "the receiving of our witness" in people's lives. It is ours to act and obey and reach out with our words and actions.

Be sensitive to the leading of the Spirit. Jesus told us in Matthew 10:32 NKJV, "Therefore whoever confesses Me before men, him I will also confess before My Father who is in heaven."

Do not hide your faith from others. Either God has placed you in the position that you are in or you got there by chance. You are not there by chance. God cares about people, and He cares about those around you. He believes they need to know the truth in love.

All our days must count for something. They must count. If we know the truth and do not do it, we are numbered in our days. We must make a difference.

Do you know that we are limiting the hand of God when we do not obey? If we obey we are actually agreeing with God and bringing good things to happen. If we obey and agree with God, we can accomplish a lot of good. Obedience is good. Obedience is king. What has God told you that you have not done yet?

The practical principles for obeying God's Word are ask, fast, obey. *If God tells you to do something, do it.* He has a reason for it. Listen up. Obey up, and keep up. Keep going and persevering. He brings blessings to us as well as to others as we obey. There is a reason. It is to bring fulfillment to God's will. If in doubt whether it is God leading, I have prayed and had God answer and then acted in obedience.

God will fulfill His purpose for me (Ps. 138:8).

The Way Jesus Did It

We looked at this passage of the woman at the well in an earlier chapter on fasting. I want to look at it again here (John 4). How did Jesus share His faith? It appears that Jesus fasted when he spoke to the Samaritan woman—the woman by the well. His disciples went to town to buy food. When they returned, after Jesus was sharing truth with the Samaritan woman, John says,

Meanwhile, his disciples urged him, "Rabbi, eat something."

But he said to them, "I have food to eat that you know nothing about."

Then his disciples said to each other, "Could someone have brought him food?"

"My food," said Jesus, "is to do the will of him who sent me and to finish his work. Do you not say, 'Four months more and then the harvest'? I tell you, open your eyes and look at the fields! They are ripe for harvest."

John 4:31-35

Interestingly, he was apparently fasting here, and he was not waiting until tomorrow to do God's will. When the disciples returned from town with food, they encouraged Jesus to eat to which He responded, "I have food to eat that you know nothing about" (Jn. 4:32). Jesus was depending on spiritual food at the time rather than physical food. He must have been fasting because he refused their food and was speaking about food that they "know nothing about." We have food as well, if we are Jesus's disciples, to do the will of God who sends us and calls us.

Do not wait until tomorrow to do God's will and to work in the harvest fields. They are ripe today. There are people waiting to know Christ today with a need for friends and coworkers and family members to pray for them and witness to them. The devil will always attempt to get you to wait to do God's will. Do now what God has told you to do now.

Jesus addressed the issue of "always waiting" before we do God's will and act. He said, "Do not say, 'Four months more and then the harvest'" (Jn. 4:35). They needed to open their eyes to the open doors of opportunity around them. The fields are ripe and ready for harvest now. How often do we say, "Oh, I'll do that in a while from now," or "I'll do that, but not this week yet. I can always wait a bit. Why rush the plan of God?" And yet there are harvest fields just waiting for us to work in.

There are opportunities all around you to share your faith and do what Jesus did. He turned down physical food to do the will of God. Fast and pray. Even Jesus did, and He shared His faith with others. And in each opportunity, He turned the conversation toward spiritual things. Do not wait for tomorrow. You do not know if it will come. Do it today. Begin now. The fields are ripe for harvest. There are people all around you who need you to reach out to them today. Fast like Jesus was here, and do God's will. The fields are ripe for harvest.

Prayer Requests for Non-Christians

Pray for their heart to be softened and open to receive Christ. Ask God to speak to people through your life and testimony.

Ask God to place a yearning and desire for Christ in their hearts and realization of their need for Him.

Ask God to do whatever it takes to bring them to salvation.

Ask God to speak to them through the day and night, that seeds that are sown from sharing, will take root and grow in their lives.

Ask God to work through your words and actions to draw them to Christ.

Ask God daily for opportunities to share your faith with others.

Ask God to open the eyes of their understanding to spiritual truths.

Ask God to give them a felt need for Christ.

Ask God to open your eyes to the needs of those around you.

Ask God to send out workers into the harvest fields (the lives of non-Christians).

Ask God to stir in their hearts His truth and love through your words and actions. Pray for opportunities to share daily and the courage and open eyes to see them and use them.

Ask God for ideas to do good deeds for God's sake.

Pray that God will do "whatever it takes" to bring the people around you to Christ.

Ask and it will be given to you (Matt. 7:7).

Break our hearts for the lost, Lord.

Pray it daily.

LOVE, PURITY, AND REASONABLENESS

"And this is my prayer: that your love may abound more and more in knowledge and depth of insight, so that you may be able to discern what is best and may be pure and blameless until the day of Christ…filled with the fruit of righteousness" (Phil. 1:9).

Dear friends, since God so loved us, we also ought to love one another. No one has ever seen God, but if we love one another, God lives in us and his love is made complete in us (1 John 4:11).

We are to walk as Jesus walked and talk as He talked, aren't we? He did walk in love and purity. So we also are to. If we say that we love God but will not walk in love, how much do we love God? Love one another for love is of God, and he who loves is born of God (1 Jn. 4:7). If we do not walk in purity, how much do we love God?

We love God, and so we decide to set ourselves apart from the crowd and from the world by choosing to "be holy" as He is holy. How do we do this? One way is to "avoid godless chatter, because those who indulge in it will become more and more ungodly. Their teaching will spread like gangrene" (2 Timothy 2:17). Then the writer gives two people's names who have wandered from the truth. This description of godless chatter sounds like gossip for one. It sure can destroy people's reputation whether or not it is true. I remember a situation of a gal talking to a guy about a lady's marriage. Someone who was in the lady's family was telling everyone about the lady's marriage and all the details of their difficulties. This gal was putting down the gossip about the lady, but in the process, she was also retelling the story.

Continue to work out your salvation with fear and trembling, for it is God who works in you to will and to act according to his good purpose (Philippians 2:12b-13). Walk in love, purity and reasonableness.

Reasonableness

I can do all things through Christ, *and* I can ask for help when needed.

We can do all things. We don't have to do all things by ourselves. We were not born alone without anyone around. We must also consider the consequences of it. Is it God's will or not?

Years ago a friend and myself were visiting the Grand Canyon. We had hiked down to a watering spot where we could rest for a bit. Then we turned around and started our way back up. As we neared the top, we came upon some kids who were leaning against the rock wall on the trail. They were out of breath and very tired. Their father was nearby. Upon talking to them they told us they had hiked (during the middle of summer) down to the bottom of the Grand Canyon and were on their way back up. It was numerous miles and a difficult climb back up, not to mention the heat. The kids were hanging on to the wall, resting against it, out of breath, and tired. They'd stop, and then they would count 300 steps at a time. Then they would rest again. Walk. Rest. I always remember the back of the dad's t-shirt. I can't help but wonder if he wore it specifically for that day. It said,

I can do all things through Christ who gives me strength (Phil. 4:13). They did make it to the top but not without a lot of work.

There are some things that God calls us to do and He gives us strength for the victory. There are other things that God may want us to ask for help with or accomplish gradually. Pray and seek the Lord about each decision. He understands our frailties as well as our needs.

A couple more thoughts on reasonableness are these:

1   How do you know the will of God? One is to follow the way of peace. It's not peace "with the world" but rather peace with God. Where do you have the most peace? God leads us in peace (Ps. 23). Even when the outside world may be full of turmoil, it is by the Spirit of God that we experience His peace as we follow Him. There are challenges, yes, and yet there is a way of peace with God that is best to follow and pursue. He is our guide even to the end. This peace from God is not the same as laxity or laziness or complacency. It is not peace to not do anything but rather peace even in the challenges of life.

2   If you are in a culture where people dress as they do, reasonableness and purity might be to not be legalistic about dress and yet dress in a way that would not be to "attract" the opposite sex to your appearance by wearing tight clothes. Don't be showy. Rather be modest.

3   If you are putting your family on the crooked, then you are not in the reasonableness of God. (Mt. 15:4-6).

The Train Track

The following chapters are from a picture God gave me of railroad ties landing one on top of the other. There were five railroad ties that fell on top of each other in this form starting with the bottom:

Kick Butt Prayer:
now titled Penetrating Prayer

Sturdy in Christ:
No Matter What Comes

Truth Stands

Faith in Something

Rock-Solid Foundation:
in the Word of God

Each of the railroad ties were labeled as such.
And they are to build a train track to run the devil over
in the nation we are in.

ROCK-SOLID FOUNDATION IN THE WORD OF GOD

The Word of God is sharper than any two-edged sword.

> For the Word of God is living and active. Sharper than any double-edged sword, it penetrates even to dividing soul and spirit, joints and marrow; it judges the thoughts and attitudes of the heart. Nothing in all creation is hidden from God's sight. Everything is uncovered and laid bare before the eyes of him to whom we must give account (Hebrews 4:12-13).

A few years ago, I awoke from a dream that was powerful. It began with a picture of thousands of soldiers marching in step. The sound was incredible. They were marching as a mighty army, in perfect unison. Then in the dream, I saw a huge sword standing straight up in front of me. It was so powerful that you could hear the power resonate from it. It was amazing. And it was the Word of God, which is the sword of the Spirit according to Ephesians 6. It is mighty and powerful for taking down strongholds. Do we use it enough?

I can't say it enough. The power from this sword was amazing. It struck me. It was audible in the dream. And it was the Word of God. God's Word is more powerful than you may believe. It is alive. It reverberates with God's ability to cut through lies of

---

the enemy that you have believed for a long time. There is power in the spirit realm with the sword of the Spirit. It is a living and active sword that defeats the enemy and its lies. The sword of the Spirit weakens the devil. It cuts it in two.

> Therefore, since we have a great high priest who has gone through the heavens, Jesus the Son of God, let us hold firmly to the faith we profess. For we do not have a high priest who is unable to sympathize with our weaknesses, but we have one who has been tempted in every way, just as we are yet was without sin (Hebrews 4:14-15).

Jesus used the Sword of the Spirit to defeat the tempter (Luke 4). He used it in a very focused and specific manner in all three of the temptations the enemy plotted against him. So we must also use it as we encounter temptation. Use the sword. Read it and memorize it. Write it down and take it with you through the day. Stick it in your pocket to take out and use against the devil when the need arises. Do not think that you have to overcome on your own against the devil's schemes. You do not have to overcome on your own. But rather we overcome with the Word of God, the Spirit of God, obedience and help from others at times.

You can do things like play it on tapes when you go to bed. I had a period that I would leave a CD of the Bible on during the night. I would fall asleep with it on. But I remember clearly a number of times that I awoke just at the right time to hear a verse that I needed. You can do this as well. Also, remember that what you think about before you go to sleep is what some researchers say tends to run through your mind all night. If this is true, then one of the best things to listen to is the Word of God. Read it. Listen to it. And fill your mind with it so that you can think like God thinks.

It is our life line. In Revelation 1:16, it is out of the Son of Man's mouth that the double-edged sword came. It is to come out of our mouths as well, having been stored up in our hearts, for times and seasons that we require it.

Increase the Word of God in your heart and you will increase the sword of the Spirit from your mouth (Eph. 6; Rev.1:16).

Therefore, take up the whole armor of God that you may be able to withstand in the evil day and having done all, to stand (Eph. 6:13). And take the sword of the Spirit which is the Word of God. All of the other pieces of our full armor are defensive. They are meant to help us stand our ground and be protected in a defensive way from the onslaught of the lies of the enemy. It is this last piece of our armor that is the only offensive piece. The Word of God is more powerful than we often give it credit.

I have sensed in the spirit realm when certain attacks of the enemy have come, the devil is actually weakened by the spoken or decreed word of God. The actual Word of God, quoted, is powerful against the devil. It does not only protect us but is effective at destroying the lies of the enemy. How does the devil gain power in the lives of believers and unbelievers? Lies are one way. We must compare what comes to mind with the Word of God.

Substantiate Everything With the Word of God

What do you believe? Substantiate it with the Word of God. Find a verse. Find a scripture or throw it out. Soothsayers tell us Jesus is not the only way to God. They say there are many ways. They make you feel warm and fuzzy. But they are leading people to hell. "Jesus answered, 'I am the way and the truth and the life. No one comes to the Father except through me.'" (John 14:6)

In some other countries churches are being turned into mosques. But it seems to be the ones that have not stayed with the Word of God. The Word of God is powerful.

We must accept the Spirit of God as well because Jesus sent Him to be our Guide, our Counselor. "When the Counselor comes, whom I will send to you from the Father, the Spirit of truth who goes out from the Father, he will testify about me." (John 15:26)

The principle is this: Substantiate everything with the Word of God. The Word of God is a rock solid foundation to build on. We stand on this. We overcome with this. It strengthens our lives as we live on it and allow ourselves to be led by the Spirit. It is never one without the other. The Spirit of God is He who gives life to the Word of God. He brings it to life and gives us encouragement through it. He will use His Word when we read it. It is the sword of the Spirit. The Spirit will take from the Word and wield it according to what we need.

When faced with decisions, we must ask the question: Does it line up with the Word of God? What verse or verses would apply to this? We make a decision accordingly. We live by the Spirit, and He guides us into all truth. Then we apply it.

A decision that I made when I first started following the Lord in late high school was to read the Bible daily, even if it was a short amount. I chose to take time to read God's Word every day at approximately the same time. It was usually first thing in the morning. If we will place God first—for 90 percent of people—reading the Bible in the early morning works best. If we don't make it a priority early, it is too easy to fill our days with other things and leave God's Word out.

I made the decision to read God's Word daily. Then if I woke up late or something happened that I missed devotions or reading, *even if I had laid down to sleep at night*, I would roll over and turn on the light to at least read a verse. Then I would go to sleep. That habit set in stone that I place God's Word as a priority. It was a way to build a habit that has been built on through the years. What does God's Word say? "So is my word that goes out from my mouth: It will not return to me empty, but will accomplish what I desire and achieve the purpose for which I sent it" (Is.55:11). Even a verse will not return void. You are investing in your life by reading God's Word daily and placing it as a priority.

Some people say that it takes around three weeks to start a habit. If you do something daily for three weeks, it begins to set as a habit that is easier to continue. Then it takes ninety days to ingrain it more firmly. Pick up the Word of God and place it first in the day. Make it a priority to read. When you wake up late, do your best to at least read a little. If you forget completely, catch up later. But keep the priority to establish the daily habit to read.

It is one of the things that makes us sturdy in Christ (as we will cover in another chapter). It builds our roots in God's Word and stores it in our heart to lean on when needed.

So our Abba Father in heaven gives us the ability to overcome this evil world. When we become a Christian, we receive power and authority that is given to us as children of God. As God's children we are heirs of the promise. What is the promise? We are no longer slaves or against God but rather children of promise and have the full rights of sons of God.

We have a Father who loves us and provides for us. He watches over us and protects us because we are children of promise. The promise is that we have authority over snakes and scorpions and to overcome all the power of the enemy. This does not mean that we ought to go out and command the wind and the storm gone or claim and slam our authority in the spiritual realm over every principality and power that we can. But rather where God calls us, He also gives us authority to trample on snakes and scorpions.

Faith is the reality by which we win. We must not only say with faith that we love our brother. We must also act on it. Some people say that you should be able to defeat the enemy always just by saying the words. Yes. We can defeat the enemy by saying the Word of God. Look at Jesus' temptation. Jesus used the Word of God to do it, and He defeated it. So we do the same thing with temptation.

> "So is my word that goes out from my mouth: It will not return to me empty, but will accomplish what I desire and achieve the purpose for which I sent it" (Is.55:11)

But submit to God also. "Resist the devil, and he will flee" means this: if the issue is pride, then you must humble yourself and ask for help. Fast and pray. God will lead you into humility through it. Ask God to defeat pride. Use the Word of God against it. Then go to a leader and submit it to them if need be. Be willing to humble yourself in public and in private. Humility is the underground building block to rising up in victory, power, and love for God. One of the common denominators in a lot of great leaders is that they are also humble.

Be led by the Spirit of God. Do not be arrogant, Neither think you can't do anything at all.

I have sensed the Holy Spirit say this: "Fast and pray, and you will hear My voice more." When we are led by the Spirit of God, we grow to overcome more and more. Strengthen the spirit and weaken the flesh by fasting and praying regularly.

The Doubts The Enemy Brings

How exactly do we defeat this evil world? Our faith is essential. We actually achieve this victory through our faith. So what do we have faith in? We have faith first that Jesus is the Son of God and that we are saved. "For every child of God defeats this evil world, and we achieve this victory through our faith" (1 John 5:4 NLT).

Faith is the shield that we hold up when the devil throws its arrows at us. One of the first things it will attempt is to cause doubts about God's Word and to divide and separate the people of God. The devil comes to kill, and destroy our faith the most. It is a main thing the devil will come after through various methods and ways. They all combat our faith in God and in His ways and will being best.

Look at the way that the devil attacked the first people, Adam and Eve. It first attacked their faith in God and in His Word. It attacked their faith in who He was. Was He a liar?

> Now the serpent was craftier than any of the wild animals the Lord God had made. He said to the woman, "Did God really say, 'You must not eat from any tree in the garden'?"
>
> The woman said to the serpent, "We may eat fruit from the trees in the garden, but God did say, 'You must not eat fruit from the tree that is in the middle of the garden, and you must not touch it, or you will die.'"
>
> "You will not surely die," the serpent said to the woman. "For God knows that when you eat of it your eyes will be opened, and you will be like God, knowing good and evil" (Genesis 3:1-3).

The first thing the serpent did was to question what God said. "Did God really say that?" Are you sure He said that? It started first by questioning if that was really what God said. The devil will try anything to get you off the Word of God, whether it is the written word of God, the Bible, or it is a personal word that was impressed on your heart by the Spirit of God. And when you doubt, your actions follow and you become disobedient. What is the Word of God that was spoken to you at the beginning of the year?

Have you ever had a word from the Lord that you first doubted and then believed? Or that you first believed and then doubted later? One thing we know is that which is of God will last—if we will obey. Obedience is king. Some things may be the will of God, but if we do not obey, will they last as well? Unity and accountability with prayer and fasting and seeking God are important with obedience.

Tests And Trials

Do you remember the story of Job? The devil brought an accusation before God that Job's love for God was not genuine. The devil claimed that Job only followed God because his life had been easy, that his love for God was not genuine.

"Does Job fear God for nothing?" Satan replied. "Have you not put a hedge around him and his household and everything he has? You have blessed the work of his hands, so that his flocks and heirs are spread throughout the land. But stretch out your hand and strike everything he has, and he will surely curse you to your face." (Job 1:9-11)

Do we love God because it is easy or do we love Him regardless? Job stayed even when times were difficult and God gave him more at the end than he had before his testing.

The devil is an accuser of the brethren. In other words, it will accuse Christians. That is its vice. It accused Job and Job loved God. Its accusations are aimed toward guilt and condemnation. You are never perfect enough. You will never be where you need to be, and on and on the accuser goes. It will accuse you of anything it can that will pull you down and lead you into living a non-victorious life. Victory comes from truth being instilled within our hearts and putting it into practice.

> Victory comes from truth being instilled within our hearts and putting it into practice.

Then we follow the leading of the Holy Spirit. "My sheep hear My voice" (John 10:27 NKJV). If you do not know the voice of the Spirit of God, seek to know Him better. Read His Word more. Pray and fast. Know that the Holy Spirit speaks in ways that do not go against the written word of God. For instance, the Holy Spirit will never tell you to cheat on your spouse, live with a partner you are not married to, or place money before obedience to God. If something is telling you to do these things, know that it is *not* the Holy Spirit. The traditions of man are out. Also, if something is telling you—whether a voice or an inclination—to do something contrary to the Word of God, then you know it is not the Holy Spirit."If you hold to my teaching, you are really my disciples. Then you will know the truth, and the truth will set you free" (John 8:31-32). Do you notice here that holding to Jesus's teaching actually comes before the understanding? If you look at the sequence, it is obey and then you will know the truth. And then the truth will set you free. There are times in my life when I have had to obey God before I understood. The understanding came after the obedience. Or sometimes it came in the midst of the obedience. The Holy Spirit leads and guides us into all truth. He is the Spirit of truth. Obedience is king. Or shall we say it this way? Our understanding and knowledge of the truth increases as we obey God and follow in His ways. Then we are increasingly led into truth, and by this we are set free.

At the risk of sounding different, I have to say here that I notice two things. Perseverance is implied in the above verse. It is "hold" to Jesus's teaching. We hold to it. We fix ourselves to it. Another word for this is being "sturdy" or fixed in our faith and obedience. We hold to it. Picture a person holding on to something, even a light pole. You hold on to it even in the storm and are protected from being blown about.

The next thing is that with the "holding" comes a knowledge of the truth. It could be an experiential knowledge of truth. And this truth "will set you free". It says it "will." It is in the future. It is to come, is coming and in process. Do not quit if it takes time. But do this. Make sure that you hold to Jesus's teaching. Act on it and continue.

We need a knowledge that is not only a mental assent but an experience in heart and commitment of will as well. For instance, we may know we are loved in our head. But our heart may not have experienced it. Heart knowledge comes with experience. For instance, are we loved? Are you loved? Yes (Jn. 3:16). You are *very* loved by God, and most likely by others as well. But the lie of the devil will always be that you are not loved or not important. But stick with God and follow Him. The experience of the love can be "on the way". If you need someone to talk to, then find someone as well. It is worth the work to do it. Love does the hard work. There is an experiential knowledge of the truth where we experience it and live by it.

He who hears the word and at once puts it into practice will find blessings (Matt.13).

We must put the Word into practice, but how will we if we do not read it? There are suggestions on how to read the Bible, but the main thing is that you read it. Don't read it just to get through twenty-five chapters, but rather read to learn. Some people suggest you read one chapter of the Old Testament, one chapter of Psalm, one chapter of Proverbs, and then finish up with one chapter in the New Testament. That is a suggestion. I have to be honest, I have worked at this in many ways and that way does not always work as well for me. I have done it but don't end up taking as much to heart from it. We are all different. It can be good to read from all of these areas, but one president read the book of John over and over. There is freedom in reading God's Word. To read the book of John first is a common recommendation for starting to read the Bible.

Allow the Word of God to soak into your life rather than just stay on the surface. "Let the Word of Christ dwell in you richly as you teach and admonish one another with all wisdom, and as you sing psalms, hymns and spiritual songs with gratitude in your hearts to God" (Col. 3:16). The key words are "dwell in you richly." And it is action that he talks about after this. Let it simmer, and then act on it. Read. Believe. Act.

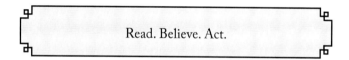

Read. Believe. Act.

You can put these on a list and read through them. Or you can find your own and read through them. But let the Word of God dwell in you richly.

Jesus said to him, "I am the Way, the Truth and the Life. No one comes to the Father but through Me."

John 14:6 (NKJV)

"Trust in the Lord with all your heart and lean not on your own understanding; in all your ways acknowledge him, and he will make your paths straight."

Proverbs 3:5-6

"The Lord is good, a refuge in times of trouble" (Nahum 1:7). Trust in Him. He loves you.

"Christ Jesus, who has become for us wisdom from God – that is, our righteousness, holiness and redemption" (1 Corinthians 1:30). Jesus Christ is our righteousness, holiness, and redemption. Personalize it with: I am made righteous by faith in Christ not because of things that I have done, will do, or am doing but because of my faith in Christ.

"This is the victory that has overcome the world, even our faith."

1 John 5:4b

"Faith comes by hearing and hearing by the Word of God."

Romans 10:17 NKJV

"For every child of God defeats this evil world, and we achieve this victory through our faith."

1 John 5:4 NLT

"And who can win this battle against the world? Only those who believe that Jesus is the Son of God" (1 John 5:5 NLT). This verse explains what we have faith in. It is the qualifier to become a child of God.

Not Live On Bread Alone

Jesus said, "It is written: 'Man does not live on bread alone, but on every word that comes from the mouth of God'" (Matthew 4:4).

I remember a friend tell me that she had the experience of feeling a drive or hunger for food. She would eat, and then she would eat again when she felt it. One day instead of eating, she tried reading the Bible once and found out that it actually satisfied the hunger feeling! It was actually a hunger for spiritual fulfillment that she was attempting to satisfy through food! It was a spiritual hunger rather than a physical hunger. Reading God's Word quenched it. So God's Word can quench your hunger. You may never know if it is a spiritual hunger unless you try reading the Word of God to quench it.

Increase the Word of God in your heart and you will increase the sword of the Spirit from your mouth (Eph. 6; Rev.1:16).

If you look at Acts 2:14ff, Peter knew the Word of God. He began to preach to the people who were in Jerusalem at the time that the Holy Spirit came in power and enabled the disciples to speak in other tongues. Peter knew the Word of God. And from this Word, he was able to defend what was happening to the crowd around them. The Holy Spirit gave him the words to speak at the time that He needed them. Read and think on the Word of God, and you will have the Sword of the Spirit upon your tongue.

Deny evil at every access by turning to the Word of God. How do I do that? I am righteous. Substantiate it with "I am made righteous by faith in Christ. Jesus Christ is my righteousness, holiness and my redemption" (paraphrase of 1 Cor. 1:30). We substantiate everything with the Word of God.

The righteous will live by faith. Heaven is real. Eternity is real. We will have a reward if we do not give up! The rewards are here on earth, having a spiritual hunger filled and the love, joy, and peace of God's Spirit in our lives. And we have rewards coming in heaven, which will be forever.

FAITH IN SOMETHING: For all eternity you will not regret what you have done for God. Remember that. Be led by the Spirit, and do not allow the things of this world to drive you away from His will. The greatest fulfillment in life is found in obedience to God. God blesses.

Wrap your mind with the Word of God. In a dream some years ago, I remember seeing a picture of my head being wrapped in something and sensing a difficult battle at the time. When I awoke from the dream, I sensed the Holy Spirit say, "Wrap your mind with the Word of God." Remember the Word. Read the Word. Meditate on the Word. Protect and guard your mind. Wrap it with the Word of God. Take Scriptures out, write them down, and carry them with you. Remember them. Use them against the enemy. Ask God to speak to your heart. And do not think that you have gotten all there is from the passage from reading it once or twice. Wrap your mind with God's Word and counter the devil's lies.

> Increase the Word of God in your heart and you will increase the sword of the Spirit from your mouth (Eph. 6; Rev.1:16).

My husband and I had a business decision to make years ago. We asked a couple financial advisors about the decision. Then we made it accordingly. But later on we discovered it was not the better decision. And we may lose a lot from it money wise. My husband sensed the Holy Spirit speak to his heart that because we had tithed and given to God, that He would take care of it. But the peace did not come for me until another week and a half at least. I was going for walks daily with the Word of God on note cards. I would read the scriptures through each day while walking. Finally, after numerous times through one scripture it suddenly dawned on me that a passage applied more than I thought. It was a passage from Proverbs 3:21-28 and struck me in the head with one verse: "Have no fear of sudden disaster or of the ruin that overtakes the wicked". It was a financial loss that could have been many, many thousands of dollars. I finally realized that I was not to fear but rather that God was going to take care of it. And sure enough He did. What could have ended up as an enormous loss was a mild loss instead.

It reminds me of Malachi 3:10-11 which says, "Bring the whole tithe into the storehouse, that there may be food in my house. Test me in this," says the Lord Almighty, "and see if I will not throw open the floodgates of heaven and pour out so much blessing that you will not have room enough for it. I will prevent pests from devouring your crops, and the vines in your fields will not cast their fruit," says the Lord Almighty" (Malachi 3:10-11).

Anchor yourself in the Word of God. It is the anchor that holds fast against the storm.

FAITH IN SOMETHING

Believe that God has something better for us than what the world has.

Believe that we have something coming in the eternal that is better than the temporal.

Believe that our desires are not always God's desires for us but submit them to God and we will come out ahead every time.

Believe that we are achieving an eternal glory that far outweighs it all.

Believe in the Lord Jesus Christ, and you will be saved.

What do you have faith in and how do you live it out?

"I overcome by the blood of the Lamb and by the Word of my testimony" (paraphrase of Rev.12:11). "I am powerful in the kingdom. I have a sound mind." Destroy the enemy's lies by truth telling. Every time it comes into a root or rite, you open your mouth and begin again by pouring out all the lies that it wants to use against you.

A root or rite is a place of access for the enemy to affect you and your thinking.

Truth is the manual. Begin truth with honesty. What is the difference? Honesty is an admission of the truth. Truth is what is true. To be honest is to admit it with another person and with God. Begin with truth. Truth is the manual. Love is the way. Truth in love is the power that God gives us to overcome the power of the enemy along with other things. The enemy will always lie and twist the truth. Get it out in the open and speak about it to someone. Compare it to Scripture. What does the Word of God say? Then pray in the opposite of the enemy's lies.

That's how you begin again. We must pour *out* rather than *in* lies the enemy has been telling. Get them out in the open and deal with them.

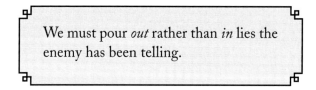

We must pour *out* rather than *in* lies the enemy has been telling.

The foundation of truth is the Word of God. We are gathering stones against the enemy, stockpiling them until we can throw them at him and crush him. It is the Word of God that is substance and abuse is to not use it. You begin using it to crush the head of the enemy.

The Word of God says, "Faith is the substance of things hoped for" (Heb.11:1 NKJV). When we hope, we have substance of the faith that causes us to hope. There is faith from reading the Word of God. There is faith in recalling the words of God spoken through His Spirit in the way that He said it, in the time and season that He planned for and works to bring to pass. We must not believe a lie that the enemy is too big to be overcome by our words and by the actions that we take through the power of the Holy Spirit. It is the Holy Spirit who enables us to overcome. We must use the Word of God and use it against the devil to discern lies from truth.

The Word of God is flawless. It destroys the accusations the enemy brings against us. Are you imperfect? Praise God. You are one of God's children, and He is able to use your imperfection for good. He does shine through us even when we are imperfect. He will use anything for good if we will allow Him. He will choose to use it for good and allow us to learn from it and grow in Him through it. It will even be a testimony, an asset that we can use to guide other people into truth and love and the goodness of God.

Does God use your life for good? Why or why not? What are you doing with it? Sitting idly by and waiting for someone to shine through? Read the Word of God and see what it says about sitting idly by. Read His Word and see what it says about working hard. What exactly does it say? It says, "All hard work brings a profit, but mere talk leads only to poverty." And "the wealth of the wise is their crown, but the folly of fools yields folly" (Proverbs 14:23-24).

Don't give up on obedience. What God has called you to do He will bring to pass if you will not quit. We must obey. Work hard. Allow God to use the difficulties or errors that you have made for good. I have had difficulties—real difficulties—but God has actually turned them around for good. He has chosen to work through them and bring good out of them. In fact, this book is a result of a difficulty that resulted in a desire and need to write. God has brought a blessing in my life and prayerfully in the lives of others as well. God will use it all if we are willing to trust Him. Turn it over to Him, and allow Him to shine through. In the hardest year of my life I began to write because I needed to. And from that came books that continue to flow. Trust in the Lord. Do not wait idly by for someone else to do what you are called to do.

Believe That Conviction Brings Something Good

For every revival that comes, there is also often in the midst of it great conviction of sin. There must be the conviction of sin to bring change. There must also be a realization of the love of God. If God is so loving, then all He does is in love.

James 4:6 says this, "God opposes the proud but gives grace to the humble." Then the passage continues and says, "Submit yourselves, then, to God. Resist the devil and he will flee from you." Then "Humble yourselves before the Lord, and He will lift you up" (James 4:10).

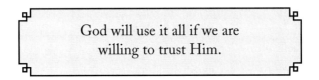

God will use it all if we are
willing to trust Him.

Notice first is "humility." Second is the gift of grace, which is undeserved favor, the promise that He will lift us up. Third is submission to God. Fourth is to resist the devil. Then the consequence is that it will flee. The last thing is to humble ourselves before God again!

But he gives us more grace.

> That is why Scripture says: "God opposes the proud but gives grace to the humble." Submit yourselves, then, to God. Resist the devil, and he will flee from you. Come near to God and he will come near to you. Wash your hands, you sinners, and purify your hearts, double-minded. Grieve, mourn and wail. Change your laughter to mourning and your joy to gloom. Humble yourselves before the Lord, and he will lift you up.
>
> James 4:6-10

We must Draw near to God, wash our hands, and purify our hearts, and it is wrapped up again with the encouragement to humble ourselves. Take it to God and draw near to God. And use prayer and fasting (which in the Bible is greater humility) as well and obedience. It takes humility to reveal our sins to someone else. It takes humility to admit and confess our sins before God. It also takes humility to change. If you have a sin or temptation that you are struggling with, take it to God. Then get it all out on the table with someone else. Confess your sins one to another, and pray for one another that you may be healed (James 5:16). *Then* it says that the prayer of a righteous man is powerful and effective.

Get everything out on the table with someone, confessing your sins before God, and have them pray for you. There must be openness and honesty and the right people to share with. We start with humility, a recognition that we need to change. Then we choose to be willing to change where needed. We overcome the devil. We purify ourselves. Then we hear the promise that as we humble ourselves before God, He will lift us up. Humble yourself. Serve and get out of the box you are in. Allow God to lift you up for Jesus did not come to be served but to serve as well (Mt. 20:28). He gave us this example and we are to follow. The blessings come in obedience.

Look at these verses that talk about humility.

"He saves the humble" (Ps. 18:27).

"He guides the humble" (Ps. 25:9).

"He sustains the humble" (Ps. 147:6).

"He crowns the humble with salvation" (Ps. 149:4).

And He gives grace to the humble (Prov. 3:34b). Grace is the undeserved favor of God. It can also apply to grace that is manifest in His gifts and Spirit. He gives grace. He supplies with favor what we have not earned nor can earn because we can never be perfect enough. God in His grace establishes us and enables us to do what He calls. Once more the humble will rejoice in the Lord, the needy will rejoice in the Holy One of Israel (Is. 29:19 NIV). There is joy that comes in humility.

If you want success against evil, humble yourself before God. Obey God.

Think of the story of King Nebuchadnezzar in the Bible. Daniel interpreted the king's dream that King Nebuchadnezzar would become like an animal in the wild until he turned his eyes to God. It happened twelve months later right after King Nebuchadnezzar showed his arrogance. But his sanity was restored when he raised his eyes toward heaven. Then he praised God and honored and glorified Him. Read Daniel 4.

So, how do we humble ourselves? Fasting is the more complete way of humbling ourselves before God.

"Humble" in the Bible also refers to fasting. Fasting is the more complete way of humbling ourselves. In fact, the verse from 2 Chronicles 7:14 is more completely fulfilled as Christians humble themselves in prayer and fasting. Of course we must also obey.

> If my people, who are called by my name, will humble themselves and pray and seek my face and turn from their wicked ways, then will I hear from heaven and will forgive their sin and will heal their land.
>
> 2 Chronicles 7:14-15

Nebuchadnezzar found the grace of God in his repentance. A great turning to God comes in the presence of conviction of sin and repentance. Conviction of sin is first. First is the realization that people need a Savior they have a need and cannot fulfill it on their own. They must realize their sinfulness to admit that they need Christ who paid for all their sin. They must humble themselves from their pride and self-sufficiency to seek God's gift of salvation. It is humility that brings us closer to God. It is the gift of life that comes through salvation when people turn to Him. There must be humility for God's grace and power and presence to be restored in the nation. People must call upon Him and ask Him to bring times of refreshing (Acts 3:19).

> So, how do we humble ourselves? Fasting is the more complete way of humbling ourselves before God.

Without conviction of sin there will be no revival. For the Presence of God does not come in the midst of sin as in the midst of repentance and holiness. People are in need of a Savior and in need of a realization of their sin so they call upon the Name of the Lord. For there is one way to God and it is in Jesus His Son. That is the only way to heaven. Many people want many ways. But it is not so.

It is we who are His people who are called to obey and follow Him in discipleship. Why do we believe that if we give something up for God that we will have less? It has never been that way. If we will sacrifice time to pray more on our own in the privacy of our own homes and also in unity with other believers, we will have more of the presence of God and the good things that He desires to give us. Martin Luther was the one who stated he had so much to do today that he must spend *more* time in prayer (three hours was one day). He needed the power of God to accomplish what he needed. Yet, when we need to accomplish more, what do we do? Look at your own life and determine if you are committed to spending time with God and in prayer on a consistent and daily basis.

Standing Rocks

What are these? These are things that remind us of the goodness of God, of His faithfulness, and what He has done in the past. In the Bible, there were times that the Israelites would set up "standing rocks" or "standing stones" as a remembrance to something significant of God's faithfulness. One of these instances was in Joshua 4. The entire army of Israelites crossed the Jordan "on dry ground" and set themselves on the other side of the Jordan River. It could only be by the hand of God that they could return to the other side since it actually took a miracle of God to pull the water back and dry the land below for them all to walk across. After this miracle of having God part the water for them and help them cross on dry land, Joshua, their leader at the time, set up twelve stones that they had taken out of the Jordan.

What are my standing rocks? They are things that we can stand up against the devil when we are discouraged. Remember the faithfulness of God through the difficulty and remember that He is faithful to the end. God is not dead. He is continuing on in the journey. He has a plan and a hope for you if you continue with Him. He has a plan. Remember what God has done in the past and how He has moved in the present. He may change in a new way in the future, but He is always faithful and will bring to pass His promises. And here now the word *covenant* also belongs. We enter into a covenant with God, where if we will trust and obey and continue in obedience to what He has said, He will fulfill His side of the covenant. If not, disobedience results in things that are not as good.

Yet, God is faithful to bring things to pass when we are not able. Trust in the Lord and continue to do good. He is the God above all who is able to accomplish His plans and will.

Stand up your standing stones as reminders of what God has done. What is it that you need to remind you of God's faithfulness? For instance, how far have you come? Where are you going?

We must place our faith in God.

TRUTH STANDS

Counterfeit vs. Reality

Bankers train their employees on flagging counterfeit money. Instead of spending their time having employees work with counterfeit money to recognize it, when someone brings it through the bank, they train them to know the real money so well that they will not be tricked with counterfeit. The bank knows it is better to have their employees be so familiar with the real that the counterfeit will jump right out as being fake. So this is the way they train employees to recognize what is real and what is not.

If we know what is real, and we trust it, we will stand up to the counterfeit and not think it looks good at all.

Train yourself in the truth so that when the lies of the devil come, you will recognize them immediately. Train yourself in God's Word so you recognize lies when they are brought against you by the devil, the world, or by the flesh.

I will give you one example. In our culture it is the norm, supposedly, to run to bed to have sex with others before marriage. But it is the counterfeit. If someone is not committed enough to you to marry then why give yourself to them? It is revealed as the counterfeit that the devil offers to people. It lacks commitment. It also produces hurts. It is not a genuine love but a selfish love. And God is against it.

We must have a rock-solid foundation in the Word of God. How do we use the Word of God? Then we ask the Holy Spirit, the Counselor and "Spirit of truth" to guide us with His truth. Believe truth and truth will come out of your mouth, will it not? Believe lies and lies will come out of your mouth. We must have our foundation in what God says.

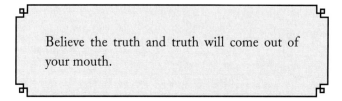

Believe the truth and truth will come out of your mouth.

I pray for truth and *honesty* in the heart. I ask the Spirit of truth to "guide me into all truth, to reveal lies that I have believed. Enable me to dwell on, follow, and to act on what is true." We are called to speak the truth in love. "Instead, speaking the truth in love, we will in all things grow up into him who is the Head, that is, Christ" (Eph. 4:15). We are called to not just cover things over but rather speak the truth *in* love. The truth is on the inside of love. Love that is genuine and true is love that will also choose to deal honestly with one another. Do not lie. If you need to address something touchy, do it patiently and in love. It will make it more difficult for the devil to get into it. Speak and act in love for one another. "Love one another deeply, from the heart" (1 Peter 1:22). Wrap the truth inside of love if it is difficult to share.

Ask God to break down lies of the enemy daily in your relationships and in your life.

Legalism Vs. Freedom

Now the Lord is the Spirit, and where the Spirit of the Lord is, there is freedom (2 Cor. 3:17).

Stand on the Word of God. Use it. And be led by the Spirit. The Spirit leads us into freedom and liberty. It is not that we do whatever we want but rather that in following the precious Spirit of God, we are led into spiritual freedom and liberty. If we do not have the Spirit of God in power in our lives to lead and guide us, we will have legalism or dogmatism, which is an unbendable way about us. We are to be led by the Spirit of God and not only by the words of man. Man's words do not have affect as the Spirit of God does. Certain denominations have more problems with legalism and dogmatism. "Legalism" is a perfectionism and rigidity. It is often guilt driven. "Dogmatism" is a stiffness. Almost like having a stiff back or stiff neck, when the Holy Spirit says be bendable and change, dogmatism will say, "Huh-uh. No way. I am staying as stiff as a board. I'm staying this way, and I ain't changing." Legalism is what the Pharisees and religious leaders were criticized for by Jesus. *Legalists are made not born.* No one is born a legalist. They are made by people's rules and regulations that are impressed upon them until they follow them. It is often guilt that is used.

Principles are good, but they are guidelines that are not to be legalized.

Now the Lord is the Spirit, and where the Spirit of the Lord is there is liberty (2 Cor. 3:17 NKJV).

What is liberty? If the Lord is the Spirit and where the Spirit of the Lord is, there is liberty, what is that? It is a freedom from captivity, from confinement, from restrictions that would seek to control. Have you ever had the precious Spirit of God lead you into something that was a new wine skin and definitely not the normal man made traditions (Luke 4:18 NKJV)?

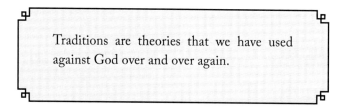

Traditions are theories that we have used against God over and over again.

Legalists are made not born. No one is born a legalist. They are made by people's rules and regulations that are impressed upon them until they follow them. It is often guilt that is used.

Principles are good, but they are guidelines that are not to be legalized.

Principles are good. The leading of the Spirit is better. Unity is best.

"Traditions are theories that people have used against Me over and over again" is what I have sensed the Spirit speak to my heart.

He leads us into freedom from the flesh that restricts. He leads us into freedom from sin and the devil's tactics, which are in part to bring legalism and stiffness. Obedience brings blessings. Disobedience brings other things. God's ways are always best, but sometimes He has to discipline His children until they follow His ways.

With the Spirit of the Lord comes freedom and liberty. Do not believe a lie that God does not want you free. God wants you free. All of His commandments are given to guide us into truth and righteousness and into the blessings that come through obedience to God. He is a great God, and He has great ability to turn things around as we fast, pray, seek His face and confess our sins. He is not limited by the confines of human construction, human gods, limited abilities, and our mistakes. Rather, he is the God who desires to bring good from human error, failings, and oopses. God desires to bring good and not evil. He is able to work good things if we will allow Him and remain with Him. The blessing of God is to break the bonds of slavery, to enable us to love one another and walk in peace. It is the blessing of God that comes upon us as we come together in prayer, in fasting, and in forgiveness. Is there someone that you hold a grudge against? Take it to God first. Then confess your sins before one another, and work through it. Get it out in the open. Work through it. Do your best. Do your part and begin again.

There are things that break off as we obey God and walk in peace. Love is the common key. God is love, and we are very loved by Him. He has a good plan for us. He will get us there. We are to love one another. We are to pray with one another. We are to follow in His ways, guided by His Spirit and His Word.

We build our lives on the Word of God. Strongholds are broken when the Word of God and the Spirit of God are obeyed.

There are things that are foundational to our Christian walk. Do not stray with the culture into patterns that say it is fine to do what you want, follow what you want, or allow sin to enter in. It is the Word of God that stands. The foundation is important.

Do you spend time in the Word of God? "Study to shew thyself approved unto God…rightly dividing the word of truth" which comes through the Spirit as well.

One is this: "Thou shalt have no other gods before Me" (Deut. 5:7).

Truth and Reality vs. Denial

What is truth? The dictionary says it is the true or actual state of a matter. It is conformity with fact or reality—an indisputable or verified fact, proposition or principle.

The truth is God loves us. God gave His Son for us. And He has a plan for us. It is the plan of victory over sin. It is a plan to do great things for God and reach people for Christ. It is a plan of victory. The Bible says, All have sinned and fall short of God's glory (Romans 3:23). All people everywhere have committed sin and are neither perfect nor without faults. Everyone has them. That is truth number one. Do not expect your brother or sister to be perfect. No one is. Jesus is. He always has been. Everyone else has fallen short. Based on this, we have the principle of forgiveness. All have sinned. Therefore, we are all in need of a Savior and in need of forgiveness. Relationally, we will all have times that we need to forgive each other. This happens. Eventually, we all have to forgive one another. That is truth, and that is how it is in life. Is it hard to forgive? It can be. Consider: what are the issues that remain to be dealt with? If there are hurts that remain, it may be good to work through them. Talk through them with a trusted friend. Forgive. And you will be forgiven. Believe that you are going forward. Believe that God is able to work even through that which is the toughest to forgive. For He is able. He is the God who is able to take what is very difficult and bring good through it.

How does truth affect us? Change us? Mold us? Help us? What do we do with truth? What does truth do for us? It sets us free. You will know the truth and it will set you free (John 8:32). Denial can be a spirit as well as an action or mind-set. It has to be dealt with by reality.

What do you do if you come up against denial? For one, you pray for reality. Speak about reality. Choose to accept reality. The opposite of denial is reality so the choice is to break it with what is real rather than what is fake or denied.

Intimidation is broken more than one way. But one way is to come close to the heart of God and accept His Spirit of grace and truth. Fear not and love God. Do not fear evil, but fear God. Do not fear what man can do but rather fear, with a loving respect, God the Father who sees all and knows all.

Reality is that the nation as a whole is immoral. It is all over the television and TV screens. It is in talk shows. It is prevalent in magazines and advertising. So, immorality is pushed on our children and our grandchildren as well as on us. Immorality is more approved of than it used to be. The standards that are culturally accepted have fallen significantly.

There Is Something Better Than

Giving Into Temptation

Playing with temptation is like playing cards at a table across from sin. You have a deck of cards between you. The longer you stay the more likely you are to lose.

You deal a hand you think you can win. But it's really sin that deals the hand.

Playing with temptation is like playing with fire. You are bound to get burned eventually. And when you do you will wonder why you took the chance you took. No one makes it out without scars.

Even Joseph had opportunity to sin. He experienced temptation when he was alone with his master's wife. But he came out ahead by resisting. It was the hand of God that pulled him ahead.

> Now Joseph was well-built and handsome, and after a while his master's wife took notice of Joseph and said, "Come to bed with me!" But he refused....And though she spoke to him day after day, he refused to go to bed with her or even be with her.
>
> Genesis 39:7-10

Joseph endured a lingering temptation. It occurred more than once. It was day after day that he had to refuse her. It was a temptation that continued more than once, but Joseph set himself to not fall into it. We all have things that are around us that can be a temptation. How do we respond? Joseph refused to go to bed with her or "even be with her." He would not entertain the temptation or even be with her. Though the temptation came to him, he would not allow himself to be enticed.

When temptation comes, do not go near it. Stay away from it. Walk the other way. Run away from it. Rather than walking toward the temptation, Joseph ran away. Run from sin. Flee. What is the temptation, and how can you run from it? Run away if you need to. Let your legs carry you when your will cannot hold you. How can you shield yourself? Often having someone else that you are friends with keep you accountable helps immensely. They can ask you about it. They can even pray for you concerning it. If you suppress evil, it will explode on you. Get it out in the open. If it is on the computer, get accountability. Be humble enough to be honest. Most temptations are cut in half if we have someone else to share it with so we are not alone.

Pray. Fast and obey.

Do you know that God rewarded Joseph for his obedience and purity in the midst of the temptation? That is God's way. He rewards us when we are obedient to keep ourselves pure and out of sin.

Obedience is king.

Finally the day came when Joseph was pushed so hard by his master's wife that he ran, leaving his cloak behind.

One day he went into the house to attend to his duties, and none of the household servants was inside. She caught him by his cloak and said, "Come to bed with me!" But he left his cloak in her hand and ran out of the house (Genesis 39:11-12).

Joseph was caught by accident in a situation that ended up causing him pain. Though he did the right thing and ran away from the temptation, even leaving his cloak behind, he was strung up on wrongful assault by her and her husband as if he had tried to rape her. From being the person most trusted by his master, he went to prison as wrongfully sinning. But God saw through it and saw the intent of his heart along with the circumstances. God was with him. In fact, this difficulty and wrongful accusation that seemed to undo so much time, work and reputation of good that Joseph had worked for, actually became the stepping-stone for God promoting him to the place where he could fulfill the very call of God in his life.

Do not forget that when man despises your beginnings or wrongfully accuses and degrades you, that it is God who holds the key to your success. He is the one who is able to work things out and bring good. He will reward you for your obedience and not succumbing to pressure.

We do not know the time frame of how long Joseph was in prison. We know that it was long enough for him to find favor and kindness from the prison warden. And it was long enough to receive the responsibility of being in charge of others in the prison. Then the next chapter explains "sometime later" and "after they had been in custody for some time." So there was probably more time there in that prison than Joseph wished to spend. Then two years after all this Pharaoh finally had the dream that brought Joseph from the prison to second in authority in the land. Now that is a promotion, isn't it? Joseph was faithful where he was even when his brothers first sold him into slavery and then he was wrongfully accused and thrown into prison.

If there are highlights in this story, remember these:

God will reward you even if man won't.

The blessings of God come with obedience even if we must wait for them.

Resist the temptation and run if you must.

Do not look at another woman to lust for her in your heart (Prov. 6:25; 1 Thess. 4:3-7). You can change the gender and also say "do not look at another man to lust for him". It applies both ways. Lust is sin, and it is a trap set by the enemy to entice you into a hardness of heart to the blessings of God. It is a trap that is set against purity. The pure of heart shall see God (Matt. 5:8). Therefore it is against you. It is also a trap that is set to cause you to falter and sin in increasing ways. What do you do when you come up against lust as a temptation? Cry out to God for salvation, and then use the Word of God directly against it. Pray. Fast and Obey. Resist the temptation and run if you must.

What is the temptation that you struggle with the most? Ask God to reveal the root cause to you. And use the Word of God to take a stand against it. If you are unsure what the temptation is, ask God to reveal it to you and the root cause for it. He knows our heart.

How Jesus Overcame

The Holy Spirit led Jesus into the desert. He went and fasted there forty days and forty nights. Then the devil showed up and began tempting him, taunting him first about food. I could imagine Jesus thinking, "I am so hungry. Why does he tempt me when God said to fast? Why does it have to be now?"

Has that ever happened to you? Has the devil ever taunted you over something that you need? "Why don't you meet your needs this way," the devil will say and will offer a counter to what God's best is.

> Then Jesus was led by the Spirit into the desert to be tempted by the devil. After fasting forty days and forty nights, he was hungry. The tempter came to him and said, "If you are the Son of God, tell these stones to become bread."
>
> Jesus answered, "It is written: 'Man does not live on bread alone, but on every word that comes from the mouth of God.'"
>
> Then the devil took him to the holy city and had him stand on the highest point of the temple. "If you are the Son of God," he said, "throw yourself down. For it is written: 'He will command his angels concerning you, and they will lift you up in their hands, so that you will not strike your foot against a stone.'"
>
> Jesus answered him, "It is also written: 'Do not put the Lord your God to the test.'"
>
> Again, the devil took him to a very high mountain and showed him all the kingdoms of the world and their

splendor. "All this I will give you," he said, "if you will bow down and worship me."

Jesus said to him, "Away from me, Satan! For it is written: 'Worship the Lord your God, and serve him only.'"

Then the devil left him, and angels came and attended him. (Matthew 4:1-11)

Does temptation to sin come from God? *No.* God does not tempt us to sin but rather provides a way of escape (1 Cor. 10:13). God can use it all for good if we are willing. Look at Job. God allowed testing. Though He did not specifically cause it, He allowed it. Jesus was tempted. God allowed it and even led Jesus into the wilderness where He fasted for forty days. But it was the devil that then tempted Him. Notice it was after his 40 days of fasting and his victory over the temptations that Jesus' public ministry began.

Look at the way Jesus used the Word of God when He was tempted by the devil (Matthew 4). He met it with the Word of God as His sword. He immediately took it up and spoke it against the temptation and the tempter. And notice it defeated the lies and He overcame. So we are also to take up the sword of the Spirit and speak it aloud to overcome the lies of the devil.

Use the Word of God against temptation. Matthew 4:1 begins this way: "Then Jesus was led by the Spirit into the desert to be tempted by the devil." Does the devil tempt people? Yes. Does the devil tempt Christians? Yes. In fact, as the verses continue, the devil is actually referred to as "the tempter."

God can use it all for good if we are willing.

A temptation to satisfy the flesh came first to Jesus. We all have this temptation. It is a temptation that is common to man. When you fast there will inevitably be times that temptations will come to not do it. So, what is the way that Jesus stood against the temptation? It was with the Word of God. He began, "It is written: 'Man does not live on bread alone, but on every word that comes from the mouth of God'" (Matt. 4:4).

He had just fasted for forty days and forty nights, and the Word of God says, "He was hungry." Notice that the devil does not tempt us as often in the area we are stronger in. But rather it looks for an opportunity and offers a temptation that would meet your fleshly desires at the time.

Imagine how hungry Jesus was when the tempter came with a temptation to make food for himself out of the stones. Have you ever fasted for forty days? Jesus had a felt desire and need for food right when the tempter brought the temptation. But it would have been leaning on his own desires rather than God's. Jesus did not sway.

The second temptation that the "tempter" brought to Jesus was to throw himself off the temple and allow the angels to rescue him. It was a pride of life temptation. What purpose was there in it other than to show that it could be done and he would be fine? Can we put God to the test? Jesus' answer was to not test the Lord. How did Jesus respond to this question?

Then the devil took him to the holy city and had him stand on the highest point of the temple. "If you are the Son of God," he said, "throw yourself down. For it is written: 'He will command his angels concerning you, and they will lift you up in their hands, so that you will not strike your foot against a stone.'" Jesus answered him, "It is also written: 'Do not put the Lord your God to the test'" (Matthew 4:7). Jesus again answered with the Word of God.

The third temptation appealed to the desire for wealth and power.

Again, the devil took him to a very high mountain and showed him all the kingdoms of the world and their splendor. "'All this I will give you,'" he said, "'if you will bow down and worship me'" (Matthew 4:8).

How did Jesus respond to this temptation? He answered with the Word of God again from His mouth.

Jesus said to him, "Away from me, Satan! For it is written: 'Worship the Lord your God, and serve him only'" (Matt. 4:10).

The devil appealed to Jesus with a temptation for power, wealth or greed. The way of God was a way that included suffering and submission to God. The devil brought a temptation with an appearance of no suffering but rather arrogance, pride, and power. How often in temptation is that the way that the lies accumulate? The devil, the tempter, and even the world will tell us that if we follow it and take of what it has, we will receive "all these things". Yet in the end is death, for he who follows the ways of the world is led right into death and into separation from the God who loves them. The ways of the world often tell people to separate and go live the good life. Go drink and party and fill up with the things of the world that look and feel good for a short time. But in the end comes the opposite of what you want. Jesus overcame the temptation for power and submitted to God with the Word of God from His mouth.

The devil offered him something other than suffering. God offered His children freedom in spirit and heaven for eternity through his Son's obedience. He was tempted to have everything he wanted without the suffering. Of course it was a lie. It is never what we want when we follow the devil's tactics into sin. It goes into enslavement and bondage. Hurts come through it. Wounds are the enemy's curse. Healing is God's blessing. When we follow God's rules, principles and leading, healing comes quickly.

Follow him into prayer and fasting as well. God promises healing with it and Jesus did it as well. (Is. 58:8)

The best things in life cannot be bought with money. Rather, they come through relationships and through the Holy Spirit of God and the things of Him. Trust in the Lord and follow Him.

Jesus used the Word of God. Is that why He was so successful? Is that the principle that we must use in our lives as Jesus's followers? When we are tempted to satisfy the lust of the flesh (whether it is food or a gratifying of passions or desires), answer with the Word of God specifically against that temptation.

For instance, if the temptation is laziness, find a specific verse from the Word of God and quote it. Do not use it legalistically as if you can never rest. Rest is of God as well. But there is a time and a place—a season for everything. Proverbs says this "Lazy hands make a man poor, but diligent hands bring wealth. He who gathers crops in summer is a wise son, but he who sleeps during harvest is a disgraceful son." (Prov. 10:4-5) Use the Word of God. Apply it. Speak it. Another Proverb concerning laziness is this one: "The lazy man does not roast his game, but the diligent man prizes his possessions" (Prov. 12:27).

Do you not know what verse to use? Get to know the Word of God and apply it. Then when you have a struggle, ask God for a Word for the day and for your specific situation. Recently I asked in prayer and the one that came was this: Dwell in the land and do good. In other words, God has placed us where we are for a season. Dwell in the land and *do good*. It comes from Ps. 37:3 "... do good; dwell in the land..."

What is the lie that God desires to deal with in your life? Why do you believe it, or why *did* you believe it? Why is God not good enough to deal with it as well as use others? The Word of God as well?

Do we know the Word of God well enough to have it at our fingertips and memory when temptation shows up? Do not put yourself in a situation on purpose just to reveal that God can get you out of it easily. Do not put the Lord your God to the test. Keep away from evil. It is evil that wants to get hooks and rites (authority and influence) against you when you walk and live for God. When you are a disciple of Christ, there are temptations and worldly attractions around that we must resist. We are to keep our heart from being so attached to the things of the world. On the other hand, we are also not to live in poverty or the other extreme. So our heart strings must be connected to God and the things of God. Then we will resist the devil. Apply your heart to instruction, to the Word of God, and to the things of God. Keep some people as friends who are not Christians.

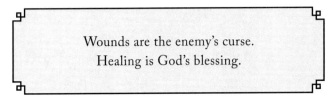

Wounds are the enemy's curse.
Healing is God's blessing.

The average Christian, within seven years of becoming a Christian, has no non-Christian friends left. Love God and love people. Follow God. Do not put the Lord your God to the test. Reach out to people, but do not put yourself in a position that condones or supports sin. Do not put yourself in a position that tests the Lord because of your inability to stay pure. It is God who leads. It is we who must follow. Believe in the Lord Jesus Christ and walk by faith.

Jesus stood his ground with God's Word. It is powerful and alive. It is alive to rebuke and comfort according to the need. It is effective, and it accomplishes in the spirit as well as in the hearts of man. It is alive. I remember again the vision I had of a huge sword that reverberated with power. In the spirit, the Word of God is alive, and it cuts right through the lies of the enemy. The enemy gains access through lies. It is the truth of God that stands.

Jesus said to him, "Away from me, Satan! For it is written: 'Worship the Lord your God, and serve him only'" (Matt. 4:10).

Do you ever feel the temptation that all these goods that the world has to offer are worth serving sin for? Have you had a temptation for power come over you? A temptation is not a sin. But giving in to it can be.

What is the basic human desire?

What is the unmet need?

The devil works to entice us into a lie that the sin is greater than purity and righteousness. The only thing giving in to the devil accomplishes is hurts. And the consequences that come are often painful and less than desired. The devil's tactic is to make sin appear enticing. It wants to cause us to lust for it, to be emotionally attached to it, to dwell on it and only see the short term pleasures of it. It wants to "sly in." It wants to work on the sly to bring you down. It wants to make sin seem compelling or attractive, but hide and minimize all the consequences of it. The world is always working to pull you away from God so they do not feel convicted or compelled to change from pleasing their sinful nature. But the bubble is bust when we give in to it, because all sin has a consequence. It also has a consequence on our relationship with God. The natural consequence of sin is pleasure for a moment but difficulty for a lifetime if you continue in it.

In His Sanctuary

"Lord, who may dwell in your sanctuary?" (Ps. 15:1a) What is a sanctuary? It is a haven for those who choose to dwell there. It is the dwelling place of God. "Who may live on your holy hill?" (Ps 15:1b) Do you notice it says "live" rather than die? Do you notice that life is the opposite of death? God brings life. The devil and sin brings death. It brings painful consequences. This verse also says "live" rather than just visit?

The answer to these questions is: "He whose walk is blameless and who does what is righteous, who speaks the truth from his heart and has no slander on his tongue, who does his neighbor no wrong and casts no slur on his fellowman, who despises a vile man but honors those who fear the Lord" (Ps.15:2-4). And the list continues. Then it says at the bottom, "He who does these things will never be shaken." First things first: Keep God first, and reject sin. Walk a walk that is blameless, and do what is right.

Speak the truth, and allow God to bless and honor you for it. He who does these things will never be shaken. Dwell in the presence of the Lord. Live on His holy hill.

Allow God to lead and direct your life; reject the enticements of the devil and the flesh and the world. What are they? Answer it.

Temptation. Is the temptation always built around lies? Typically, yes. It has to be or it wouldn't be tempting.

Sexual immorality is one sin that the devil lies about. The world says it is fun and expected. God's Word says it brings sin and pain. The pleasure of sin is fleeting. The devil says it won't be gone tomorrow but it is. The pain it brings can last much longer than expected.

> For everything in the world—the cravings of sinful man, the lust of the eyes and the boasting of what he has and does—comes not from the Father but from the world. The world and its desires pass away, but the man who does the will of God lives forever.
>
> 1 John 2:16

Everything you want that God does not want is flesh, of the world or things that will end in compromise. Things that provoke you to stare at sin are flesh. Jesus said, "the Spirit gives life" (John 6:63).

Get to know the truth so you recognize the lies when they are brought against you by the devil, the world, the flesh or others. Use the Word of God like Jesus did.

Matthew 4:4:

Jesus answered, "It is written: 'Man does not live on bread alone, but on every word that comes from the mouth of God.'"

Jesus fasted and when temptation came he overcame with the Word of God. Then his public ministry began and he is described as being "in the power of the Spirit" (Luke 4:14).

Resist vs. Ignore

Anger, if not dealt with, can give the devil a foothold. Anger that is destructive has different results from righteous anger. Jesus was angry at the temple. Jesus was angry about being told not to heal on the Sabbath. It was a righteous anger. Selfish or destructive anger can give the devil a foothold.

I want men everywhere to lift up holy hands in prayer, without anger or disputing (1 Timothy 2:8). Rather than disagreeing and having anger against one another, we are to pray and worship God. God is able to heal better than devils. Whatever the devil says to do, do the opposite. "Anyone who has been stealing must steal no longer, but must work, doing something useful with their own hands, that they may have something to share with those in need" (Eph. 4:28).

Do not only ignore the devil, but resist it. "Submit yourselves, then, to God. Resist the devil, and he will flee from you" (James 4:7). Submit yourself to God in heart, in mind, and in soul. When He says to rid your life of things, then do it. Obey immediately. Do what God says. Come near to God and he will come near to you (James 4:8).

If He says to speak the truth in love, then speak the truth in love. "Whoever says to the guilty 'You are innocent' peoples will curse him and nations denounce him. But it will go well with those who convict the guilty, and rich blessing will come upon them" (Pr. 24:24-25).

"An honest answer is like a kiss on the lips" (Pr. 24:26).

As He leads, obey. "But you have an anointing from the Holy One, and all of you know the truth… As for you, the anointing you received from him remains in you, and you do not need anyone to teach you. But as his anointing teaches you about all things and as that anointing is real, not counterfeit—just as it has taught you, remain in him" (1 John 2:20,27).

Where the Spirit of the Lord is, there is freedom. "Now the Lord is the Spirit, and where the Spirit of the Lord is, there is freedom" (2 Cor. 3:17). We all know people who have "shined" with the presence of the Lord. Even Moses's face shone after being in the presence of the Lord (Ex. 34:34). The next verse says that we are being transformed into his image "with ever-increasing glory," which comes from who? From the Lord, who is the Spirit. In other words, when we come to Christ and receive Jesus Christ as our Lord and Savior we receive a portion of the Holy Spirit. The book of Acts specifically describes a filling of the Holy Spirit that results in new tongues. Did that only apply then and not apply now? Freedom comes with the Holy Spirit.

People who struggle with sin still have a portion of the Holy Spirit but sin can result in the presence of the Lord leaving some. God does not dwell with sin. If we have a mixture of water and wine, or oil and wine, do they not separate?

Breaking Strongholds

How do you break strongholds? There are a few ways. Follow the leading of the Holy Spirit and have others help you if need be. There is blessing in unity. There is strength in unity and in the Word of God. There is power in agreement. The anointing of God breaks strongholds, too. Do not fear God's anointing. Rather, fear (respect) God. Do not fear evil. Fear God.

Sin causes strongholds to remain. Suppression is sin. It loses its power by being open and honest.

If you want to combat a stronghold, begin by acting on the opposite. If the stronghold that you are working on is fear, begin by addressing the issues that cause you to have fear. Dig into the reason for it and address it. Then replace it with the opposite: love. Deal with the root cause.

Fast and pray to dig those roots out.

Strongholds are broken with prayer and fasting. Then accountability and uniting with others is a second key. Humble yourselves before the Lord, and in due time He will raise you up (1 Peter 5:6). Pray and fast. Continue to pray and fast regularly. Do not give up. Follow the leading of the Holy Spirit. If thoughts or ideas are coming to mind, ask the Lord to remove it if it is not from Him. Then ask Him to strengthen it if it is from Him. I have seen this blessed by God time and again.

"Lord, if this idea _____ is from You, I ask You to strengthen it. And if it is not, I ask that You remove it, in Jesus's name."

Pray and fast and listen to the Holy Spirit. How do we listen to the Holy Spirit? Allow ourselves to be led by the Spirit rather than the flesh or human nature. It takes practice or discipline. We must choose willingly to follow the Holy Spirit rather than our fleshly desires, which includes food at times.

What does fasting and prayer do? It intensifies our ability to hear the Holy Spirit. The flesh is denied its normal comforts and enticements as we lean on the Holy Spirit.

Pray and search out what the stronghold or issue is. Follow the leading of the Holy Spirit. We do not "outsmart" the devil. God outsmarts the devil. We must follow His leading and guidance in our lives. Be sensitive to the Holy Spirit. How many times in hindsight I see that the leading of the Holy Spirit would have corrected me before the enemy hit harder. Many times in my life I see that following His Spirit has protected me from things that I myself did not have the foresight to see ahead.

Follow the Word of God. Follow the leading of the Holy Spirit. It will protect you from many things you do not expect.

You can use other people as well. Do not always do it on your own. For perfect love casts out all fear. "There is no fear in love. But perfect love drives out fear, because fear has to do with punishment. The one who fears is not made perfect in love" (1 John 4:18).

Such love has no fear because perfect love expels all fear. If we are afraid, it is for fear of judgment, and this shows that his love has not been perfected in us (1 John 4:18 NLT).

Dressed For Battle

God has spiritual armor or protection for us. Ephesians 6 speaks of putting on the whole armor of God. Pray and ask God to put His full armor on you daily. Ask God to teach you what it means to walk in the full armor of God. One thing is to forgive our neighbor so that the devil will not get a foothold. Next, the separate parts of the armor that the Word of God speaks of in Ephesians 6 are as follows:

Belt of Truth:

First things first, read and memorize the Word of God. Read it often. Meditate on it. Take time to ponder it in your heart and mind. Even write it on a 3x5 card and take it with you through the day, in the car, on your walk, etc. Then also ask God to reveal truth to you and apply the truth you've learned.

Ask God to demolish arguments and every pretension that sets itself up against the knowledge of God and help us take captive every thought to make it obedient to Christ (2 Cor. 10:5).

Breastplate of Righteousness:

Jesus Christ has become "our righteousness, holiness and redemption" (1 Cor. 1:30). He has paid the price for all of our sin. Our standing of being righteous before God comes first by faith in Christ having paid the price for us. He makes us righteous. We could never work enough to earn it on our own. Stand on it. Quote it and remember that God does want us to "walk in it".

So also ask Him if there are areas He desires you to change. It is Jesus Christ who is "our righteousness, holiness and redemption."

Feet Fitted with the Readiness
of the Gospel of Peace:

Be able and ready to give an answer to everyone who asks you to give the reason for your hope in Christ. (1 Peter 3:15) Share courageously and boldly about your relationship with God (Phil.1:14b). Be willing to share. Read and practice sharing your testimony, in a few minutes, with your friends and family. Receive their input. We are to be prepared.

Shield of Faith:

It is the shield of faith that we hold up "to quench all the fiery darts of the wicked one" (Eph. 6:16 NKJV). One of the first things that the spiritual enemy will do is try to convince us that following God, serving Him, and seeking Him earnestly in prayer and even in fasting is a waste of time. Doubt is a number one tool in the enemy's arsenal. Read Hebrews 11, and ask God to increase your faith! Faith comes by hearing and hearing by the Word of God. Hold up the shield of faith to quench the devil's darts. Doubt the devil not God.

Helmet of Salvation:

"Take the helmet of salvation and the sword of the Spirit" (Ephesians 6:17).

It is salvation here and now. It is also salvation to come. Believe in the Lord Jesus Christ, and you will be saved. We walk in the power of God and our salvation comes from God through Jesus Christ.

Our head is important in battle. A head blow is serious so guard your thoughts. If a thought does not line up with the Word of God, kick it out. Speak the opposite, the truth, over your thoughts and take every thought captive. What is a first thing that the spiritual enemy, the devil, will bring against your mind? First is the doubt that God's Word speaks and is powerful. God's Word is powerful. It is alive in the spirit realm. Guard your head by guarding your thoughts.

Salvation is of the Lord.

Sword of the Spirit:

"For the word of God is living and active. Sharper than any double-edged sword, it penetrates even to dividing soul and spirit, joints and marrow; it judges the thoughts and attitudes of the heart" (Hebrews 4:12).

The greatest offensive weapon is the sword of the Spirit, which is the Word of God. If you do not read the Bible regularly, you will never be as effective for God.

Do you notice what this passage says? "I write to you, young men, because you are strong, and the Word of God lives in you, and you have overcome the evil one" (1 John 2: 14b). Three things go together in this verse. Being strong, the Word of God living in you and overcoming the evil one are combined in this verse. *Substantiate everything with the Word of God.*

Then also *allow the Holy Spirit* to dwell in you, guide you, and teach you all truth. For the sons of God are led by the Spirit of God (Rom. 8:14). What things are important to God? Place God first. Repent and turn to God that your sins may be forgiven and that times of refreshing may come (Acts 3:19). What comes with repentance? Your sins are forgiven. Accept forgiveness. Receive forgiveness. Forgive yourself. Forgive others.

Use the full armor. Pray and ask God for it daily.

Stronghold? What Is That?

A stronghold is a place that the devil bunkers in. A stronghold is often fortified by its holder. It sits on the inside and attempts to strengthen or hold its place. It protects its valuables. The devil does it through lies and hiding things that need to be dealt with.

Strongholds are made of things that are invisible. They are not seen to the naked eye but are spiritually discerned. One does not even know sometimes when a stronghold is there unless God reveals it. We work to break strongholds so that we can experience the freedom, joy, love, peace, and blessings that God desires for us. Strongholds tend to cause pain and difficulty in our lives as well as in our relationship with God and others.

Here are a couple definitions of strongholds:

Strongholds: a well-fortified place, resistant to attack.

A stronghold is a place that is fortified like a fortress against outside attack. "It is a place we hold strongly. Strongholds are often attitudes of the heart and actions. Consistent attitudes are strongholds. They can be good or bad. We are speaking here of ungodly strongholds, something that the devil has "bunkered in".

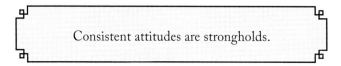

Consistent attitudes are strongholds.

A stronghold can be a *position, belief, soul rite, mind rite- whether good or bad. It is a refuge, fortress, center or area of dominance. It is a place that is resistant to attack, a "strong hold".*

I want to say first that I don't believe we will ever have it all "pinned down" and never have things to learn. We are not smarter than the devil but God is and His Word is.

The first thing in spiritual warfare is know the Word of God and grow in obeying the Spirit of the Living God. He is alive and real. He does lead and direct. We are to be led by the Spirit as well as the Word. Jesus was and we are to be as well.

> "Then Jesus was led by the Spirit into the wilderness to be tempted by the devil" (Matt. 4:1).

> "Jesus, full of the Holy Spirit, left the Jordan and was led by the Spirit" (Lk. 4:1).

> "For those who are led by the Spirit of God are the children of God" (Rom. 8:14).

> "But if you are led by the Spirit, you are not under the law" (Gal. 5:18).

We must be led by the Spirit of God and the Word of God.

The more obedient we are, the more able we are to overcome the enemy's tactics and the greater authority we gain over it. We must be led by God. Obedience is key. Blessings come through obedience. And it is strongholds that often make it more difficult to obey. In prayer and fasting we seek God to break these holds the enemy, or wrong thoughts and attitudes, have in our lives.

What are strongholds? They can be roots and rites, places of access the devil gets in to influence us. These cause an open door for the enemy, our spiritual enemy, to get through.

We may have personal strongholds that are difficult to break through. In my experience, when you break a stronghold, it needs to be replaced with something new. In this case it would apply to replacing it with God, His truth, His priorities, His people. We must replace it with something.

The things of God must be established in our lives in a godly way. They must be laid layer upon layer. We build principle upon principle, truth upon truth. Godly affections must take the place of ungodly affections. The only way to rid poverty is to replace it with something else. And yet the opposite end from poverty can lead to gluttony. So in between the two lies a balance that we must come to. We must be led by the Spirit of God and by the principles in God's Word.

Another example is this: Wealth is to be a blessing for those that have it. Yet, when we hoard wealth we run into problems. The principles of God's Word lead us in how to handle it. A way to break strongholds that may come through having wealth is to give. "Give and it will be given to you. A good measure, pressed down, shaken together and running over" (Luke 6:38). Do not hold onto it so tightly that it gains control in your life. We are to give. Then, expect God's blessings! God promises to provide for your needs. Give and it will be given to you. He may show up when you give with a generous attitude and bless you with wealth *to give for the kingdom.*

Strongholds In The Bible

Strongholds are a center of something, whether good or evil. It can be a spiritual stronghold or a physical place. Looking through the Bible, David had strongholds to run to when King Saul chased him down to kill him. They were physical places that he would run to, to hide from his enemies. David stayed in the wilderness strongholds and in the hills of the Desert of Ziph. Day after day, Saul searched for him, but God did not give David into his hands (1 Sam. 23:14). It is interesting that David ran to the strongholds in the wilderness when chased by Saul. It was a physical place that was a strong place of protection against his enemy. Jesus went often to pray in the wilderness. God is also to be our stronghold.

David referred to Jerusalem having a stronghold around it. "Pray for the peace of Jerusalem: 'May those who love you be secure. May there be peace within your walls and security within your citadels' (Ps. 122:6-7). A citadel is a place that is strongly fortified, or a "stronghold".

Sodom and Gomorrah were definite centers or strongholds of wickedness. The Lord sent two angels to destroy them but warned Lot to leave the city with his wife and daughters. So they left. "Then the Lord rained down burning sulfur on Sodom and Gomorrah – from the Lord out of the heavens" (Genesis 19:24). Their evilness had come up before God. They were strongholds or centers of evil.

Columbia had a stronghold of drugs. United prayer and fasting was the key ingredient that began to crumble the stronghold. What police and authorities- man- could not do, prayer and fasting that reached the throne of God, did. It took down the evil drug dealers in this fortified center of drugs.

Each area has its stronghold. Some areas it is wealth which can bring with it gluttony. Wealth can bring a struggle with sin that poorness does not. To be well fed and righteous is a blessing but handle it with generosity. Different strongholds come with different areas.

When strongholds are broken, they must be replaced with something godly or the original stronghold can likely come back. Twenty-one days is the time it takes to begin to establish a new habit. Ninety days is the time it takes to set it. Do something for twenty-one days, and you will start a new habit. If you quit your Bible reading for that long, you start the habit of not reading God's Word. The Bible says this:

> The weapons we fight with are not the weapons of the world. On the contrary, they have divine power to demolish strongholds. We demolish arguments and every pretension that sets itself up against the knowledge of God, and we take captive every thought to make it obedient to Christ.
>
> 2 Corinthians 10:4-5

> For the weapons of our warfare are not carnal but mighty in God for pulling down strongholds, casting down arguments and every high thing that exalts itself against the knowledge of God, bringing every thought into captivity to the obedience of Christ.
>
> 2 Corinthians 10:4-5 NKJV

What are the weapons of our warfare? Prayer is one. Fasting is another. I would even say that obedience is the one that is best. Some strongholds take a lot of effort to break.

Ungodly strongholds are land mines that have the potential to destroy God's will in your life. They come through believing lies, most. When we believe a lie it sets up a stronghold in our life if it is consistently believed.

For though we walk in the flesh, we do not war according to the flesh, for the weapons of our warfare are not of the flesh, but divinely powerful for the destruction of fortresses (2 Corinthians 10:3-4 NASB).

"Fortress" here in the Greek is (according to NASB) is a castle, stronghold, fortress, fastness; anything on which one relies; of the arguments and reasonings by which a disputant endeavors to fortify his opinion and defend it against his opponent.

> Ungodly strongholds are land mines that have the potential to destroy God's will in your life.

God can be our stronghold, but these verses also say that we have weapons to demolish strongholds. A stronghold is similar to a fortress. It is a place that is well-fortified either by good or evil. It is a place that serves as the center of a group or belief. God gives us divine power to destroy strongholds that are ungodly. They can be areas of sin that we or our family struggles with. Greed or worry can be strongholds. It could be difficult to share with other people or trust God. But the weapons we fight it with are not the weapons of the world.

PRAYER:

Ask God to demolish arguments and every pretension (false claim) that sets itself up against the knowledge of God, and lead us to take every thought captive to the obedience of Christ. Then, pray it for your loved ones or family.

The weapons of this world have no power to destroy spiritual strongholds. It must be in united prayer and fasting and obedience that these things are destroyed and broken. And we need strongholds of righteousness established in their place. We must have the commitment. Are we committed to make a change, or are we just looking for a quick fix? If we do not go forward—to make a difference—we go backward. Ask God to correct our thinking and guide us into abundant life!

The Bible makes use of the picture, comparing God to this structure of survival and refuge. It reads: "The Lord is my rock, my fortress, and my savior; my God is my rock, in whom I find protection" (2 Samuel 22:2 NLT). "My fortress of safety" is one way to put it. God becomes our stronghold. So when ungodly strongholds are broken in our lives, God is able to fill them up with His Spirit and strengthen them with His truth instead.

> Are we committed to make a change, or are we just looking for a quick fix?

A stronghold is a fortified defensive structure or, a place of strength and safety. Strongholds and Fortified places were built in war to fulfill several purposes.

To avoid a surprise attack and to give warning.

To hold the enemy back until reinforcements came which at times took weeks, depending where it was located.

To save manpower. They didn't need as many soldiers if it was well fortified.

To give it time to rebuild.

What did Jesus say about strongholds or strongmen?

"Or again, how can anyone enter a strong man's house and carry off his possessions unless he first ties up the strong man? Then he can rob his house" (Matthew 12:29).

"When a strong man, fully armed, guards his own house, his possessions are safe. But when someone stronger attacks and overpowers him, he takes away the armor in which the man trusted and divides up the spoils" (Luke 11:21).

God has given us strength in numbers as well as reinforcements in prayer and fasting. Find others to help as well if it is a stronger stronghold than you can break on your own.

"Here now is the man who did not make God his stronghold but trusted in his great wealth and grew strong by destroying others" (Psalm 52:7).

David said "I have become a sign to many; you are my strong refuge" (Psalm 71:7).

Referring to Jesus, "Therefore I will give him a portion among the great, and he will divide the spoils with the strong, because he poured out his life unto death, and was numbered with the transgressors. For he bore the sin of many, and made intercession for the transgressors" (Isaiah 53:12).

Plead the Blood of Jesus

When you are unable to discern the will of God or make heads or tails of a situation, the blood of Jesus is powerful. Try praying something like: I plead the blood of Jesus *through* my ability to discern what is of God. I plead the blood of Jesus *through* my ability to discern right and wrong.

How many times speakers have encouraged people to plead the blood of Jesus over things. The Scripture for this was that in the Old Testament—the Hebrews placed the blood of the lamb over the doorposts and the angel passed over the Hebrew's houses and did not touch their firstborn (Exodus 12). In the houses of the Egyptians that did not have the blood on the doorposts as God had commanded, the firstborn died. It was the blood of a lamb that was used. Later, when Jesus came in the New Testament, He became the Lamb of God to take away the sin of the world. And His blood paid for all our sin, to those who receive His gift. It is His blood that cleanses us from all sin. (1 John 1:7; Ephesians 1:7; Heb. 9:14; 1 Peter 1:2; Rev. 12:11). The blood of Jesus is protective and cleansing. He has shed His blood for us and there is something in the spirit realm that occurs when we plead the blood of Jesus over and through us.

I went through a season that I had times when it was difficult go to sleep. I began to plead the blood of Jesus *through* my ability to go to sleep and *through* my ability to rest. I seemed to relax after praying it out loud. There were times that it helped me sleep better. I would pray, "I plead the blood of Jesus through my ability to go to sleep and through my ability to rest."

At one point my child of five years old went through a time of waking up with nightmares. I began to plead the blood of Jesus through all her dreams during the night when she went to bed. I also taught her to do it. They did improve. If your child is having problems with nightmares, try having them plead the blood of

Jesus *through* all their dreams during the night. Pray it when they go to bed. If they are too young, you can do it for them as well. But train the children up early in life.

Also command any spirits causing it to be gone. Pray for the peace of God to well up within them instead.

I have also applied this to other things such as my ability to discern. In a moment when I was unsure what of my thoughts was actually of God, I pled the blood of Jesus through them and noticed that it helped me discern more clearly. If you continue to do it, it does weaken the enemy. There is nothing that the devil cannot stand more than the blood of Jesus. You can even plead the blood of Jesus *through* your relationship with your spouse or child or other person. If you are having difficulty in your relationship, it can help for a bit.

You can try this as well:

I plead the blood of Jesus through my thinking and through my mood.

The blood of Jesus is powerful!

Meat

You will not die immediately if you eat meat, even if some may think so.

The Spirit clearly says that in later times some will abandon the faith and follow deceiving spirits and things taught by demons (1 Timothy 4:1).

They forbid people to marry and order them to abstain from certain foods, which God created to be received with thanksgiving by those who believe and who know the truth. For everything God created is good, and nothing is to be rejected if it is received with thanksgiving, because it is consecrated by the word of God and prayer (1 Timothy 4:3-5).

I eat meat because I feel better. The symbolism of meat in the Bible is "the Word of God." In other words, in the Bible the symbolism of meat is not negative. The Word of God uses it to symbolize something that is good. It is something that is beneficial. I do not see anywhere in the New Testament where it tells us explicitly to stay away from meat. Do you? The Old Testament had laws in effect so that the over a million Jews in the wilderness would not become sick or spread disease. In the New Testament, the apostle Paul speaks about eating with faith, that anything God has made is good. It is given to us to eat and to thank God for it (1 Corinthians 10:25).

Jesus did not say anything about not eating meat. If it was an issue to be extra concerned about surely He would have addressed it. But Jesus did say this, "What goes into a man's mouth does not make him 'unclean,' but what comes out of his mouth, that is what makes him 'unclean'" (Matt. 15:11). Jesus was responding to the religious leaders following man's traditions rather than God's commands. It is not what goes into a man that makes him unclean but rather what comes out.

What did God send when Elijah needed food? He sent meat as well. It doesn't specify what kind of meat.

The word of the Lord came to Elijah: "Leave here, turn eastward and hide in the Kerith Ravine, east of the Jordan. You will drink from the brook, and I have ordered the ravens to feed you there." So he did what the Lord had told him. He went to the Kerith Ravine, east of the Jordan, and stayed there. There ravens brought him bread and meat in the morning and bread and meat in the evening, and he drank from the brook (1 Kings 17:2-6).

A first point is that God provided meat for him to eat. It was not a bad thing. God's food for Elijah included meat. In fact, it was provided at each meal that God gave him. For Elijah it included reality. If it hadn't been beneficial for him, God wouldn't have given it to him. God decided Elijah needed meat.

If you look at the priests in the Old Testament, God also provided meat for them. Out of the sacrifices that were presented and burned before the Lord, the priests were allowed to take a portion of the meat for themselves.

Nowhere in the New Testament do I see Jesus against eating meat. I do find it interesting that a culture that is full of immorality is the same culture that accepts meat as being not as good to eat. The timing of the two is interesting. There are people who find their spiritual strength increase when eating more meat. Daniel did not even abstain from meat forever. It was for a time (Dan. 10:3). The same culture that promotes immorality and anti-Godism is the same culture that tells us not to eat meat much at all. Is that because it strengthens us spiritually and allows us freedom?

Do we have to eat meat? No. But there are people who notice their spiritual strength increase when they eat it.

Seized by Temptation

"No temptation has seized you except what is common to man" (1 Cor. 10:13). What does "seized" mean? It means "taken hold of." The temptation has taken hold of you. It has not just passed by and gone on to the next person. But rather it grabbed you and made you shudder, stop, shake, or dwell on it. Be careful when this happens. If need be reach for the phone and call a friend. Run in the opposite direction. The Word of God says, "Flee from sexual immorality" (1 Cor. 6:18). Flee from it. Turn and move in the opposite direction *hastily*. Do not even take a second look. Berrate it with love for God. Tear it down hastily with your love for God.

How do you rate on this? When the TV is on and lustful things flash in front of you, what is your reaction? Turn away! Turn it off. Get out of the room. Direct your thoughts and eyes on other things that are beneficial. Do not bring it back up in mind. If the temptation seizes you, run away from it. Don't just stand there and stare at it. Find someone to share it with. It will tend to break 50 percent of the temptation (or more often) if you have honesty in your relationship with others, so you can share it. It may be your spouse or loved one, but it does not always have to be. Find someone to share it with, even a friend or pastor or respected elder. Humble yourself that in due time *God may exalt you.*

Take another look at the word "seize." If you look at seizures, what are they? They are something that interrupts a person's life. An epileptic seizure will make the person shake. So, when sin comes knocking at your door, deny self and run away. Flee from it. Do not allow the enemy to gain a foothold. Remember Joseph. He ran from the master's wife who called to him to go to bed together. He was disciplined wrongly by man, but he was blessed and promoted by God.

"And God is faithful; he will not let you be tempted beyond what you can bear. But when you are tempted, he will also provide a way out so that you can stand up under it" (1 Corinthians 10:13). But it is our responsibility to flee. Keep others that you are accountable to as well. Pray through it that God will strengthen you and replace it with the opposite, such as purity.

Jesus had twelve disciples, and of these three were the closest. You must have accountability, and you must have honesty.

Generally when you are married and love your spouse, you will naturally dislike something about a coworker or person of the opposite sex who is very good looking. Even so, do not even take a second look if sin comes knocking at your door.

Repent and renounce sin.

One thing a friend used after he accidently happened upon pornography on the computer was to come before God and repent and renounce what he saw. "I repent of seeing those graphic pictures today and renounce it as sin. Be gone, in Jesus's name." And the pictures left his mind. Or you could also, pray: I plead the blood of Jesus through the images and pictures that come in my mind. Command the mountain gone and plead the blood of Jesus *through it.*

While to be tempted is not sin, to give in to it is. Do not pay attention to the devil's doubts or let them settle in your mind-set. Rather focus on what has been done by God and continue to walk forward. The flaming arrows of the evil one are doubts that the devil sets in our way to stumble us about from accomplishing what God desires.

So do not throw away your confidence; it will be richly rewarded. You need to persevere so that when you have done the will of God, *you will receive* what he has promised. For in just a very little while, "He who is coming will come and will not delay. But my righteous one will live by faith. And if he shrinks back, I will not be pleased with him." But we are not of those who shrink back and are destroyed, but of those who believe and are saved (Hebrews 10:35-39).

"Now faith is being sure of what we hope for and certain of what we do not see. This is what the ancients were commended for" (Hebrews 11:2).

We continue by faith. God is love. God's love is secure. He is faithful and continues to be. Do not quit. His love never quits. When you feel like quitting, He is still here, waiting for us to receive His love. He is there. Do not believe a lie that God is not able to do what He has planned. He has His ways. We must obey. Our God is a covenant God. As with Abraham, God made a covenant. No, Abraham was not perfect, but he continued with faith and trusted God. So we must continue with God's Word, which says: "Ask and you will receive." Do not believe that your prayers are not working. They are working. God is at work and is answering. Do not quit. Many times God's timing is different than ours.

He has a perfect plan to make it happen. He loves us. God's plan is perfect. *He is love.*

Unmet Needs

If you have temptation that continues, it is due to an unmet need. What is the need? Do you know or do you need to pray and ask God about it? Accountability may be part of the need as well. When you are too alone, the enemy will attempt to go after you more. When you have the fellowship of other believers and accountability, there is strength. And the Spirit of the Lord is present when two or more are gathered in His name (Matthew18). *Find out what the unmet need is*, and begin to meet it in righteous ways.

Find a way.

Paul wrote this in 1 Corinthians 10:12-13: "So, if you think you are standing firm, be careful that you don't fall!" It is when we are the most confident that we can be overcome and humbled greatly. It is also when we don't have the accountability and fellowship of others around us that we will be the most lonely, needy, and squished by the enemy more. We need the fellowship of others. We must have love and good works. It is important to have someone who you can share anything with.

Do not look at the culture to decide if you are right but rather look at God's Word. Then, apply it specifically. Do we struggle with lying? Do we have a temptation to say things that are not true so we look better? First, find scriptures that speak directly to it. One scripture for an example is this: "You shall not steal, nor deal falsely, nor lie to one another" (Leviticus 19:11 NKJV). Speak it out loud when the temptation arises.

You can even speak to the difficulty "Grace. Grace. Grace."

Isolation, secrecy, and intimidation is what many people experience when going through difficult things. Get everything out in the open. *Find* someone to share it with. There are people who are able to listen.

Love breaks the yoke of bondage off of our lives.

Making Spiritual Warfare Simple

So, what is spiritual warfare? It refers to the battle that we wage in the spiritual realm between God's ways and the devil and its ways. Do we have a battle? Have you ever had a difficulty understanding spiritual warfare? The Word of God says in Ephesians 6:10-13:

> Finally, be strong in the Lord and in his mighty power. Put on the full armor of God, so that you can take your stand against the devil's schemes. For our struggle is not against flesh and blood, but against the rulers, against the authorities, against the powers of this dark world and against the spiritual forces of evil in the heavenly realms. Therefore put on the full armor of God, so that when the day of evil comes, you may be able to stand your ground, and after you have done everything, to stand.

How many people do not believe that we need to deal with spiritual warfare at all? As I look in the Bible, especially the New Testament, I am struck by how many verses have to do with it (around 109 in the New Testament). Many of these (around eight-one) occur in the gospels. What am I saying by this? Jesus did not deny that the devil was there. Neither did He focus on that only.

A couple scriptures on it include:

Cast all your anxiety on him because he cares for you. Be alert and of sober mind. Your enemy the devil prowls around like a roaring lion looking for someone to devour. Resist him, standing firm in the faith, because you know that the family of believers throughout the world is undergoing the same kind of sufferings (1 Peter 5:7-9).

"In your anger do not sin. Do not let the sun go down while you are still angry, and do not give the devil a foothold" (Ephesians 4:26-28).

"Get rid of all bitterness, rage and anger, brawling and slander, along with every form of malice" (Ephesians 4:31).

A Few Strongholds

Freemasonry restricts the Spirit in this nation more than you know. We must pray and fast daily and in unity to overcome it. It is throughout the country and must be destroyed by fasting. The most efficient against the strongman is fasting; the most efficient against the general (the spirit that is the brains of the operations) is unity. Unity and intimacy is the first thing to use against it. The body of Christ united in fasting and prayer.

Appolyon calls itself a wisdom of the ages. It is false wisdom. It is ungodly and demonic wisdom. It is not wisdom at all but is sin. It is anchored against Christ. One of the most effective things against it is unity and intimacy. It is the general behind the group. It directs the others and will hide until found out. Its goal is legalism. It will cover things over as right, but in reality, it is angled to legalism.

If people who are affected by this false wisdom pray for wisdom, it will attempt to slide in and cause them to misunderstand and receive ungodly wisdom. It will attempt to mislead them. If something bothers you when you pray for wisdom, then pray for counsel. Counsel is to know what to do, when to do it and how to do it. It is specific guidance. The strongman in it is *abbadon* and has to do with destruction. Fasting is the most effective weapon against it. Remember also to pray and obey the leading of the Holy Spirit. But fasting is what seems to weaken it the most.

There is also a false trinity group that affects people from freemasonry. It attempts to mimic or fake the true God. *One* of the tactics this group will use is *guilt*. It will attempt to *guilt* people into legalism and other things. It will guilt people to obey it and it is against God.

When these spirits disempower, they actually break in spirit and a "thud" is heard by some people. And it will often be around three days until they leave. When they are disempowered it becomes far easier for people to obey God.

It affects the nation more than we know. We must overcome it with prayer and fasting and unity.

I once fasted every breakfast for four months in obedience to God, and found it more effective than other things. I found it made a difference. And it broke strongholds in my life I did not even know were there.

It added a power punch that did not come without it. That was not the only thing I did, but I found fasting was effective. It added a power punch that was not there without it. It's like prayer on steroids, if I can put it that way.

Be united in prayer and fasting and obedience to God and we can disempower the enemy's hold in our lives and our churches and families. It will require fasting with prayer to kick out and break some of the bigger strongholds more quickly. Strongholds cause disunity. If we kick out (disempower) the big ones, we will have more peace and joy in our nation as well as in our families and our churches.

The less open to the Holy Spirit the church is, whether Pentecostal or not, the more likely the devil can gain power in it in some way. It will try to influence people to apply the Word of God with legalism, for instance.

Secrecy is sin. That is a goal of satanic ritual abuse—to bring secrecy. This spirit will tell people they have to go it alone and not tell a thing about their problems. The opposite is openness and honesty. Honesty is godly which is an opposite of its goal.

Paranoia will always try to get you to focus on detail. And it will do it over and over until it gets authority by a person being worried or paranoid. It will push people to worry about details and it will gain more authority (ground or influence) when people give in to it. It may push people to check the door three times to make sure it's locked. If you have this problem, pull out of detail and resist it. Use the Word of God. Trust Him and His ability to protect and take care of things.

Rebellion will always try to hold you back from obeying God. You can pray over your children daily and command it out of their lives and out of your life. If I place my hands on my child, I will cover myself as well by praying, "I command rebellion off and out of this child's life and off and out of my life as well in Jesus' name." And do it daily until it is gone. Then repeat it if it comes back at all. Pray for them to obey God and to love Him more daily. Pray over people's sheets or bed if needed.

The opposite of suppression is truth. The opposite of denial is reality. The opposite of mind-set wrong would be mind-set right. Do the opposite of what the devil wants. Do it daily. Pray specifically against things if possible. If not, pray with common sense and the leading of the Holy Spirit.

Pray and fast more to break strongholds. And stick with it until it is done. The opposite of these few strongholds here is godliness and openness, submission to God, truth and reality. Pray in the opposite of what you see in your children's lives or others as well. But pray and fast and you will break more strongholds than without by far.

Spiritual Warfare

If Christians have no need for protection and no spiritual battle, why would Jesus give us the example in the Lord's prayer to pray for protection from the evil one? Yes. There is a spiritual battle. Do not be unaware of the devil's schemes. Yet on the other hand do not make it bigger than God and do not fear it.

"If you forgive anyone, I also forgive him. And what I have forgiven—if there was anything to forgive—I have forgiven in the sight of Christ for your sake in order that Satan might not outwit us for we are not unaware of his schemes" (2 Corinthians 2:11).

In other words, the devil does have schemes. What are schemes? Schemes are underhanded plots against the people of God. It tries to rob, steal, cheat, lie and kill, etc. Whatever is not of God is what it will try to bring. Unbelief is one as well. One of the devil's first schemes is to bring unforgiveness in the relationships. This is what was addressed here by the apostle Paul. Everybody sins and everybody makes mistakes, but it is God's will that we lay it down and choose to forgive one another out of love for God and out of a realization that God has forgiven us even more. He has forgiven us completely. Love and forgiveness helps to overcome the devil's plans against you.

If you have unforgiveness toward someone, keep in mind two things. You need to work through it and you need to choose to forgive for your own health as well as for your own freedom. It is not only something that will hurt you emotionally and mentally and cause problems for you and often those around you, but it also gives an open door to the devil.

But it must be healed by God. Unforgiveness allows the devil an access point or entrance into your life because it is sin. So take time to ask God if there are any people in your life that you need to forgive. Do it regularly, and ask if he can remove everything or he might send you to people to help. Do not be unaware of the devil's schemes. One of its schemes is to get us to not focus on God and to not ask for help when needed. But ask godly people. In other words, if you have a difficult time forgiving people because the hurt is deep, then talk through it with others and pray daily that God will give you increased grace to forgive and have someone pray with you about it. Address it daily with God, and get help from others as needed. Speak to the mountain, "Grace. Grace. Grace." I remember the story of a missionary who had a family break up and used this.

If you want to get good at spiritual warfare, the first thing is to forgive well and encourage others to do so. It is one of the first things the devil attempts to gain access through in the body of Christ. If it can get Christians to become bitter and angry toward one another, it can also destroy the Christian testimony to non-Christians around. "Forgive as your Father in heaven forgave you" (Matthew 18).

Faith Is Needed As Well

A Temptation of doubt. The enemy attempts to get us to disbelieve God and doubt His Word. It is the very Word of God that destroys the enemy. Jesus spoke of "little faith" and "no faith." Without faith it is impossible to please God. With faith all things are possible if God is God.

> Later Jesus appeared to the eleven as they were eating; he rebuked them for their lack of faith and their stubborn refusal to believe those who had seen him after he had risen.

> He said to them, "Go into all the world and preach the gospel to all creation. Whoever believes and is baptized

will be saved, but whoever does not believe will be condemned. And these signs will accompany those who believe: In my name they will drive out demons; they will speak in new tongues; they will pick up snakes with their hands; and when they drink deadly poison, it will not hurt them at all; they will place their hands on sick people, and they will get well."

Mark 16:14-18 NIV

Jesus was speaking to the disciples and told them to "go into" all the world. Do you notice the first part of the sentence is a command of action? We do not sit back and do nothing and have people come to us very often. We must get out and go into the world around us.

This verse applies to "whoever believes" (v.17). These signs are to accompany those who believe. What does "accompany" mean? It means to join in action, to go along or in company with. So these signs are to join in activity or be associated with "believers." Believers are to be associated with these signs. Where are they is my question.

Now in the morning, as they passed by, they saw the fig tree dried up from the roots. And Peter, remembering, said to Him, "Rabbi, look! The fig tree which You cursed has withered away."

So Jesus answered and said to them, "Have faith in God. For assuredly, I say to you, whoever says to this mountain, 'Be removed and be cast into the sea,' and does not doubt in his heart, but believes that those things he says will be done, he will have whatever he says. Therefore I say to you, whatever things you ask when you pray, believe that you receive them, and you will have them.

And whenever you stand praying, if you have anything against anyone, forgive him that your Father in heaven may also forgive you your trespasses. But if you do not forgive, neither will your Father in heaven forgive your trespasses."

Mark 11:20-26 NKJV

Look at what Jesus said. They noticed His words had caused the fig tree to wither by the very next morning when they passed by it again. His comment to them was clear: have faith in God. He also told us to say it and not doubt in our heart. Then He told us that whatever we pray, we are to believe that God will answer. After this Jesus mentioned again the issue of forgiveness. Faith and forgiveness are two keys.

Pray and believe; then also forgive. Love. Love never fails (1 Corinthians 13). God is love, and if God is love, the devil is the complete opposite of it. It is evil and opposes God in every way it can. So, to win against the devil's schemes, one of the fortresses to use against it is the common denominator of love. "Whoever does not love does not know God, because God is love" (1 John 4:8). "And so we know and rely on the love God has for us. God is love. Whoever lives in love lives in God, and God in him" (1 John 4:16). The first thing we know is that love and forgiveness opposes the devil.

Forgive well and love well, and you will be able to kick the devil out of a lot of things. Those are two of the basics to overcome the devil. Of course another is truth. Love overcomes fear, and it overcomes a lot of things that are not overcome easily. Love is the rubber that meets the road to kick the devil out quickest. It is the place where truth is allowed and people are accepted as people anyway. It is the place where agape is. It is the unconditional love of God.

Do we believe, forgive and love? It will drive the enemy berserk. Then add prayer and fasting to break strongholds and we will raise a banner of a testimony to Jesus.

Does It Work Through People?

And the devil does work through people.

But Elymas the sorcerer (for that is what his name means) opposed them and tried to turn the proconsul from the faith. Then Saul, who was also called Paul, filled with the Holy Spirit, looked straight at Elymas and said, "You are a child of the devil and an enemy of everything that is right! You are full of all kinds of deceit and trickery" (Acts 13:8-10a).

The devil's tactics are to pervert the right ways of the Lord. The devil is full of all kinds of deceit and trickery. It tricks people into thinking a lie. It is a lie to believe that God does not heal, that He is not able to deliver His people. God is a good God. He is pure and right and true. Truth is His counter to the devil's lies. The devil would like us to think we can't do what God has called us to do.

But our battle is not against people. It is against the devil. There are thirty-three references to "the devil" in the New Testament (NIV). Jesus obviously realized it was there and neither denied its reality nor succumbed to its temptations or pressure. He did not say it was not real. Neither did he say that we should fear it. Rather, we must be aware that its tactics are to pervert God's ways. But remember that the Lord works through you. His will is to work through you, through your words, through your life, and through your love for Him. He is able at every access point to bring someone to stand in the way and cause problems for the enemy if he so desires. Begin to pray for protection and for power, insight, and understanding, and count on God.

God is able to save a nation from impending doom by the obedience of His people. And do not think that your faithfulness will go unrewarded. Do not give up. God is able to reach in and bring miraculous things as His people obey His call to fast and pray. It is a powerhouse, and God always answers the prayers of His people. Do not look at the physical results you see from your physical eyes. Rather believe and seek Him earnestly for He is able.

Are You Depressed?

What do you do when you feel depression? What did David do? He sought the Lord in the Psalms.

1. Get it out in the open. Pray about it. Share it with someone. Do not keep it all to yourself. Do not hide from people. Do not tell people that you are not depressed. Do not lie but tell the truth. Do not hide from people.

2. Then do something for yourself as well.

3. Use the Word of God. It is not the only thing but it is an important thing. For example, what would I use from God's Word for depression?

   I will live and not die and I will declare the works of the Lord (Psalms 118:17).

   Jesus came that I might have life and have it more abundantly (John 10:10).

   I will be rewarded by God (Colossians 3:23-24).

From where does my help come from? It comes from the Lord, the Maker of heaven and earth (Psalms 121:1-2).

Look up others that are encouraging to you such as Psalms 42:5. Then also, get out in public as well. Do not hide from people *and* use the Word of God.

4. Fast and pray. Actually, fasting is effective for some people for pulling up depressive rites. Rites are places of access for the devil to affect us. For some people prayer and fasting works very well. It is one way that overcomes the power of the enemy and brings great breakthrough if followed through on. It also can overcome the abuses of the enemy. It is one way that brings success. Even Jesus said in Matthew 17:21 KJV, "Howbeit this kind goeth not out but by prayer and fasting." There are strongholds that can be broken through it. Even thought patterns or habits can be broken and overcome with prayer and fasting that cannot be broken any other way. Add it to your regimen, and see what God will do for you. *If you are under a doctor's orders, be sure to check with them or your medical caretaker first. They know your situation.*

Pray for the opposite of whatever you are tempted by or struggling with. Reject and renounce it. Command it gone. Pray for the opposite of it and the blessing of God instead.

If there is a stronghold, have others pray with you as well. You must look for the heart issue. And fast and pray, as well.

Do not be unforgiving or continue in sin (Ephesians 4:25-26). Speak the truth with your neighbor and put off falsehood. Verse 27 says, "and do not give the devil a foothold." Get your struggles out in the open with people. Remember that temptations tend to be cut in half if you have someone to share it with. Trustworthy people are healthy and helpful. God gives us people to share it with for a reason. You must have others that you can be honest with. Find them. We are stronger when we are united. Pray, fast, and obey.

We grow when we have others around us that are trustworthy and genuine. We must learn to grow together in unity and support one another. Strengthen the feeble knees. And pray Ephesians 3:16-18 daily. Do you notice that the prayer is for God to strengthen them and then that they will have power established in love and together with all the saints?

The Highway

"My way is the highway" says God. I remember seeing this on a t-shirt. I jumped up and talked to the friend and told them I had been hearing God say this to my heart recently. He had been telling me, "My way is the highway". His way is certainly the better way, with less thorns and roadblocks on it.

"The way of the sluggard is blocked with thorns, but the path of the upright is a highway" (Proverbs 15:19).

God's way is the way to go! "Pass through, pass through the gates! Prepare the way for the people. Build up, build up the highway! Remove the stones. Raise the banner for the nations." Isaiah 62:10

Do things God's way and we will avoid a lot of hurts.

Be angry and do not sin (Ephesians 4:26 YLT). Temperance is best when it comes to anger. The temptation is to overdo things. It is to go extreme. If God says to wait or stay, the temptation is to jump and go. The enemy will always bring a temptation to do the opposite of what God's plan is. It is God's plan that stays. It is God's plan that is sturdy and trustworthy. It is God's plan that works in the long run as well. Stay the course. Forgive when you are hurt by man's ways. It may not always be their actions or words that cause it. It may be both of yours. It is a blessing to forgive for God did the same for us. So we also must forgive and love each other. Love one another and choose to forgive so that the enemy, the tempter, cannot get in between you two. Choose to forgive because God has forgiven you much. Soften your hearts and begin again. When you are choosing to forgive, pray for the Spirit of truth—God's Spirit—to guide you into all truth and to direct your hearts in love. Pray through it. Ask for the love of God to fill you up.

"Forgive us our sins, for we also forgive everyone who sins against us. And lead us not into temptation" (Luke 11:4).

Do you notice what comes after this verse? Then he said to them, "Suppose one of you has a friend, and he goes to him at midnight and says, 'Friend, lend me three loaves of bread, because a friend of mine on a journey has come to me, and I have nothing to set before him'" (Luke 11:5-6). The human answer is to say "Don't bother me. I am sleeping and can't get up and give you anything." Yet, because of the boldness of the man, he gets up and gives in. Then Jesus compares this to prayer. "Ask and it will be given to you; seek and you will find; knock and the door will be opened to you. For *everyone* who ask receives; he who seeks finds; and to him who knocks, the door will be opened" (Luke 11:9-10). Related to forgiveness, if the bitterness or anger is difficult to let go of, do not give up in asking God for help. Do not give up asking God to help you with it.

Do not go it alone or put yourself in a rocky position just to prove that God can get you out. It is sin. Jesus also taught us to pray about temptation. "Now that you have purified yourselves by obeying the truth so that you have sincere love for your brothers, love one another deeply, from the heart" (1 Peter 1:22). Love one another from the heart. We must love one another from the heart which implies a genuineness of heart. Ask God to show you how to love one another deeply from the heart.

Look at the passage in Matthew 13:37 and following:

He answered, "The one who sowed the good seed is the Son of Man. The field is the world, and the good seed stands for the sons of the kingdom. The weeds are the sons of the evil one, and the enemy who sows them is the devil."

As we look at this passage, we see an analogy of the world being a field. God sows good seed that stands for the children of God, the sons of the kingdom. ("Sons" refers to both genders.) The weeds are the sons of the evil one, and the "enemy" who sows them is the devil. The devil sows followers of itself in the world among the children of God. As Christians we must resist the tempter and stand with God.

Do you notice what Jesus said will be weeded out? "The Son of Man will send out his angels, and they will weed out of his kingdom everything that causes sin and all who do evil" (Matthew 13:41). The angels will weed out all who do evil. Choose your close friends carefully. If they lead you into sin, do not keep them so close. You can be a witness to them, but do not mesh with them. Where we rid ourselves from sin and choose to follow the leading of the Spirit, we grow in Christ and learn to live in freedom and life.

Do we sit in front of the tube and watch flicks or programs that do not contribute to righteousness? Do we mesmerize ourselves with sin or laugh at it? If we are to be close to God, pull these things out. Pluck them out, and find something more beneficial to do or watch. Allow God's ways to guide your decisions even in front of the tube. Pull up or remove everything that causes sin.

So how do we deal with temptation? First use the Word of God. Here are some examples of scriptures to use directly with temptation or accusations that come.

It is written: "Man does not live on bread alone" (Luke 4:4). Is it hard to stop eating or difficult to restrain yourself?

It is written: "Worship the Lord your God and serve him only" (Luke 4:8). Is money the battle? "Thou shalt have no other gods before Me" (Exodus 20:3).

It is also written: "Do not put the Lord your God to the test" (Matthew 4:7). Are you being pushed into a situation that would be evil or increase temptation?

"I will set before my eyes no vile thing" (Psalm 101:3a). I will have nothing to do with evil (Psalm 101:4b). When you are tempted to watch something that is not pure, use this verse. Speak it out loud, and apply it.

It is written: "A new command I give you: Love one another" (John 13:34). Do you have a tendency to be unloving at times?

It is written: "Do not steal." (Romans 13:9).

It is written: "You shall not covet" (your neighbor's house, wife, etc.) (Exodus. 20:17; Romans 13:9).

It is written: "You shall not murder" (Exodus 20:13; Matthew 5:21).

It is written: "Do not lie to each other" (Col.3:9; Lev. 19:11). Speak honestly. Tell the truth. "Speaking the truth in love" (Ephesians 4:15).

It is written: "And do not be drunk with wine … but be filled with the Spirit. (Eph. 5:18 NKJV)

"You shall not commit adultery" (Exodus 20:14). Jesus said not to even look at a woman to lust for her in your heart (Matthew 5:28 NKJV).

Do not slander. (Proverbs 10:18 NKJV; Proverbs 30:10; James 4:11).

"If you have anything against anyone, forgive him..." (Mark 11:25 NKJV). We are to forgive that our Father in heaven will also forgive us.

"Do not worry" (Matthew 6:34). Do not Fret. Not worry.

"So I say, live by the Spirit, and you will not gratify the desires of the sinful nature" (Galatians 5:16). I choose to be led by the Spirit and not fulfill the lusts of the flesh.

My body is the temple of the Holy Spirit (1 Corinthians 6:19 NKJV).

"All who belong to the Lord must turn away from evil" (2 Timothy 2:19 NLT). Avoid evil.

"Do not lust in your heart after her beauty" (Proverbs 6:25).

"Give and it will be given to you" (Luke 6:38 NKJV). "Bring the whole tithe into the storehouse, that there may be food in the house. Test me in this..." (Malachi 3:10).

"Fear not for I *am* with you" (Isaiah 41:10 NKJV).

What is it that you struggle with? Ask God for verses that pertain to it. What is the opposite? Is it trust? Find the opposite.

For instance, "Trust in the Lord with all your heart" (Proverbs 3:5).

Seek The Lord Earnestly

When you are down, ask God to bend you. Ask Him to change you, and see if He will. Humbly come before God, and submit to Him. He knows the path that comes with humility is better than pride. Humble yourselves before God's mighty hand, and He will lift you up in due time. He is the one who knows how to heal, to fix, and to change what needs to be changed. He is also the God who is able to provide for all your needs if you ask Him. He is our Jehovah Jireh, our provider and help. Do you know that life is not perfect? It changes. But God knows the changes that come and how to bend us with the changes for good and not for evil.

So take God's word to heart. Get to know it and realize that God's plan is for good and not for evil. There are times that I pick up the Bible and read during the day quickly and come to a verse and just sense the Holy Spirit say, "That is your word." Or there is a verse that has a light bulb attached to it. It seems to stand out.

How do we let ourselves be led by the Spirit? We trust God. We take what He gives us and do good with it. We must depend on the Word of God as our foundation. We will be able to judge what is the Spirit of God versus what is not by whether or not it lines up with the Word of God.

The Word of God is powerful, and the Spirit of God gives us understanding of the Word. We must have both. One without the other is not what God intended. So we allow the Spirit of God to take the Word of God and lead us into truth and application and clarity of mind. The Holy Spirit takes the Word that we have read and learned and brings it back to mind throughout the day, week, or year to speak to us and guide us into truth and His ways. It is the Holy Spirit who also speaks to our hearts and minds and draws us to His path. Do not be stuck in making things legalistic, though. God guides through the Word. He also uses people, circumstances, and otherwise. What do you sense the Spirit of God saying?

We must not be passive in spirit but rather active. We must not be passive in mind but rather active.

Hebrews 4:12 says, "For the word of God is living and active…"

The Word of God is powerful. It is living. It is full of life and defeats the arrows and the lies of the evil one. It is the Word that we stand on and root ourselves deeply in and firmly upon to establish us well. We must build our foundation on the Word of God, which is dependable and forceful. In fact, the promise is that God's Word will not return void. Whether we use it to stand against temptation and the lies of the evil one or we use it to share Christ with others, it is active. And it is living. It is the Word of God that has force and authority. "Sharper than any double-edged sword, it penetrates even to dividing soul and spirit, joints and marrow" (Hebrews 4:12). We must wield the Word of God rightly. Build your foundation on the Word of God.

Then, as the Word of God directs, allow yourselves to be "led by the Spirit" of God (Romans 8:14). For it is the Spirit of God who directs and enables and empowers us to live according to the Word of God. It is the Spirit of God who gives discernment and understanding. Jesus was "led by the Spirit" (Matthew 4:1). He was led into a time in the wilderness without food. Then He was tempted and overcame using the Word of God as His sword to cut through the lies of the tempter.

Ask God for a verse, and He will typically give you one. But if you do not know the Word of God enough, there is a limited amount of encouragement that He can give through it. If it is our sword of the Spirit, then it is not only the handle of the sword but rather it *is* the sword. It is important. It is a tool that the Holy Spirit can use to bring truth against lies that are cultural, spiritual, and for our demise. We must have the sword of the Spirit healthy and strong. So we must get to know the Word of God and read and reread it. Grow and meditate on it until it becomes a part of who we are.

How do we apply the Word of God specifically? Are you tempted to lie or "tell a fib"? Speak the truth in love instead (Ephesians 4:15). The blessings of God come as we obey the Word. Are you tempted to be flaky and change quickly with situations that come? Then look at the Word, "fixing our eyes on Jesus the Author and Finisher of the faith who for the joy set before Him endured the cross, scorning its shame and sat down at the right hand of the Father" (Hebrews 12:2). There is a reason that Jesus endured it. It was because of His love for us and for the Father.

Hold your ground when the enemy tells you to change and to be flaky or to not stand your ground and share your faith for Christ. What did Jesus say? "Whoever denies me before men will be denied before the angels of God." (Luke 12:9 NKJV). Do not be shy to share your faith. Let people know that you are a Christian, and not just someone who says it but someone who lives it.

We must have the Spirit of truth to guide us into all truth and to bring understanding. We also have safety in numbers. If you are a lone wolf, you are not nearly as safe as abiding in the presence of God's children who are mature and growing in the Lord. There is safety in numbers, and likewise there is safety in accountability. Present your disagreements to one another, and work through them. Work through your questions, and continue to ask God to lead and guide you into all truth. The Word of God says this about truth, "You will know the truth and the truth will set you free." Jesus said, "If you hold to my teaching, you are really my disciples. Then you will know the truth, and the truth will set you free" (John 8:31-32). When Jesus said this, He was speaking to the Jews who had believed him and put their faith in Him. There is truth in Christ. Read the Word of God. Sharpen your sword of the Spirit and keep it sharp.

Isn't it interesting that Jesus said first to the new believers: "If you hold to my teaching, you are really my disciples." Obedience is king. Obey and hold to the truth. Then you will know the truth, "and the truth will set you free." There are times in the Christian walk that we obey before we understand. We obey by faith. How often do we say that we love God but disobey? Disobedience has consequences. Consequences are not fun. As we grow up in God, we must grow up in faith and obedience as well. We hold to his teaching and are set free.

Pray For Truth

Sin is what allows the devil in.

All roots and rites that the devil is able to have in people's lives are through deception and sin. One of the most common ways that the devil will work to obtain access is in the lives of Christians is through bitterness, unforgiveness, and relational problems. It can be your sin or someone else's sin. Abuse can also be an issue, but it may be someone else's sin initially. Sin and deception allow the enemy access into our lives. Pray for truth and reject sin.

Have you ever had a situation where it seemed that words were actually being twisted when talking to another person? The enemy can be coming between you and another person to cause dissension, distractions, and difficulty. What are our weaknesses? It will often play on them. That's where it will go first. We must take personal responsibility to respond in godly manners, but also remember that the devil will attempt to cause misunderstanding and provoke anger. The devil always attempts to lead you into sin. That is the only way it can get a stronghold in mind, in heart, or in your life. Sin and deception is the access point. Lies are of the devil. They are the access point for a lot of people. If it can get you to believe lies, then it can get in to establish strongholds more.

The Bible says the devil comes to steal, kill, and destroy. Jesus said, "The thief comes only to steal and kill and destroy; I have come that they may have life, and have it to the full" (John 10:10). Jesus actually said that the thief, who is the devil, comes only to steal, kill, and destroy. There is nothing else that it attempts to do but that. It is only evil, and it is completely evil. Every lie that it brings against you and others is only to pull you down and cause difficulty. There is nothing good about its intentions, its temptations, or its tactics. Remember that when you have difficulties in relationships.

Remember that when you have temptations that are looking pleasing to the eye or satisfying to the flesh. Which direction does the tempter want you to go? It always desires us to go in a way that is opposite of God and what is good. God's way is good and loving and pure and right. The devil comes to steal what is pure and right. It attempts to deceive you and pull you away from the God who is the giver of life, contentment, peace, and love. He is the God who desires you to love Him purely and not with sin in the way. The devil will attempt to deceive you with a lie that God does not desire the best for you.

Who is he who will dwell on his holy mountain (Psalm 15:1)? It is he who keeps himself from sin. Keep yourself pure and avoid temptation. Do not put yourself in a position that tests God because you want to be close to sin. Run from it. We are human. We are fallible. But if we stay close to God, we realize success in His ways and through the power of His Spirit that does not come in any other way. Keep accountable to those around you that God has placed in your life. Do not be a lone ranger.

"Send forth your light and your truth, let them guide me; let them bring me to your holy mountain, to the place where you dwell."

Psalm 43:3

Have you ever prayed this verse as a prayer? Consider putting this on a 3x5 card and praying it. Light is the opposite of darkness. One more prayer is this one. Consider praying it daily.

"And this is my prayer: that your love may abound more and more in knowledge and depth of insight, so that you may be able to discern what is best and may be pure and blameless until the day of Christ, filled with the fruit of righteousness."

Philippians 1:9-11

STURDY IN CHRIST NO MATTER WHAT COMES

When the enemy comes in like a flood, go to God. Go to others when needed. And pray and fast. Fast more than usual is what I will do. Or I will eat more meat when I do eat. I usually pray and ask God what to do. And I also can ask others for help as well. "Where two or more are gathered in My name I am there in the midst of them" (Mt. 18:20 NKJV) is the promise of the Lord, the Holy One of Israel. We are God's children.

I ask God for the full armor according to Ephesians 6. I pray like this: Lord, I ask for Your full armor of godliness according to Ephesians 6. I ask for the helmet of salvation, the sword of the Spirit, the breastplate of righteousness, the shield of faith, the belt of truth and feet shod with the preparation of the gospel of peace. And I pray that You teach me and remind me of how to use them and walk in them effectively in Jesus's name.

"Now the Lord is the Spirit, and where the Spirit of the Lord is, there is freedom" (2 Corinthians 3:17).

The point here is that where the Holy Spirit is, there is freedom. Do not be legalistic or religious. He is not religious as in adhering to laws and things that are the standard practice that do not have life in them. Religious is to adhere to something or hang on to something that has no life in it. It is standard or it is rote. It is not done because of our love for God but rather just because it might still be "the acceptable thing to do." Pray on your knees.

It is not a have to. It is one way to pray. You can pray standing up. You can pray walking around. You can also pray kneeling, but it is not the only way. Pray in the bathtub. There are other ways as well. When the "life" leaves it, try another way. And see if it helps.

Now for instance, worship can have life. The life comes through the Spirit. When it is dull or drab, it is either possibly religiously being practiced or we need a new refreshing and revival. How does that come? It comes by asking God to refresh it. Pray for God to refresh your hearts and give you a desire to worship. Sometimes we need an extra hand to help us worship God in heart. Then rise up and be honest. Honesty is essential. Worship your way out or be honest with God. Don't fake it.

Is He the law giver? Does He say to worship? Worship also comes in the way of obedience. If we only lip sync, we are having a form of worship but not the substance thereof. Ask God to put it in your heart to worship Him. We worship God with our lives. It is the substance thereof by which we walk out our love and gratefulness for what God has done for us. What does He desire for us to do? Walk it out by faith and begin to do it. Find a way to reach a relative with the love of God. Make the time to go out of your way and reach your neighbor. Talk to them and begin to grow a relationship that will witness to them. Do not hold a grudge if they fail and make fun of you. It is obedience to God that is worship. If we only lip sync, we are missing the point of worship. Worship is also obedience. It comes through our actions. The fruitfulness of our faith and commitment to God comes in the way of our actions. We can praise God with our mouth. And that is powerful. It is something that will usually lift up your heart. But remember that praise with our mouth is not the ending point of worship. It is to be walked out in our life and through our actions by sharing our faith with others, for one. For example, do we really worship God when we fail in kindness to one another or sharing our faith with our neighbor?

Sturdy As An Oak Tree

The apostle Paul was even through persecution.

So we are to be sturdy in Christ regardless of the situations or circumstances around us. Our lives may have challenges at times, but we remain sturdy or strongly built. As a trunk of a great oak tree remains fixed and neither moves nor shakes in the wind and storms, so we are to remain fixed in Christ. Regardless of what is around us we know that we continue to remain in Christ. We must have our roots set deep.

How do we become sturdy? We must have a commitment that is set deep for one. How is this built? Sturdy is built several ways. One is time. Another is storms. A third is perseverance. We must persevere and continue even when the storms and difficulties of life come. We remain. Stand your ground. Remain fixed in the shelter of the Most High.

"Let us fix our eyes on Jesus, the Author and Perfector of our faith" (Hebrews 12:2).

Faith first. Then walk it out in action and persevere. Continue to walk with Christ in truth, love, and power. That's how you become sturdy. In the Christian life there will be times that the rudder hits the road, when we have to put it into action. We must put feet to action and trust Him to work things out in the end.

Do you remember those giant oak trees with trunks that are sturdy and unbendable in rain and wind? That is how we are to be in Christ. We must be "stayed in Christ" through the difficulties as well as the times of refreshing. When the winds blow, we do not move much. Our roots are fixed. Our trunk is stable, and we remain in Christ.

Who comes to mind when you think of sturdy? Sturdy is someone who stays the course even when the hurricane hits. We remain fixed in Christ. We remain and stay. Our roots are firmly established through commitment. A picture of this is an oak tree that has rooted its roots in the ground and grown sturdy. It charts its course and goes up and out. It grows up in Christ and spreads out in growth. So our lives grow up in Christ and spread out in affecting others and doing the will of God.

> You will see down the road everything He did for you in that tapestry to bring about fruitfulness, belief, and love for God.

A common answer among men, when asked what has caused them to grow the most in Christ, has been tests and trials. Some women have answered more with reading or studying the Word. Regardless of what it is, we can be committed to Christ in good times and in bad times. Either way, we choose to follow Christ through it all. We love one another and grow together and remain sturdy and fixed in Him.

When the winds blow and we draw close to God during it, surrounding ourselves with people who are godly and love God, we grow up in our faith and in our salvation, and our roots begin to grow deeper. It is similar to an oak tree that is sturdy with deep roots. Compare our sturdiness to the trees. The older they are the more sturdy we assume they become, but that is not always the case. Sturdy comes from reading the Word of God as well as applying it.

What causes us to become sturdy? A couple things cause this.

A depth of commitment to Christ brings sturdiness. Do we expect everything to be easy? Or are we committed for the long haul?

To place God first brings sturdiness. Remain obedient to God regardless. The hard knocks of life may threaten us, but we hold onto God regardless and choose to continue with Him. His ways are best, you see. You will see down the road everything He did for you in that tapestry to bring about fruitfulness, belief, and love for God. "Now we know that all these things work together for good to those that love God, to those who are called according to His purpose. In all these things we are *more than conquerors* through Him who loved us" (Romans 8:37).

Not tossed to and fro with every wind of doctrine, we hold to our faith in God and who He is regardless. Even when life is difficult or situations are owies, God is good. He is loving even if life isn't.

> Study to shew thyself approved unto God, a workman that needeth not to be ashamed, rightly dividing the word of truth.
>
> 2 Timothy 2:15 KJV

Do not be unknowledgeable of God's Word. Study the Word of God. Read it. Simmer it. Dwell on it, and study it. Allow it to be central to your life. What does the Word of God say concerning this? When questions come and assaults come, ask God for a verse that applies. Ask the Spirit of God to speak to your heart.

Psalm 1 has principles of sturdy and safety.

> Blessed is the man who does not walk in the counsel of the wicked or stand in the way of sinners or sit in the seat of mockers. But his delight is in the law of the Lord, and on his law he meditates day and night. He is like a tree planted by streams of water, which yields its fruit in season and who leaf does not wither. Whatever he does prospers. For the Lord watches over the way of the righteous, but the way of the wicked will perish
>
> Psalm 1:1-6

Sturdy: stalwart, robust, strongly built as an oak tree whose roots go deep and does not shake.

We are to be sturdy as an oak tree, "oaks of righteousness" (Is. 61). Oak trees are known for being tough and strong, or durable. They make it through tough times. The wood is dense, very hard and very resistant to the attacks of insects and fungus. Oak trees are a well-known symbol for strength and durability.

A Two Sided Agreement

Joshua erects a stone under an oak tree—the first covenant of the Lord (Joshua 24:25-27). They used stones that they stood upright as a remembrance or sign of what God has done or of their covenants with the Lord. What is a "covenant"? It is a two-sided agreement. Both parties choose their way and decide accordingly, and it is signified in a covenant between them. It's like shaking hands only more committed. People in the old days used to make a deal on a handshake. Or even in Bible days they would at times take off one of their shoes, and the two people would actually exchange shoes as an agreement between them. That was their sign—their covenant.

When Boaz agreed to redeem Ruth, he first went to the man who would have first rights according to their culture and was closer in relation. The man did not want to risk his own marriage, it seemed, by marrying Ruth as well as receiving the property that would come with her, so he allowed Boaz the right to redeem instead. (Ruth's husband had died, so she was a widow.) So they exchanged sandals in public agreement before the elders and people that Boaz could marry Ruth. "So the kinsman-redeemer said to Boaz, 'Buy it yourself.' And he removed his sandal" (Ruth 4:8).

God makes a covenant with us to bless us, and we make the covenant with Him to remain fixed with Him and in His Son, Jesus. He makes the covenant to take care of us.

> And why do you worry about clothes? See how the lilies of the field grow. They do not labor or spin. Yet I tell you that not even Solomon in all his splendor was dressed like one of these. If that is how God clothes the grass of the field, which is here today and tomorrow is thrown into the fire, will he not much more clothe you, O you of little faith?
>
> Matthew 6:28-30

And we make the covenant to seek first His kingdom. We do not go for public approval, although we do strive to have peace with others. As you continue down the passage, Jesus explains two things. They were worrying about their welfare when God promised to take care of them. Also, the covenant is: Seek first the kingdom of God, and all these things *will be added to you.* We must make Christ first and central in our lives. We follow Him and seek what is of Him, and all these things will be added to us.

Jesus said, "But seek first his kingdom and his righteousness, and all these things will be given to you as well. Therefore do not worry about tomorrow, for tomorrow will worry about itself. Each day has enough trouble of its own" (Matthew 6:33-34).

Focus on God, and allow Him to take care of the rest. Do not be consumed with worry.

Determine to stay in Christ for the long haul. Sturdy refers to being built strong. You do not break apart when the winds blow. Rather, you cling to the Word of God and stay firm in Christ. In Christ we live and move and have our being (Acts 17:28). We are children of God made perfect in Christ.

Read The Red

What did Jesus say? Read the words of Jesus. They are red in some Bibles. *Try it and see what happens for two weeks.* Then pray for increased understanding and power.

Read them and apply them in your life. Jesus Christ is our "righteousness, holiness, and redemption." It is upon him that we place our faith and build our love. We are his offspring. We are his disciples. As his disciples, we are to mimic him. What he did, we do. What he exhorts us to do, we put into example. Keep your eyes on Christ, and follow him. What did Christ do when people came against him? He spoke the truth in love. Mimic him. He was angry at sin. Read what he said and put them into practice in your life.

What does Jesus say? For instance, He said, "Can you make the guests of the bridegroom fast while he is with them? But the time will come when the bridegroom will be taken from them; in those days they will fast" (Luke 5:34-35). He told those who questioned him that no, his disciples were not doing the typical fast while he was with them. But he declared that the time will come after He was gone that his disciples "will fast." And fast they did. After Jesus went to heaven and sent the Holy Spirit, power came upon his disciples, and they surely did fast. In fact, most understand that the early church disciples fasted more than once a week. Jesus also did fast. Read through the gospels and ask God to speak to you through it. Follow it.

> He replied: I saw Satan fall like lightning from heaven. I have given you authority to trample on snakes and scorpions and to overcome all the power of the enemy; nothing will harm you. However, do not rejoice that the spirits submit to you, but rejoice that your names are written in heaven.
>
> Luke 10:18-20

I tell you the truth, anyone who has faith in me will do what I have been doing. He will do even greater things than these, because I am going to the Father. And I will do whatever you ask in my name, so that the Son may bring glory to the Father. You may ask me for anything in my Name, and I will do it.

John 14:12-14

Then he said to them, "Whoever welcomes this little child in my name welcomes me; and whoever welcomes me welcomes the one who sent me. For he who is least among you all—he is the greatest."

Luke 9:48

When they had finished eating, Jesus said to Simon Peter, "Simon son of John, do you truly love me more than these?"

"Yes, Lord," he said, "you know that I love you." Jesus said, "Feed my lambs."

John 21:15

Read the words of Jesus and pray for understanding and God's enablement.

Even Through Difficulties

The remembrance of people watching us encourages us to be sturdy in Christ. Therefore, since we are surrounded by such a great a cloud of witnesses, let us throw off everything that hinders and the sin that so easily entangles (Hebrews 12:1). We are not to be tossed to and fro by every wind of doctrine but rather to be strong in Christ no matter what comes our way. Christ is the central theme in our faith. We build our lives on the facts of the Word of God.

Have you seen people that do not shake in the wind? Watch those people. What do they do when difficulties come? Where have they been, and what have they learned? The godly remain. The ungodly run away when things get tough.

How do we become sturdy, that no matter what comes, we remain stayed in Christ? When you know that God has spoken to you (given you a word about what to do), obey. Get up and do it. Trust and obey. Trust in the Lord and "do good." Continue. The faithfulness of God is rich and pure. He is faithful to His promises. If you need change, ask God to bring change. If you need help, ask Him to bring help. Where you need finances, ask and you shall receive. And there is a time and a place for asking others as well. We ask God. We ask others if needed. And we ask for wisdom. God is able to provide. He is able to look through the glass and see where we are in heart when we do not know.

In order to be sturdy in Christ, we want our roots deep. *Fast, pray, and obey.* Walk the walk and talk the talk. Decide beforehand that you will stand as Christ's follower when persecution comes. Make a decision in your heart before it comes. If you are a Christian and doing God's will, trust God. "On my account you will be brought before governors and kings as witnesses to them and to the Gentiles. But when they arrest you, do not worry about what to say or how to say it" (Matthew 10:18-19). Allow the Spirit of God to guide you and direct you in it. Remain sturdy in Christ. There are rewards in the end and joy in the midst.

Strongly built means built up in the faith, built up in unity, and built up in love for God and for people. Love, action, and discipline. Love binds. Dissensions and factions separate and weaken. Proverbs 17:9 says this, "He who covers over an offense promotes love, but whoever repeats the matter separates close friends." Sturdy includes being united with others in Christ. We have accountability and we choose to grow up in Christ in all things. We must have people around us who will stand with us when times are rough, similar to a tree that has trees leaning up against it or a tree that has been transplanted. One of the principles to being sturdy is to surround ourselves with godly people.

Deny Evil At Every Access

Blessed is the man who does not walk in the counsel of the wicked or stand in the way of sinners or sit in the seat of mockers (Psalm 1:1 NIV). Deny evil at every access, every door, it tries to come in. Flee from evil. Love the good. Be filled with the Spirit. The Author and Perfector of our faith did it, and so we must also. Faith is the substance of things hoped for—the evidence of things not yet seen. It is substance and evidence. We do not believe in nothing. Rather, we have faith in something that is real and is credible. The Word of God stands alone.

We substantiate everything with the Word of God. Deny evil at every access by turning to the Word of God. How do I do that? I am righteous. Substantiate it with: "I am made righteous by faith in Christ." "Jesus Christ is my righteousness, holiness, and my redemption." "The righteous will live by faith." Heaven is real. Eternity is real.

Deny evil at every access, every door that it attempts to come in. The devil will try to get a stronghold in your mind or in your emotions. It can try in other ways as well. But if it can get a "rite" of access in your life, it can attempt to get in more.

The first area it will attempt to get into is the mind-set. If it can push your mind-set out of holiness, godliness, reality, truth, honesty, and the fruit of the Spirit, it can begin to develop a stronghold that is more difficult for you to break. For instance one of these strongholds could be depression. Depression is something the devil can attempt to bring through suppression of truth, through lies that it attempts to feed you. It will attempt a mind rite and then try for an emotional rite (get emotions into it as well).

Emotional root is what the devil will also attempt. The devil will attempt to convince you of a lie by concealing or distorting the truth. It will attempt to pull our emotions in ways that are dangerous or difficult for us to uproot from. What is the issue that the "tempter" uses against you? Address the issue with truth, with reality and with the Word of God. There are specific verses that apply to different tactics of the enemy.

If you need counseling, get counseling. Please find a *Christian* counselor and/or pastor to help.

PENETRATING PRAYER

"The god of this age has blinded the minds of unbelievers, so that they cannot see the light of the gospel of the glory of Christ…"

2 Corinthians 4:4

How will revival come? It will come through the grace of God, through the power of His Spirit, and in answer to the earnest prayers of His saints.

Why would national repentance come? We are going to pray for things that we have never prayed for before and see what God does. We will *fast and pray*. And we will do it in unity because there is increased power in unity and agreement. I have seen God answer the prayers of His people in increasing measure as they gather together in prayer.

There is power in spirit when you fast and pray. There are several factors that must be taken care of for revival to come in our own lives, families and nation. Conviction of sin is good for a nation to repent. If we want repentance in the nation, we must begin by asking God to bring conviction of sin and truth and love. A common factor during many revivals is the conviction of sin. Where there is moral laxity in a nation, there must be something that opens hearts to change. First is the Holy Spirit. He is able to bring people to change. Sometimes it is through His people's mouths, hands, and feet as well. But it is ultimately the Holy Spirit that must confirm and convict people of guilt in regard to of sin, righteousness, and judgment (John 16:8). And it is often preceded by His people asking Him to bring it in prayer and in fasting.

Only God truly sees the heart of man. Only God truly knows the heart of leadership in the country, in our churches, and in our own states. It is God's way to turn the heart of man and then the actions will follow. He works on the inside of man. It is the Holy Spirit that illumines the heart of man. God sees what we don't. He knows where the change is needed.

In order for there to be lasting change, there must be a conviction of sin that is found through the Holy Spirit's prompting. People and leader's eyes and minds must be opened to see right from wrong (2 Corinthians 4:4). We do not always realize our sin until the Holy Spirit grants conviction. And if we do not have conviction, will we change? Will leadership change? Will the unsaved change? And how would they? We need conviction in the country to do the right thing and to see immorality for what it is. If we do not have conviction of sin through the power of the Holy Spirit, we will not have revival. It will take a massive conviction of sin to change the morality of the nation.

Have we ever prayed for conviction of sin before on a large scale? Why or why not?

We must also ask the Lord of the harvest to send out workers into the harvest field to speak, to preach, and to minister to people's needs. People need the Lord, and they need His presence.

The only way for the presence of God to come in a manifest way is if people respond to the wooing of His Spirit. It is holiness that God desires. "Be holy, because I am holy" (1 Peter 1:16 NIV). Sin is the opposite of holiness. Sin separates us from a loving God but repentance turns us toward Him and brings the presence of God. God will not dwell with sin. If we desire God's presence in the nation, we must pray for conviction by the Holy Spirit.

Praying for A Wall of Fire

Have you ever heard of praying for a wall of fire? It is taken from Zechariah 2:5.

> Then the angel who was speaking to me left, and another angel came to meet him and said to him: "Run, tell that young man, 'Jerusalem will be a city without walls because of the great number of men and livestock in it. And I Myself will be a wall of fire around it,' declares the Lord, 'and I will be its glory within.'"
>
> Zechariah 2:3-5

The context of the passage is that the people had returned to Jerusalem, but there were too many of them and their livestock to fit inside the city walls for protection. So some of them were open to their enemy's attacks with no protection. That is when God sent his angel to say that He Himself would be as a wall of fire around them and the glory within. God became what they needed at the time they needed it. He was holy, righteous, and true, and He stands corrected not at all for what He plans and prepares to come.

Pray for God to be both a wall of fire around you and the glory within. This is one of the ways to pray for protection from the evil one. For example, you can pray like this:

God, I ask that You would be a wall of fire around myself, _____ (add other people or your loved ones if you desire), and around all that you have given to me to manage. Be a wall of fire around us and the glory of God within, a canopy over and protection below. In Jesus' Name we pray.

The "canopy and protection" I just add on. I was awake at night a few months after moving into a different house and sensed a strong spiritual battle going on in the house around me. I asked Him what I should pray, and immediately this Scripture came concerning God being a wall of fire. So I actually asked God to be as a wall of fire over the floor, up the walls, and over the ceiling in the house. I have seen God use this prayer to protect people's finances as well. Within a couple weeks, they had provision that hadn't been there.

It is biblical to pray for God to be a wall of fire around His people, or more specifically, around you, your family, or loved ones and around everything that God has given you to manage. Why everything God has given you to manage? Sometimes the spiritual enemy or even natural things can come at our finances, business, joy, or even ministries that He has given you to oversee. Why not pray for protection over these as well?

Ask God for protection. Even Jesus taught us this. When asked by the disciples how to pray, He added this in the Lord's prayer: "And lead us not into temptation, but deliver us from the evil one" (Matthew 6:13). Jesus also gave us this example when he prayed for His disciples, "My prayer is not that you take them out of the world but that you protect them from the evil one" (John 17:15). If it was not important enough to pray for, Jesus wouldn't have spent time on it in prayer either. Be aware and pray. But don't fear.

Ask God to break down lies of the enemy daily in your relationships and in your life.

Get to know the truth so you recognize the lies when they are brought against you by the devil, the world, the flesh, or others.

To Convict The World

Conviction of sin is the job of the Holy Spirit. He came to "convict the world of guilt in regard to sin, righteousness, and judgment." (John 16:8) The "world" in this verse ties in to the unsaved, the worldly. That is part of what the Holy Spirit does in the lives of non-Christians. If they never realize that they need Him by His conviction and power, how will they ever turn to Him? In America where we are so blessed by things and stuff that can temporarily fill our felt need for God, we must have conviction of sin for repentance to come. People will not come to Christ without the conviction that they need Him. We do not have the sight or understanding to place other things below God without the realization of our need for Him.

Leaders must have the conviction of the Holy Spirit to change their hearts. Our job is to pray for those in authority. And our job is to pray that God will bring conviction of sin and righteousness upon the leaders that affect us.

God, we ask that you convict men and woman across the nation of sin. Convict them of their need for you and that Jesus is the only way, truth, and life. There is no one that comes to the Father but through Jesus.

We need massive illumination and conviction of sin by the Spirit of the Living God.

Yes, people and those in authority do need to know and realize the love of God as well. But how often have we prayed for God to bless and guide and direct and reveal His love to leaders? The way to bring change quicker if it is the will of God (which we know that it is according to the word of God for non-Christians) is also to pray repeatedly for conviction of sin upon them. Some people change with softness and change quickly. Others like Jonah in the Bible—changed when they had difficulties and God got in their way. If the ground is soft in the hearts of those in authority, the conviction of sin will be quick. They will move to repentance quickly and they will receive the blessing and peace of God through it.

For those in leadership over us that are hard hearted to the will of God and completely unwilling to change, there must be the working of the Holy Spirit upon them—whatever it takes—

to bring about change in their lives. If that is the only way that there will be change *and* it is the will of God, then that is what we must pray for.

Leadership in a nation has a dramatic effect upon the people in it. It can also affect whether God's hand of blessing is upon it. Look at David in the Bible. He sinned, and God disciplined the people under him as well as him (2 Samuel 24). When David disobeyed God's command and counted all the fighting men in Israel, God sent judgment on the nation not just on David. It affected many more than the king only. So in a nation such as this we as the people will be both affected by the choices of those in power and will be held accountable for what we did or didn't do in the time they were there.

Look at our children and grandchildren as well. The leadership in the nation now will make determining choices in the future of our children. We must pray for conviction of sin in the lives of all those in authority over us. Think of five thousand people praying in agreement, for this request alone. What would the effect be? God is able to reach those in power, but we *must* begin to pray for it. Again the verse, "Ask and you shall receive." We will ask until God moves in the hearts and lives of those in leadership. While they are on their bed at night, while they are sleeping or awake, the Holy Spirit will answer our prayers and convict them both of their need for Him as well as their sin that is affecting our nation. Selfishness will be dealt with. Morality issues will be dealt with as well if we will pray for those in authority like this. People must come to salvation for there to be dramatic or noticeable change in the nation. There are too many people that don't know Christ. And we must pray that people in leadership come to salvation as well. How do we do this? We pray for the Holy Spirit to do His work of "convicting the world of guilt in regard to sin and righteousness and judgment." And "that they will know the greatness of God's love for them".

The Holy Spirit loves people, and we must believe that if the Holy Spirit came in power on Pentecost when the disciples were united in the upper room that the Holy Spirit will also come as His people gather now. As His people gather in prayer and in one mind and one heart to pray for this, the lives of people in the nation *will be* revolutionized. In revivals through and through, one of the common factors in them is that people are convicted of their sin. When done by the Holy Spirit this leads people to repentance and grants them life and love and joy. Times of refreshing are what come as we in unity turn to God to repent before Him for our sin, for the sin of our families and nation (Acts 3:17-19).

Remember to take time to ask God daily and repeatedly—as you watch the news, read the newspaper, and as you watch children in your neighborhood—to convict them of sin as needed and open the eyes of their understanding to truth, love, and their need for Christ. Pray it regularly and often, and allow God to deal with the specifics.

Also, the Word of God says our battle is not against flesh and blood, but it is rather against spiritual hosts of wickedness in the heavenly places. When these spiritual hosts of wickedness lose their effects upon people's lives is when people often have an easier time becoming freer from sin. Sin is what gives the devil a foothold. In order to remove the control or strongholds that the devil has upon a nation, we must target our prayers to pray that God will bring conviction of sin, as needed, in the lives of ungodly leaders who are in authority and power. Open the eyes of their understanding that they may see and desire godly ways. I see a revolution in the making as God's people unite in prayer for these things. Add fasting and we will break strongholds even more.

If we just pray for guidance for those in leadership, God may guide. But will they listen or pay attention? But if we pray for conviction of sin, God will send His Holy Spirit to convict them first of sin. Have you ever had God convict you of sin and His love? Breaking free of sin will bring freedom in your life as well. This verse from John 16:8 says the Holy Spirit came to convict the world of guilt in regard to sin, righteousness, and judgment. Massive conviction of sin brings the opportunity to realize the need to turn.

What To Pray For:

Ask God to hound people into the kingdom, if needed, and into His ways.

Ask God to increase a revelation of His truth and love in our lives, churches and people in the nation.

Ask God to turn hearts to repentance increasingly and convict the world of guilt in regard to sin and righteousness and judgment. (John 16:8-11)

Ask God for His will to be done and kingdom to come on earth and in our leadership as it is in heaven.

Ask God to bring national repentance, an increased turning to Him more and more.

Ask God to bring people to salvation, whatever it takes in their lives.

Ask him to illumine their understanding and bring them to a saving knowledge of the Lord Jesus Christ.

Ask God to send workers into the harvest fields and shine through them.

Ask God to work miracles that will draw people to Him.

Everyone who asks receives.

Rooted In Sin

Every spiritual root and rite that is against the power of the Spirit is rooted in sin. Sin in people's lives is what gives the enemy a foothold. If we will regularly pray for conviction of sin, the Holy Spirit will bring conviction in the lives of leaders and people in the nation. In fact, if people are not willing to change with ease, then pray that they will change with the Holy Spirit convicting them.

We must have the power of God to change a nation. It comes through prayer and fasting first. Then it comes through unity. United, Christians stand and blaze a light to unbelievers that is a witness to the truth of God's Word and to the belief in Jesus being God's Son. We must pray for this unity as well For it is the plan of the enemy to divide Christians over small, divisive things. It is the plan of the enemy to cause bitterness and factions. Remember that our battle is *not* against flesh and blood (people) but rather against the spiritual forces of wickedness in the heavenly places.

Some people wonder why we pray for conviction of sin in people's lives. Is it right or is it wrong? First, Jesus said that this is what the Holy Spirit comes to do. It must be God's will to do so. So we can also pray for it. If it brings people to conviction of sin, it may lead them right to the Savior. If they are aware of their sin, two things can happen. First, they can turn from it. He who does not know that he needs help will not ask, will he? He who does not know that he does wrong will not turn to righteousness (right living).

But the power of the Spirit can bring change that is needed. It is God who knows our deepest needs and hurts and desires to get us free. Without massive conviction of sin people will not know their need for a Savior. It is the future of this nation that is at hand. And it is the future of many lives for all eternity ahead.

As a body of Christ, we must be mission minded for the gospel of the glory of Christ. We must see outside of ourselves and outside our circumference.

Pray also for "conviction of sin" in the lives of ungodly leadership that affects us. And pray for an increased understanding of God's love in their lives. Because of my own experience with being convicted of sin I also like to suggest to pray for a deeper revelation of God's love in their lives.

If we want principalities removed, pray for conviction of sin. Every principality is rooted in sin. What is a principality? It is a stronger spirit or group of demonic spirits. Pray. Then add fasting as well.

Praying For Individual People

When you are dealing with sin or spiritual strongholds in someone's life, do it in love. Pray for discernment. Follow the Holy Spirit, for we are to "be led by the Spirit of God."

Remember that God looks at the person's heart and sees the broken pieces or places. He looks to heal and to reveal truth in love. He looks to bring healing and restoration to the deepest parts of a person's life and heart and mind and soul. It is here that roots are set that must require the love of God to heal. He often uses His people as well. Do not forget that.

Pray for healing.

Pray for love to fill up the person and be poured into their heart and soul.

Ask God to reveal truth.

Remember to use the love of God when you are dealing with people. They are people that God has made and they may be deceived. Wrongness in dealing with people can create bitterness or a hardening of their heart. God deals with people in love, remembering that they are "dust" (Psalms 103:14 NIV).

Ask and pray for truth as well. Truth is in love. Notice the scripture says "speaking the truth in love" (Ephesians 4:15 NIV). It is to be wrapped in love. There are times and places to speak firmly, but most people are won over through it being saturated in love. Love without truth is floppy. There must be the combination, but hard heartedness is to be reached and changed through the truth being spoken and acted out in love.

For God has given us the Spirit of truth, to guide us into all truth, and truth is the Word of God.

The Hound Of Heaven

Pray for God to hound people into the kingdom. The Holy Spirit has been referred to at times as the "hound of heaven." It is not to imply a disrespect for Him but rather to recognize that He is able to hound people right into the kingdom. The precious Spirit of God is able to continue and persevere in people's lives until they change their hearts and minds to receive Jesus and change their ways.

This is what we ask the Lord to do and the reason why is this: If people do not go to heaven, they go to hell. If they go to hell, they will live forever without God. It is all eternity to come, and it is also the rest of their lives here on earth without the blessings and love of God. There is power in praying for this.

I remember praying in a group for the Holy Spirit to hound people into the kingdom. I prayed it generally, thinking especially of people in the city. But what I prayed generally, God applied specifically. Later that afternoon I visited a friend who was older. I sat and talked to them for a few minutes and my mouth about dropped open. I was amazed. He was being "hounded" by God. I mean *hounded*. And before I left that day he asked me what he needed to do to change his life with God. I told him in simple words what to pray to accept Christ and left it with him. The next time I saw him, he looked dramatically different. He had prayed and accepted Christ in his late fifties. Great is the Lord and greatly to be praised (Psalm 145:3 NKJV).

"For we do not wrestle against flesh and blood, but against principalities, against powers, against the rulers of the darkness of this age, against spiritual hosts of wickedness in the heavenly places" (Ephesians 6:12 NKJV).

"For our struggle is not against flesh and blood, but against the rulers, against the authorities, against the powers of this dark world and against the spiritual forces of evil in the heavenly realms" (Ephesians 6:12 NIV).

If we do not think that we have a spiritual battle as Christians, then we have not read these verses. Even Jesus acknowledged that we need protection from the evil one and gave us the example in the Lord's Prayer to pray for this protection. He was also tempted by the devil and prayed again in John 17 for protection of believers.

Do we focus on the devil? No. But we acknowledge that it is there and pray for protection. Even when praying for the unsaved, people who do not know Christ, one of the ways to pray is for the eyes of their understanding to be opened. 2 Corinthians 4:4 tells us that the "god of this age has blinded the minds of unbelievers, so that they cannot see the light of the gospel of the glory of Christ." So we must pray for their eyes of understanding to be opened as well.

There are many prayer requests through the chapters in this book. Take them out. Write them down or put a bookmark in the sections and begin to pray them regularly.

Consider This

Above all, we need to humble ourselves before God more so He can lift us up in due time. When He lifts us up we will be a people and nation more healed and revived in spirit. Will you join with us more earnestly than ever to fast, to pray and to unite together to seek God for a new day for the sake of our children, our own lives and our nation? We must have the blessing of God in our nation. It must come through humility. It must come through a deeper commitment to God. And it must come through united obedience to Him.

"Call to Me and I will answer you and tell you great and unsearchable things you do not know." Jeremiah 33:3

Will you join us to seek God, to discipline our bodies and unite together to bring spiritual awakening in our own lives, regions and nation? It will be the greatest adventure of your life!

A PRAYER FOR ALL PEOPLE

Father in heaven, we praise You and adore You for who You are and how great You are. You are holy, holy, holy and there is none like You.

Help us, God, to walk in Your ways. May people turn to You increasingly in our nation, in our neighborhoods and in our communities. We ask that You turn our hearts to You more and more. May we prioritize Your will, Your desires and what is best.

Bring unity in Your body, amongst Christians all over, that we will shine for You in the nation we are in. May our witness stand out as distinct and draw people to You, Lord.

Bring salvation to the unsaved, Lord. Reveal to them their need for You. Give them a felt need for Christ and open the eyes of their spiritual understanding that they will see the light of the gospel of the glory of Christ. (2 Cor. 4:4)

Increase a passion in the hearts of believers to reach people for Christ. And open doors of opportunity daily and weekly to share the gospel with those around.

May Your will be done and Your kingdom come in the nation we are in, in our own lives and in our relationships. Give us courage and boldness to share our faith.

In Jesus's Name we pray. Amen.

Look for the book of quick, powerful prayers for ourselves, our loved ones and our nation titled, "A Touch of Prayer".

For more information visit cordof3.net.

BIBLIOGRAPHY

1. Revival 101 by Dale Schlafer, Copyright © 2002 NavPress Publishing.

2. Transformations, a documentary by Global Net Productions copyright 1999 The Sentinel Group

3. Bill Bright, www.CRU.org website: www.ccci.org/training-and-growth/devotional-life/personal-guide-to-fasting/01-message-from-bill-bright.htm–2010-04-23 *Accessed Sept. 2012*

4. Cornerstone Church Network. "Useful Statistics for Church Leaders" published on 16. Aug. 2010 by ccnetadmin in All, Current News, Ministry Tips. Accessed September 30, 2012. http://www.ccnetonline.org/2010/08/16/useful-statistics-for-church-leaders/.

listen|imagine|view|experience

AUDIO BOOK DOWNLOAD INCLUDED WITH THIS BOOK!

In your hands you hold a complete digital entertainment package. In addition to the paper version, you receive a free download of the audio version of this book. Simply use the code listed below when visiting our website. Once downloaded to your computer, you can listen to the book through your computer's speakers, burn it to an audio CD or save the file to your portable music device (such as Apple's popular iPod) and listen on the go!

How to get your free audio book digital download:

1. Visit www.tatepublishing.com and click on the elLIVE logo on the home page.
2. Enter the following coupon code:
   6035-11cf-3e13-dca5-8914-3e40-b194-2e93
3. Download the audio book from your elLIVE digital locker and begin enjoying your new digital entertainment package today!